Erich Maria Remarque

American University Studies

Series I
Germanic Languages and Literature

Vol. 65

PETER LANG
New York • Bern • Frankfurt am Main • Paris

Harley U. Taylor, Jr.

Erich Maria Remarque

A Literary and Film Biography

PETER LANG
New York • Bern • Frankfurt am Main • Paris

Library of Congress Cataloging-in-Publication Data

Taylor, Harley U.
Erich Maria Remarque : a literary and film biography / Harley U. Taylor, Jr.
p. cm. — (American university studies. Series I, Germanic languages and literature ; vol. 65)
Bibliography: p.
Filmography: p.
Includes index.
1. Remarque, Erich Maria, 1898-1970. 2. Authors, German—20th century—Biography. 3. Remarque, Erich Maria, 1898-1970—Film and video adaptations.
I. Title. II. Series: American university studies. Series I, Germanic languages and literatures ; vol. 65.
PT2635.E68Z89 1989 833'.912—dc19 88-8890
ISBN 0-8204-0636-8 CIP
ISSN 0721-1392

CIP-Titelaufnahme der Deutschen Bibliothek

Taylor, Harley U.:
Erich Maria Remarque : a literary and film biography / Harley U. Taylor, Jr. – New York; Bern; Frankfurt am Main; Paris: Lang, 1988.
(American University Studies: Ser: 1, Germanic Languages and Literatures; Vol. 65)
ISBN 0-8204-0636-8

NE: American University Studies / 01

Printed by Weihert-Druck GmbH, Darmstadt, West Germany

Contents

Preface

The columnist George Will once wrote that "Wanting to know an author because you like his writing is like wanting to know a cow because you like its milk." Despite the oversimplification involved, I must plead guilty.

Several years ago I had the pleasurable experience of discovering for myself the novels of Erich Maria Remarque. As my interest in his literary works grew so also did my interest in learning more about their author. Unfortunately, that was not to be a simple matter of consulting a few reference works or reading a biography. Attempts at that time to obtain biographical information about Remarque usually produced minimal, often erroneous, information. There were no biographies. This despite the fact that the phrase "all quiet on the western front" had become part of the language and most literate adults could identify Remarque by association with his internationally famous book.

Information concerning Remarque has become somewhat more available in recent years with the publication of two studies. The first of these, Franz Baumer, *E. M. Remarque* (Berlin: Colloquium Verlag, 1976) is in German and has 87 pages of text. The second study, Christine R. Barker and R. W. Last, *Erich Maria Remarque* (London: Oswald Wolff, 1979) is in English. The Barker-Last work is far more comprehensive than the Baumer book and has 141 pages. It deals primarily with the novels and themes of Remarque's work. There is also one chapter of 27 pages entitled "Life".

My own biographical research efforts began in earnest shortly before Remarque's death in 1970. The immediate motivation was the acquisition of background information for a graduate literature seminar on Remarque which I intended to teach at West Virginia University. Through subsequent years my interest in Remarque remained strong and my fund of information about him grew greatly. Because of the new material I had acquired, I felt justified in undertaking a book length study dealing with Remarque's life and works.

When I made my decision to write a book about Remarque, I wrote to his widow, Paulette Goddard Remarque, to tell her of my intention and to ask if she would be willing to talk with me. There was no answer to that letter—or to a second letter. I did receive a letter of inquiry from Dr. R. Neven Du Mont of the Kiepenheuer and Witsch publishing house in Köln asking for information about my work. He indicated that Mrs. Remarque had forwarded my letter to him. My response to Dr. Du Mont led eventually to a very pleasant and productive visit with him in October, 1976 during a research trip to Germany. After our visit, Dr. Du Mont wrote a letter in which he suggested the name of a person with whom a meeting with Mrs. Remarque might be arranged. By that time, however, I had decided, perhaps unwisely, to avoid whatever obligations might be inherent in a possible "authorized" biography. I must add that there was never any hint that that might have been a possibility in any case.

The Remarque study I have written is essentially biographical with detailed information about his literary works and the movies based upon those works. There are also chapters dealing with those posthumous events which have a bearing on the man, his possessions, or his writings. It has been my intention to provide the single most comprehensive source of information regarding all aspects of Remarque and his works. To that end, I decided it was necessary in some cases to give rather detailed accounts of novel story lines in order to provide an adequate perspective for every reader.

Even with the abundance of information presented, there are areas of the coverage of Remarque's life which have remained less complete than I would have wished. Despite this shortcoming, which I prefer to think is inherently unavoidable in any biographical work, the reader may nevertheless be reminded of the story of the man who had heard a lecture on whales and when asked what he thought of it replied that he had learned more about whales than he cared to know. I hope that will not also be the feeling of most readers in regard to what they learn of Remarque and his works.

Acknowledgments

One of the most gratifying aspects of my research work for this book has been the gracious and helpful response from other persons to whom I have turned for information or other assistance. Almost without exception, everyone with whom I have talked, or with whom I have corresponded, has been very encouraging and helpful.

I have often thought with amusement that the biographer's situation is well expressed by Tennessee Williams' character Blanche Du Bois who claimed that she had "always depended on the kindness of strangers." Although I can't speak for Blanche, I have rarely found that kindness lacking.

I wish particularly to acknowledge my debt to Remarque's friend Hanns-Gerd Rabe who has done more than anyone to preserve Remarque materials and provide answers to many of the problems dealing with Remarque family history and Remarque's early life in Osnabrück. He has been a tireless and successful advocate in the struggle to ensure proper recognition for his friend. The Remarque materials collected by him and made available in the Niedersächsisches Staatsarchiv in Osnabrück have been used with profit by me and other Remarque scholars. The Rabe collection continues to be the single most important source of material for Remarque scholarship.

On a more personal level, I am also grateful to Mr. Rabe for his generous hospitality during my visit to his home in Osnabrück. My conversations with him were informative as well as very enjoyable for me.

I would also like to express my gratitude for the help of

several other persons whose lives or careers have in some way touched those of Remarque and his wife Jeanne. In particular I am indebted to the kindness of Mr. Lew Ayres, the distinguished actor and star of "All Quiet on the Western Front"; Dr. R. Neven Du Mont, Business Director of the Kiepenheuer and Witsch Verlag in Köln; Mrs. Lion Feuchtwanger, widow of the emminent German exile author and Remarque friend; Mr. John Gavin, star of the Remarque movie "A Time to Love and a Time to Die" and former United States Ambassador to Mexico; the exile author Hans Habe, Remarque friend and neighbor in Switzerland; Mrs. Ursula Hammil, friend of Jeanne Remarque; Dr. Robert M. W. Kempner, Remarque's friend and attorney; Mr. Denver Lindley, Remarque friend and translator; Mr. Stefan Lorant, distinguished author and Remarque friend; Dr. Walter Rauer, Jeanne Remarque's attorney and friend; and finally, the eminent writer Peter Stone who did the English-language adaptation of Remarque's only play.

Others whom I wish to thank for their kindness in responding to my requests for information are: Mr. Jack Franses, Lord Lew Grade, Dr. Jürgen Kalkbrenner, Mr. Otis Meyer, Mr. Philip Scheuer, Ms. Dorothy Spellman, Mr. Earl Wilson, and Mr. William Wyler.

I would like to single out for special thanks Remarque's friend Mrs. Ruth Marton who was very generous in sharing with me her extensive knowledge of Remarque and of the persons in his world.

Several officials of the Federal government have also been quite helpful in making available to me records pertaining to Remarque and his wife Jeanne. I wish particularly to acknowledge the assistance of the following: Mr. Elliott B. Light, attorney in the Department of State; Mr. Stanley E. McKinley, Associate Commissioner, Immigration and Naturalization Service; and Mr. Edward M. Milburn, American Consul in Genoa, Italy.

My research has also profited greatly from the cooperation of a number of archives and publishing houses. The Niedersächsisches Staatsarchiv which houses the Rabe Remarque collection was very helpful during my visit and also later sent photocopies of additional requested material. The Archives of the Continental Gummi-Werke Aktiengesellschaft in Hannover also supplied copies of those Remarque writings which could be salvaged after the extensive damage caused by war-time bombings. Generous assistance was provided as well by the Staatsbibliothek Preussischer Kulturbesitz, *Der Spiegel*, Ullstein Verlag, Droemer Knauer Verlag, and the Kiepenheuer and Witsch Verlag.

I also wish to express my appreciation for the West Virginia University Faculty Senate Research Grant which helped to support a sabbatical research trip to Germany and Switzerland.

I am grateful for the support I received from my friends and colleagues in the Department of Foreign Languages at West Virginia University. In particular I wish to thank Dr. Robert J. Elkins who was unfailingly supportive and encouraging throughout all stages of the book's progress. I would also like to express special thanks to Mrs. Bonnie C. Anderson for her efficient, cheerful, and conscientious work in the typing and preparation of the final draft of the manuscript.

The most important acknowledgment of my gratitude and affection must go to my wife Charlotte who typed the first draft of the manuscript and, more importantly, was always supportive and encouraging throughout the entire project. I have never known my favorite collaborator to be otherwise.

It is also a pleasure to acknowledge the individuals and publishers who have graciously granted permission to quote from their works or from the works for which they control the rights.

Three Comrades (Matthew Bruccoli, Editor)
Turner Entertainment Company

Don't Say Yes Until I Finish Talking, Mel Gussow
Doubleday & Company, Inc.

Erfahrungen, Hans Habe
F. A. Herbig Verlagshandlung

Marlene, Charles Higham
JCA Literary Agency (acknowledgment is printed on the copyright page)

"Road & Track" (Richard A. Bartkus, Publisher)
"Reprinted with permission of 'Road & Track' magazine"

Papa Hemingway, A. E. Hotchner
International Creative Management, Inc.

Madame Sphinx, Marthe LeMestre
Ballantine Books

I Was Hitler's Prisoner, Stefan Lorant

Bring On The Empty Horses, David Niven
"Reprinted by permission of The Putnam Publishing Group from *Bring On The Empty Horses* by David Niven. Copyright © 1975 by David Niven"

European of Yesterday, D. A. Prater
Oxford University Press

"Three Comrades" (screenplay)
"© 1938 Loew's, Incorporated
Ren. 1965 Metro-Goldwyn-Mayer, Inc.
Turner Entertainment Co."

"Full Circle," Erich Maria Remarque, adapted by Peter Stone
"From 'Full Circle' by Erich Maria Remarque,
copyright © 1974 by The Estate of Erich Maria Remarque and Peter Stone; Introduction copyright © 1973, 1974 by Peter Stone. Reprinted by permission of Harcourt Brace Jovanovich, Inc."

The Black Obelisk, Erich Maria Remarque
"From *The Black Obelisk,* copyright © 1957 by Erich Maria Remarque. Reprinted by permission of Harcourt Brace Jovanovich, Inc."

Shadows In Paradise, Erich Maria Remarque
"From *Shadows In Paradise* by Erich Maria Remarque, copyright © 1971 by Paulette Remarque; English translation copyright © 1972 by Paulette Remarque, Executrix of The Estate of Erich Maria Remarque. Reprinted by permission of Harcourt Brace Jovanovich, Inc."

A Time To Love And A Time To Die, Erich Maria Remarque
"From *A Time To Love And A Time To Die,* copyright © 1954 by Erich Maria Remarque. Reprinted by permission of Harcourt Brace Jovanovich, Inc."

Heaven Has No Favorites, Erich Maria Remarque
"From *Heaven Has No Favorites,* copyright © 1961 by Erich Maria Remarque. Reprinted by permission of Harcourt Brace Jovanovich, Inc."

I am particularly grateful for the cooperation and courtesy shown me by Mr. Richard L. Kay and Mr. Robert Stein of the law firm of Pryor, Cashman, Sherman, and Flynn representing The Estate of Erich Maria Remarque.

The Estate of Erich Maria Remarque controls the complete or partial literary rights to novels from which I have quoted such as: *All Quiet On The Western Front, The Road Back, Flotsam, Heaven Has No Favorites, Three Comrades, A Time To Love And A Time To Die, Shadows in Paradise, The Black Obelisk,* and "Full Circle."

1

Remarque Family Origins

Erich Maria Remarque was born Erich Paul Remark on June 22, 1898 in the town of Osnabrück in Lower Saxony. His birth took place in the Provincial School of Midwifery and Childbirth on Knollstrasse.[1] Erich was the second son, and third child, of Peter Franz Remark and Anna Maria, née Stallknecht, Remark. The oldest Remark child was a daughter, Erna. The older son, Theodor Arthur Remark, was born July 9, 1896 and lived only until October 30, 1901. The youngest of the Remark children was a second daughter, Elfriede, who was born March 25, 1903. The four Remark children were baptised in the Roman Catholic faith of their devout parents.

The Remark family origins are French. The spelling of the name adopted by Remarque during his residence in Berlin after World War I is an earlier French form and does not represent the affectation sometimes suspected.[2] It has occasionally been speculated that the family made its way to Germany from France to escape the turmoil caused by the French Revolution. Erich Remarque believed this might be the case. However, because of the persistent research efforts of Remarque's devoted friend Hanns-Gerd Rabe, this possibility now appears to be in serious doubt. Rabe has traced the Remarque line back to a great-great-great-grandfather named Toussaint Remarque who lived in Aachen.[3] This earliest ancestor was occasionally listed in registry records as "Tossanus Remacle". Unfortunately, other than his birthdate of 1720, there are no dates, or other hard biographical information, concerning the first Toussaint Remarque (or Tossanus Remacle) and his wife Maria Lejeune. They had a son, also named Toussaint, who married

Catharina Courteaux of Aachen. This Toussaint Remarque was born in 1757 and died May 6, 1827. The records list him as a mason and her as a spinner at the time of their marriage. On the basis of 1789 as the beginning date of the French Revolution, it is apparent that this Toussaint is the Remarque who would have emigrated to Germany if the French Revolution were the cause of the move. Unfortunately for the theory he spent his entire life in Aachen. It appears likely that this also was the case with his father. The Remarque family is undoubtedly of French origin although the move to Germany was made earlier than the French Revolution.

Toussaint Remarque and Catharina Courteaux Remarque were the parents of a son, Johann Adam Remarque, born October 28, 1789 in Aachen. He was married on August 26, 1829 to Elisabeth Frenken, also of Aachen, who was born January 1, 1809. Johann Adam Remarque, who was Erich Maria Remarque's great-grandfather, left Aachen and worked as a master nailsmith in Kaiserswerth on the Rhein. Johann Adam Remarque had a son, Peter Aloys, who also worked in Kaiserswerth as a master nailsmith. At this time, whether through family choice or as the result of a clerical error, the surname was indicated as "Remark" in official records. Erich Remarque was of the view that it was his grandfather Peter Aloys who changed the French spelling to "Remark."

Peter Aloys Remark and Adelheid Bäumer, whose profession was listed as seamstress at the time of their wedding, became the parents of Peter Franz Remark on June 12, 1867. With Peter Franz Remark's marriage to Anna Maria Stallknecht, and the move to Osnabrück, the stage was set for the appearance of Erich Paul Remark, who unfortunately was to be the last male of his line.

2

The Early Years in Osnabrück

The Osnabrück of today with its population of approximately 176,000 is the third largest city in Lower Saxony. It is a thriving and progressive industrial city which also has been successful in preserving and restoring much architectural evidence of its rich historical past. The city has essentially completed its recovery from the almost total devastation caused by the Allied bombing raids in 1945. As a result of those raids almost seventy percent of Osnabrück was destroyed. A population of 100,000 in 1939 dropped to 60,000 by the end of the war.

Osnabrück is a very old city. It was established as a bishopric in 782 by Charlemagne and its official existence dates from that time. However, archeological evidence indicates the presence of human habitation approximately 4,000 years ago. The Emperor Barbarossa granted Osnabrück important city privileges in 1171 and in 1246 it became a member of the Westphalian City Union and of the Hansa. Undoubtedly Osnabrück's greatest claim to historical fame is the fact that the Westphalian Peace negotiations which terminated the 30-years war took place in the Town Hall (Hall of Peace). The peace was proclaimed from the steps of the Town Hall on October 25, 1648.

When Peter Remark came to Osnabrück in 1895 from his hometown of Kaiserswerth on the Rhein the city still retained much of its medieval charm and flavor even though industrialization was well underway. This city of two worlds was later to become a treasured memory for his son Erich Paul with an impact exceeding the usual nostalgia for the scenes of boyhood.

During the childhood of Erna, Erich, and Elfriede, the Remark family was in an essentially lower-middle class financial situation. Frugality was practiced partly by necessity and partly by choice because Peter and Anna Remark were not given to extravagance. Peter was employed as a book binder, and later master machinist, by the Prell firm on Krahnstrasse. His income in the early days was modest but dependable.

Possibly as a result of their modest financial circumstances the Remarks were a well-traveled family in Osnabrück. When Erich was born in 1898 they lived at Jahnstrasse 15. From 1900 through 1901 they were at Jahnstrasse 21. In 1902 Schinkelerstrasse was home. During the years 1903 to 1917 they resided for varying periods of time at Herrenteichstrasse 16, Gertrudenstrasse 17, Klingensberg 7, Jahnstrasse 29, Jahnstrasse 23, again to Jahnstrasse 29, Luisenstrasse 28, and finally to Hakenstrasse 3 to an attic apartment in which they lived until 1935. The house at Hakenstrasse 3 was owned by the Prell firm by which Peter was employed.

Hanns-Gerd Rabe in his biographical sketch "Remarque und Osnabrück"[1] speculates that the reason for the unusually high number of family moves might be the practice of charging lower rents for new or "wet" houses. When the plaster dried, and the structural soundness of the dwelling had been demonstrated in accordance with legal requirements, the house was "dry" and higher rents were then authorized. Frequent moves would have allowed the financially shrewd Peter Remark to save an appreciable amount of money by taking advantage of these legal provisions.

The numerous family moves gave young Erich an excellent opportunity to become well-acquainted with his hometown. If one uses the "Innenstadt," that is, the old inner or central part of the city, as a point of reference it can be seen on a map of Osnabrück that all but one of the Remark residences were located north, northeast, or northwest of that area. The only exception is Jahnstrasse which is located to the southwest near the outskirts of the city. It is an important exception, however, because it was this area of Osnabrück which was apparently closest to Erich's heart.

A very short distance to the southwest is an area designated then, as now, as the "Wüste" (a wilderness area) which at that time was in the undeveloped condition indicated by its name. The "Wüste" with its interesting varieties of plants, birds, and animals was a wonderful place for young Erich and his friends to spend the long days of childhood. Between the "Wüste" and Jahnstrasse was another childhood attraction, the "Pappelgraben". The "Pappelgraben" (the poplar ditch or canal) with its stately trees is mentioned in *Im Westen nichts Neues* (*All Quiet on the Western Front*), twice directly, and once indirectly, when it is used as the basis for the description of a similar locale in France. The Remarque protagonist in the novel, Paul Bäumer, gives us a nostalgic look at the importance of this childhood memory.

> "Between the meadows beyond our town there stands a line of old poplars by a stream. They were visible from a great distance, and although they grew on one bank only, we called them the poplar avenue. Even as children we had a great love for them, they drew us vaguely thither, we played truant the whole day by them and listened to their rustling. We sat beneath them on the bank of the stream and let our feet hang over in the bright, swift waters. The pure fragrance of the water and the melody of the wind in the poplars held our fancies. We loved them dearly, and the image of those days still makes my heart pause in its beating."[2]

It was here that Erich developed an interest in butterfly collecting and fishing. He not only fished for sticklebacks in the Poggenbach near his home but also occasionally carried home specimens for his aquarium. This boyhood interest continued throughout much of his life. However in later years the limited varieties of fresh water fish were replaced by exotic tropical fish in elaborate aquaria rather than in glass jars.

Although the boyhood pleasure of roaming the meadows and fields near Jahnstrasse in search of butterflies to add to his collection was limited to the span of a few years it made a lasting impression. The hobby is mentioned at various times in his novels and is of particular interest in *Im Westen nichts Neues*. The movie version of the novel gave the point special emphasis because it portrayed Paul Bäumer's death as the result of a sniper's bullet when Paul reached out in front of his trench to pick up a butterfly which was resting on a sandbag.

The first school Erich attended was the Catholic Volksschule, the "Domschule" which he entered in 1904 when his parents lived at Herrenteichstrasse 16. When the family moved from the northern part of the city in 1908 to Jahnstrasse 29 south of the "Innenstadt" he entered another Catholic Volksschule, the "Johannisschule".

Throughout the course of his early education Erich's academic performance was generally very good. He was a bright, perceptive student for whom learning was easy. His occasional clashes with teachers were largely due to his own independent interpretation of rules and his tendency to be overly free with critical observations. Remarque's lifelong inability to suffer fools gladly was often evident in his youth. He could be a good comrade and loyal friend and was generally popular with his peers.

Although Erich appears to have had an essentially cheerful and happy disposition, there was also a darker side of his nature. He was an idealistic boy who sometimes became discouraged and depressed when he realized that the reality of life often fell short of his idealistic expectations. An indication, perhaps an exaggerated one, of Remarque's unhappiness with some aspects of his youth can be found in Harry Kessler's published diary, *In the Twenties*, in his entry for Friday, August 30, 1929.

> A visit by Erich Maria Remarque to discuss his contracts. He came at Hutchinson's suggestion and stayed an hour and a half. He has the head of a Saxon peasant boy, an incisively contoured face with furrows, fair-haired with blue eyes beneath fair eyebrows. A firm expression that sometimes slips into lyricism. He told me his story in great detail and almost without a pause for breath. As a boy, from a lower-middle-class home in Osnabrück, he was very unhappy at the lack of any intellectual mentor. At fifteen he swotted his way through the *Critique of Pure Reason*, though without much appreciation. It always seemed to him extraordinary that he should exist at all. He spend a disconsolate youth interspersed with thoughts of suicide.[3]

Actually, apart from this retrospective view, there is little to suggest that Remarque's boyhood was as disconsolate as Kessler reports. It certainly had its share of pleasurable and fulfilling interests and activities. Along with the nature study of his early youth, and the related interests in fishing and butterfly collecting, Erich had an avid interest in stamp collecting. He also had an interest in magic and even tried his hand at hypnotism. For a while he was devoted to gymnastics and in 1911 he was an active member of the Osnabrück Gymnastics Club. Gradually, however, all these pleasant, youthful diversions were supplanted by more significant and lasting interests in music, art, and literature.

It is not certain how his strong interest in music developed but it became one of his most important and fulfilling avocations prior to his departure for military service in 1916. At an early age he began receiving instruction in piano and later progressed to playing the organ. He achieved a high degree of proficiency with both instruments and because of his success decided to give piano lessons as a means of supplementing his rather meager pocket money. During 1915 and 1916 he gave lessons to several young people, most of whom were girls. He was considered an excellent teacher and was well-liked by his pupils. However, "well-liked" does not go far enough in describing the effect Remarque had on some of his female pupils who were very attracted to their handsome and personable young teacher.

Remarque felt confident enough in his musical talent to consider seriously a career in music. This prospect was eliminated in 1917 because of a shrapnel wound he received just above his right wrist which impaired his playing.

Some of his additional income from the lessons was used for the purpose of dressing better than he otherwise could have afforded. Even at this time there was some evidence of the later well-known Remarque vanity in the matter of dress. However, most of his money was spent to satisfy a second great love of his youth, the love of literature. He was an avid reader of German literature as well as world literature in German translation. He not only bought books to add to his sizable personal library but also took advantage of the opportunities offered by his father's job as a bookbinder to read newly-bound books.

His parents were generally supportive of their son's literary and intellectual interests although they didn't always understand them. However, even though there was not always complete understanding but there was always love. This was particularly true of his mother to whom he was very close.

His mother, Anna Maria Stallknecht Remark, was born in 1871 at Altenessen in the Landkreis (district) of Essen. Her parents were Gottfried and Elise Poeppinghaus Stallknecht. There is unfortunately no other information available concerning her family background. Anna Maria Remarque was a loyal and devoted wife as well as an understanding and loving mother whose bond with Erich was made even stronger by the loss of her young son, Theodor Arthur.

As with many other facets of Remarque's life, the reader of his novels can get an accurate impression of Remarque's affection for his mother by examining the way he treats the mother-figures in his stories. The best and most accurate portrayal is that of Paul Bäumer's mother in *Im Westen nichts Neues*. The low-key, but emotionally moving descriptions of the mother-son relationship during Paul Bäumer's furlough from the front help to provide a strong reader identification with the novel. In this novel, which was the first after his own mother's death from cancer, there is true poignancy in the understated descriptions of Frau Bäumer's illness and the awareness that when Paul and his mother part it will be for the last time. The reader can be certain that any reference in a Remarque novel to the protagonist's mother will be a positive one.

Remarque's relationship with his father was considerably more problematic. Peter Remark was from all indications not an easy person to know or, on occasion, to get along with. He has been described by a former acquaintance, Johannes Spratte, as being taciturn with a thorny, often unfriendly manner. Peter Remark was indeed not an easy person to get to know.

However, longer acquaintance enabled one to discover the sensitive and decent human being he really was. He was also a proud and thoughtful man who took great pride in his professional ability and had little sympathy for fellow employees who gave less than their best effort. Spratte, as quoted by Hanns-Gerd Rabe, provides an interesting insight into one of his rather bizarre avocations:

> "Peter Remark liked to concern himself with occult things. I can still see how he attempted with his pocketwatch to conjure up things which are between heaven and earth. If one showed him a photograph of a person whom he did not know he allowed his watch on the chain to swing over this photograph and then said, often suprisingly correctly, who was dead or was still living."[4]

There is no direct evidence of significant conflict between Erich and his equally strong-willed father although their interests and philosophies were quite different. If one again attempts to determine Remarque's attitudes by turning to his treatment of the father-figure in the novels it becomes readily apparent that Remarque did not have the same concern and affection for the father that he had for the mother. A father-figure is found only in the novels *Im Westen nichts Neues* and *Der Weg zurück* (*The Road Back*). There is no significant conflict between father and son in these stories but there is also no real understanding. The relationship of Paul Bäumer and his father in *Im Westen nichts Neues* not only shows the gulf of misunderstanding between the combat soldier and the civilian but also the basically undemonstrative, somewhat wary, attitude of a father and son without essential closeness who are linked together through family ties and particularly a shared concern and love for the wife and mother in her illness. The father of Ernst Birkholz, the protagonist in *The Road Back*, appears to be drawn exactly from life. Although the father again does not figure significantly in the action of the novel the limited portrayal is completely accurate. The scene in which Ernst's father asks him why he has given up his teaching position offers the best insight Remarque could possibly provide of the basic attitudes and values of the two men.

> "Have you really given up your position as a teacher?" he asks.
> I nod.
> "And why did you do that, may I ask?"
> I shrug my shoulders. How should I even begin to explain it to him? We are two utterly different men and have got along well together thus far only because we have not understood each other at all.
> "And what do you propose doing now?" he goes on.
> "Oh, anything," I say. "It's all one to me."
> He looks at me shocked and begins to talk about a good and respected calling, about getting on and making a place in life for myself. I listen to him sympathetically but am bored. How strange that this man on the sofa here should be the father who formerly regulated my life! Yet he was not able to look after me in the years out there; he could not even have helped me in the barracks—any N.C.O. there carried more weight than he. —I had to get through as best as I could by myself and it was a matter of entire indifference whether he existed or not.[5]

Ernst tries to make clear to his father that his experiences in the war have made him content with very little. He further assures him that he can easily scrape together enough for his modest needs and that he has his whole life before him to worry about the rest.

> "Yes," he objects; "but that is no life, a bare hand-to-mouth existence like that."
> "Every man to his taste," I say. "To me it would seem no life to be able to say at the finish that I had entered every day for thirty years the same schoolroom or the same office."
> Rather astonished, he replies, "It's twenty years now that I have been going to the carton factory, yet I have always contrived to be my own master."
> "I don't want to contrive to be anything, Father; all I want is to live."
> "And I have lived, and uprightly and respectably too," he says with an accession of pride. "It wasn't for nothing I was elected to the Chamber of Commerce."
> "Then be thankful that you have had it so easy," I retort.
> "But you must do something, you know," he confirms.
> "I can get a job for the present with one of my army pals; as a matter of fact, he has already offered me one," I say. "That will bring in all I need."

"He shakes his head. "And for that you would give up a good civil-service job!"

"I have often had to give up things before now, Father."

He puffs away at his cigar distressfully. "And even assured of a pension too!"—

I smoke away thoughtfully and look at my father. I still see that this is my father, but also I can see he is just a kindly, somewhat older man, rather cautious and pedantic, whose views have no longer any meaning for me. I can quite well picture what he would have been at the Front; somebody would always have had to be looking after him one way or another, and he would certainly never have become an N.C.O.[6]

The quotation contains a degree of bitterness not present in the young Erich of pre-war days and the exchange shows clearly the gap which existed between the two men.

For a young man of Erich's economic and social situation prospects for advanced educational training were rather restricted. There were, however, two possibilities of which he could avail himself. Traditionally, superior students of limited financial means were able to receive state support in the areas of theology and teacher training. To the Remarks this seemed an ideal arrangement. Erich's mother and father had long encouraged him to become a teacher because of the practical advantages of job security and professional prestige. However, those aspects of a vocation which his parents saw as desirable held little appeal for their son who felt no real attraction to teaching. He was, however, very eager to grow intellectually. And although the field of pedagogy was not his true interest it did represent to him the most agreeable means of continuing his education. Therefore, for lack of a more appealing alternative, Erich acquiesced in his parents' wishes and was prepared for, or perhaps resigned to, the prospect of a career in teaching. Therefore, after he had completed his work at the Johannisschule in 1912 he enrolled in the Catholic Training College for Teachers to qualify for admission to the Lehrerseminar, the seminar for teachers. In 1915 he began the training program for elementary school teachers at the Lehrerseminar and remained in the program until his studies were interrupted by military service. In the final two or three years before he was drafted into the army Remarque's early literary interests broadened and his creative writing efforts intensified. At this point his extra-curricular reading of world literature had become more important and satisfying for him than the curricular expectations of the school. More importantly, his long-standing involvement in creative writing was at the point of producing some tangible results.

In the 1915–16 years Remarque's artistic and literary interests led to acquaintance and friendship with a group of like-minded young people who occasionally met to discuss literature, to offer each other encouragement in their creative efforts, and, also, to lament the sad state of parental, academic, and governmental authority. The acknowledged intellectual mentor of this group of enthusiastic and idealistic young people was the Osnabrück painter and literary light Fritz Hörstemeier. Hörstemeier, who was thirty-three years old at this time and several years older than most of his admirers, had led an interesting life which seemed exotic in comparison with the lives of his younger friends in Osnabrück. His earlier vagabond travels through Germany and Italy and his subsequent success with various types of painting were impressive credentials for him in their eyes. More important, however, was the fact that Hörstemeier was apparently a very decent person whose humanistically oriented philosophy with its love of nature and religion free of institutional dogma was very appealing to Erich Remarque and his friends.

Remarque used his experiences with the Hörstemeier group as the basis for the first novel he wrote. This novel, *Die Traumbude* (roughly, "The dream house" or "dream pad"), which was published in 1920 by the Verlag der Schönheit in Dresden, was a romantic depiction of the young idealists who had been very important to him during one of the most meaningful and pleasant periods of his youth. The significance this association had for him can not be overemphasized because it reinforced his commitment to literature and intensified his interest in other areas of artistic creativity as well.

Die Traumbude was later to become a literary embarrassment to him after the overwhelming success of *Im Westen nichts Neues*. In order to spare himself odious critical comparisons regarding the two works, and because he no longer saw himself as the same person he was when he wrote the earlier novel, Remarque asked the Ullstein Verlag, the publishers of *Im Westen nichts Neues*, to buy up all available copies of *Die Traumbude*. On March 9, 1929 Ullstein bought up all the copies in the possession of *Die Schönheit* publishing house with the intention of destroying Remarque's romantic and somewhat juvenile first major literary effort. Ullstein was apparently very thorough in its efforts because now copies of this first novel are almost impossible to find.

Although *Die Traumbude* had its genesis in events and friendships of Remarque's youth the novel itself was written later. However, the honor of being recognized as his first published work belongs to a more modest literary effort. In 1916 he took part in a prize contest in which the winning essay on the Jugendwehr (the youth defense association) was to receive a prize of thirty Marks. His article "Aus der Heimat" (from home), subtitled "Von den Freuden und Mühen der Jugendwehr" (regarding the joys and trials in the youth defense association) was published in the *Heimatfreund*, a paper for the youth of the Osnabrück governmental district.

3

Military Service

During the first two years of the war Erich and his family remained relatively untouched by its effects. The real tragedy at that time for the Remarks was Mrs. Remark's illness from cancer. The traumatic effect of that illness can best be appreciated by reading in *Im Westen nichts Neues* the account of the Remarque surrogate Paul Bäumer's furlough home from the western front. Even with the understated Remarque style the reader can not fail to appreciate the impact on Paul (Erich) of the impending loss of the mother who provided his principal emotional support.

In 1915 three of Erich's classmates in the seminar volunteered for army service. However, even though there was some feeling of societal pressure to join those who had gone ahead, Erich and his other classmates continued their studies until 1916. On November 21 of that year he and other physically fit classmates who were born in 1898 were drafted from school into the army. Some of the young men were caught up in the spirit of the great adventure and welcomed the opportunity to serve the "Fatherland". Others, such as Remarque, loved their country no less but entered its service with a less naive view of what such service would entail. Even that more realistic view, however, could not fully appreciate the horrible reality of actual combat.

At first the transition was relatively painless. The group was sent for recruit training to the Caprivikaserne (Caprivi barracks) on the Westerberg. The Westerberg is an area of rolling hills located two or three kilometers northwest of Osnabrück. At the camp on the Westerberg Remarque and his fellow recruits were given an accelerated basic training course which was rigorous but tolerable. His account in *Im Westen nichts Neues* of the petty indignities suffered by Paul Bäumer and his comrades at the hands of the martinet Corporal Himmelstoss remains essentially fiction although abuses of power were certainly commonplace, if not routine, in the Prussian military establishment.

After a brief period in a replacement battalion at the Klosterkaserne he was assigned to a military camp at Celle in lower Saxony for further training. It was fortunate that Celle, which lies east-northeast of Osnabrück, was not far from his home because his mother's terminal illness caused him to return to Osnabrück frequently. By this time the family had moved to Hakenstrasse 3 and was occupying the top floor apartment of a house owned by Peter Remark's employer, the Prelle firm.

Following the training period at Celle Remarque was sent toward the western front. On June 14, 1917 he was assigned to the second company of the field recruit depot for the Second Guard Reserve Division. Hanns-Gerd Rabe's research has placed this unit at this time in Ham-Langlet on the "Canal de la Sensee" behind the Arras front. From that point the unit marched to the town of Aubigny-au-Bac, thirty kilometers east of Arras, from which they were transported by rail to Flanders. In Flanders, which was on the point of erupting once more in a major outbreak of fighting, the destination of Remarque's group was an area located between the Belgian town of Thourout and the Houthulst forest roughly ten kilometers to the southwest. Remarque was assigned to duty in a sapper, or engineer, unit which had the task of fortifying positions east of the Houthulst forest. Here they were engaged in laying barbed wire and building gun emplacements, bunkers, and dug-outs. The work was difficult, dirty, and often dangerous. Much of it was necessarily done at night. In *Im Westen nichts Neues* Remarque captures some of the atmosphere and danger involved, with his descriptions of a sapper group's activities while laying barbed wire.

According to Rabe there were several others from Osnabrück in Remarque's sapper outfit.[1] Among them were Theodor

Troske, Georg Middendorf, Wilhelm Katschinsky, Seppel Ollfke, and Detering. All of these comrades had their fictional counterparts in *Im Westen nichts Neues*. On July 25, 1917, while on a sapper assignment, Remarque's friend Troske was wounded by shell fragments. Remarque carried him out of the enemy fire. Troske was sent to a hospital in Detmold. There he died of his wounds and was returned to Osnabrück for burial.

Remarque and his comrades had been sent to Flanders as part of a massive build up of German reserve strength which was to be used when the long-awaited British and French major offensive took place. At this time the British army under the command of Field Marshall Douglas Haig had reached peak efficiency and strength and was well-supplied with record numbers of field guns, tanks, and airplanes. Haig's force was made up of 62 infantry divisions and was supplemented by the French First Army under General Francois Anthoine.

The German Fourth Army, under the command of General Friedrich Sixth von Arnim, had completed its defense preparations under the direction of von Arnim's chief of staff Colonel von Lossberg who had greatly strengthened the German system of trenches and pillboxes. His strategy emphasized, in general, a defense utilizing strong points rather than relying heavily on fixed concentrations of troops. This strategy was based essentially on the premise that more flexibility and effectiveness could be achieved by the use behind the lines of reserve groups of troops which could be deployed to crisis areas as needed. The largest reserve groups in this system were placed the farthest to the rear. The reserve groups were also often used for sapper activities as in the case of Remarque and his unit.

The British and French artillery bombardment preparatory to the offensive began on July 15 and gradually increased in intensity until by July 22 the continuous exchange of allied bombardment and German counter-bombardment was of unparalled ferocity. For three days prior to the July 31 attack British and French assault units moved forward to their attack positions. At approximately 3:45 A.M. on July 31 the attack began.

The weather conditions were incredibly bad for the launching of the offensive. Heavy rains on a terrain already devastated by saturation bombardment made progress very difficult. Nevertheless Field Marshall Haig's forces began their advance on an offensive front which extended a distance of fifteen miles. General Anthoine's First French Army occupied the northernmost position. Directly to the south came the Fifth British Army of Sir Hubert Gough in the Ypres area. To the south of Gough was Sir Herbert Plumer's Second British Army. Plumer's Army was in position opposite the German lines north and south of Warneton.

With the joining of the battle five months of nightmarish horror began. Very little of real military significance was achieved in the ensuing slaughter which raged over the sodden quagmire of the Flanders battlefield. In Britain the great expectation of a major victory, which had been encouraged by military and newspaper reports of the first weeks, was bitterly disappointed when government officials and the public came to realize the truth. Gradually, accurate reports from numerous quarters made clear the hell of the Flanders No Man's Land and raised questions concerning both the wisdom and the conduct of the military operation there. However, nothing could equal the negative impact on British civilians of the sight, and stories, of British soldiers and airmen who had been shipped home because of their war injuries.

The British War Office indicated in statistics released in 1922 that British casualties between July and December of 1917 (which would include the Flanders campaign and the fighting at Cambrai) amounted to 448,614.[2] French losses for the same campaign were not indicated in these figures of course but were estimated by the Flanders military historian Leon Wolff to be around 50,000. On the basis of these statistics the price the Allies paid for the Flanders campaign was approximately half a million casualties. The Germans, in essentially a defensive posture, suffered 270,710 casualties.

One of those German casualties was Musketier (musketeer, private) Erich Paul Remark. On July 31, 1917, the very first day of the Battle of Flanders, he was seriously wounded by shell fragments from English long-range artillery shells. His wounds were in the neck, the left leg above the knee, and the right forearm just above the wrist. Remarque and his sapper unit had been working east of the Houthulst forest, south of Handzaeme, when the shelling started. He and three other seriously wounded soldiers were taken by wagon to a collecting point at Geite St. Josef. From here they were taken to Field Hospital 309 in Thourout. There it was decided that his wounds were serious enough to warrant transport by hospital train to the St. Vincenz hospital in Duisburg. For Remarque the shooting was now over.

Apparently the period of convalescence at Duisburg bore little resemblance to the traumatic experience of Paul Bäumer in *Im Westen nichts Neues*. Remarque's stay at the St. Vincenz hospital was relatively pleasant. He worked part-time as a clerk in the office and also had time to flirt with the daughter of a hospital inspector. There was also a lot of leisure time to continue his interest in creative writing, particularly the writing of poetry. Also very important for his good morale was the opportunity to become reacquainted with music. Access to a piano allowed him to play for his own pleasure, to spend some time on musical composition, and even to give some piano lessons.

On September 9, 1917, his mother's long struggle with cancer finally came to an end and Remarque received leave from the hospital to attend her funeral in Osnabrück. With her death the family had lost its emotional mainstay. The family would unfortunately also never again have quite the same significance for Erich.

Despite the many pleasant features of life during this convalescence in Duisburg reminders of the war were constantly present. Rabe, in his work dealing with Remarque and Osnabrück, quoted a Remarque letter of January 10, 1918 to his friend and front comrade Georg Middendorf in which he expressed his sympathy for the hardships experienced by Georg and his fellow soldiers. Remarque then continued:

> "A short time ago we received a hospital train from Cambrai. The fellows complained greatly about the cold and ice at the front. There were terrible wounds among them: amputations, wounds as large as babies heads, nasty bone wounds and the like. Sometimes it seems criminal to me that I sit here so nice and dry—where were you Christmas and New Year? I wasn't on leave because of the suspension of leave. However, Christmas here was also nice. Many a man wiped his eyes with his hand and I saw old fellows who cried like children and sobbed their heartsickness into their pillows.
>
> Both of us will certainly not forget this Christmas: You in the rubble, blood, shit, and death, I in the hospital. Soon the war will be over and then we will meet again. When I get to the replacement battalion I want to see if I can report to your unit."[3]

Remarque signed his letter "Schmieren" which was a nickname from his schooldays. "Schmieren", which essentially means to smear, or spread, comes, by extension, to mean to scrawl or scribble. The nickname dates back to the criticism by his teachers who thought his penmanship and neatness left much to be desired.

"Schmieren," or "Kamerad Schmieriges" (comrade messy) as he also signed himself on occasion, obviously had a bad conscience because he was enjoying the safety and relative comfort of the hospital while his comrades were still exposed to the incredible hardships and danger of the Flanders front.

While Remarque was still in Duisburg he learned of the death of his close friend and former mentor Fritz Hörstemeier in Osnabrück on March 6. Remarque received leave to go to Osnabrück for the funeral and played the organ for the service. For Remarque, Hörstemeier's death was like a death in his own family.

Although Hörstemeier was dead and the other free-spirits of the idealistic group were scattered their influence on Remarque remained. His interest in writing was growing stronger and his desire to see his works published was growing apace. During his period of recovery at the St. Vincenz hospital he submitted a sketch, a short story, and a poem to the Richard A. Giesecke periodical in Dresden, *Die Schönheit*. They were all accepted for publication and appeared in the magazine in 1918. The first, the sketch "Aus der Jugendzeit" (From the Time of Youth), was an overly romantic, maudlin exercise in nostalgia for a lost love. The second, "Die Frau mit den goldenen Augen" (The Lady with the Golden Eyes) described an imaginary episode with a dream girl. The third work, "Ich und Du" (I and You), is a poem of only three stanzas expressing the author's yearning to be united with his love. All three of these published efforts suffer from excessive romanticism. At this time Remarque also was writing his first novel *Die Traumbude* which suffered from the same excess of sentimentality. *Die Traumbude*, which did not appear until 1920, was also published by the Giesecke publishing house.

On October 13, 1918, he was released from the hospital after being declared fit for garrison duty and assigned to the First Replacement Battalion of Infantry Regiment 78 in Osnabrück. On November 7 he was examined by the battalion physician and pronounced fit for field duty. The timing couldn't have been better for Remarque because on November 11, 1918 the guns fell silent. The armistice ended the fighting and dying—but not the hating.

4

From Field Gray to Mufti

War's end brought only cold comfort to a Germany exhausted by the years of suffering and deprivation. The national tensions and unrest which ended in post-war turmoil and revolution were well advanced even before the signing of the armistice and, indeed, were largely responsible for the end of the war. From the beginning of 1916, with the establishment of the Spartacus League by left-wing extremists, German war aims were under attack. Revolutionaries such as Karl Liebknecht and Rosa Luxemburg successfully went about their work of producing the chaos which they hoped would ensure the downfall of Imperial Germany and the rise of a new proletarian government.

The first major domestic threat to the continued rule of the imperial government came on October 30, 1918 when the fleet at Wilhelmshaven mutinied. By November 3 the mutiny had spread to Kiel and Hamburg. In Bavaria the Socialist Kurt Eisner organized a revolution which overthrew the monarchy and proclaimed on November 7 the establishment of a separatist government. Thoroughly alarmed, the Kaiser turned to his generals only to learn that the army would not support him. It was now clear that only his abdication would satisfy the country. In a rapid series of events power was passed from Prince Max to the Socialist leader Friedrich Ebert and the republic was established. The former emperor Wilhelm II left Germany on November 10 for exile in Holland.

The most dramatic and violent confrontation of this turbulent period occurred when 3,000 sailors occupied the former imperial palace in Berlin ostensibly to protect the new Ebert government. The situation got out of control when the sailors began looting. The sailors refused government demands that they leave and even took hostages. Ebert then requested help from the army against the rebellious sailors. General Gröner agreed to send troops and on Christmas Day 1918 a division of soldiers outside the palace began shelling the palace and its navy defenders who soon surrendered. The importance of this episode lay in the fact that it hardened political convictions and made enemies of some socialist groups because the independent socialists and Spartacists did not approve of the action of Ebert's majority socialists in sending German soldiers to attack German sailors.

It was to this volatile and vitriolic situation that Remarque and his comrades returned. Remarque was never directly involved in any of the bloody street fighting such as the battles between the Spartacists, who now called themselves Communists, and Gustav Noske's "Freikorps" (volunteer corps) which was composed of former soldiers under the leadership of former officers of the imperial army. Remarque, who placed a very high value on comradeship, was appalled by the sight of former comrades who had survived the horrors of the war now opposing each other in combat. This important concern is expressed in *Der Weg zurück* (The Road Back), his first novel after *Im Westen nichts Neues*, which makes just as important a statement about the post-war problems of the returned soldier as *Im Westen nichts Neues* made about the soldier in combat. Adjustment to civilian life was not easy for Remarque and his friends and he does not make it easy for the veterans in his stories.

The date on which he was discharged from the army in Osnabrück can not be determined because the military records of the former imperial army which were kept in army archives in Berlin were destroyed in February 1945 as the result of a bombing raid. In fact, it can not even be determined that Remarque was discharged. It may well be that in the confusion of November, 1918, he simply went home as thousands of others did.

More intriguing questions about another aspect of Remarque's military record are raised by a post-war picture of him in uniform which accompanied an item in an Osnabrück newspaper. The picture, which was taken in the Schulz photographic studio in Osnabrück, showed him standing in front of a studio backdrop which depicted a forest scene. Remarque was wearing on his military tunic the Iron Cross First Class, the Iron Cross Second Class, and the badge worn by German soldiers to indicate war wounds. In his left gloved hand he held the leash attached to the neck of his shepherd dog "Wolf". It was a very impressive looking picture of the dashing and handsome young veteran home from the war. The main question, in addition to the matter of a few non-regulation items of attire, was the wearing of the Iron Crosses. Hanns-Gerd Rabe found the newspaper item in the "Osnabrücker Tageblatt" of November 26, 1918 which stated "The seminarian Erich Remark was awarded the Iron Cross, First Class".[1] It may very well be that in this case, as with all modern wars involving large bureaucratic organizations, the award was authorized earlier but not conferred until after the conclusion of hostilities. It may also be that the awards were self-conferred. This is a more likely possibility. In any event, the fact that the newspaper report mentioned the Iron Cross, First Class, whereas there was no mention of the Iron Cross, Second Class even though he is pictured wearing both awards, shows that more explanation is needed.

Unfortunately there are two further reports which cast considerable doubt on the validity of Remarque's "military honors". In November of 1918 his former classmate and fellow soldier Christian Kemmerich met "Gefreite" (Lance Corporal) Remarque in Osnabrück. Remarque was wearing the Iron Cross, First and Second Class, and the Oldenburg Cross, First and Second Class. Subsequently Kemmerich learned that the batallion commander had sent out a patrol from local military headquarters to bring Remarque in to question him about his "promotion" and decorations. There is no information regarding the resolution of the matter.

The next year Remarque was seen in Hannover in the uniform of a Lieutenant, wearing the Iron Cross, First Class, as well as a monocle. This report is given a measure of credence by the detail of the monocle because Remarque was known to have affected a monocle in his later Berlin days.

Even if one discounts some of this information, it is almost impossible to avoid the conclusion that, on occasion, Remarque wore military attire and decorations for which he had no authorization. If this is true, the most logical explanation appears to be the Remarque vanity and ever-growing hunger for recognition. Apparently at this time his later well-known penchant for flamboyance was beginning to assert itself. Perhaps his feelings of guilt for having spent such a sizable part of his military service in the safe haven of a hospital also played a part and he felt a need to embellish his military accomplishments. If the last possibility is the case there was certainly no reason for that feeling because he had served honorably and well.

In January of 1919 Remarque returned to his unfinished educational program at the Catholic Lehrerseminar in Osnabrück. Although Remarque and his comrades had received enough "education" to last a lifetime, unfortunately it was not of a type for which academic credit could be given. So the returning veterans found themselves in an anomalous situation. They were older than their non-veteran classmates. Their own outlook on the world was also basically different from that of the innocents they had been when they left the training program for the war. Their teachers apparently could not appreciate the fact that their comfortable, traditional routine would no longer work with these students who had familiar names but decidedly changed attitudes. Young men who had survived the most horrible example of man's inhumanity to man did not intend to acquiesce in the re-imposition of an institutional routine which treated them like juveniles. The degree of bitterness felt by the veterans for their inflexible faculty was great. This was particularly true in regard to the Director Wess.

The situation was much the same for the students in Osnabrück's other teacher training seminar, the Evangelical Seminar. Remarque's friend Hanns-Gerd Rabe was the dominant figure among the students at that school. Rabe had a distinguished military record. He had been a combat company commander on the Western Front and had also served as an ordinance officer on the staff of a General. He had twice been personally decorated by the Emperor. Rabe spent the last part of his war service as a pilot-observer in the German Air Corps and participated in 160 combat flights. It would be ridiculous to relegate a man such as Rabe to the status of "Zögling" (pupil, student), a term applied to teacher-trainees in the seminar.

At the heart of the problem was the fact that the teacher-student relationship had been basically altered and could never be restored with the group of student-veterans. In *The Road Back* Remarque treats the seminar situation at some length. As usual, because of his strongly autobiographical approach, there is very little deviation from the true situation. In the protagonist Ernst Birkholz's comment about the faculty at the Teachers' Seminar there is a statement about older civilian authority in general.

> I look at the group of masters. For us they were once more than other men; not merely because they were in charge of us, but because, however much we may have made fun of them, we believed in them. Today we see them merely as so many somewhat older men, of whom we feel mildly contemptuous.
>
> There they stand now and propose to teach us again. But we expect them to set aside some of their dignity. For, after all, what can they teach us? We know life now better than they; we have gained another knowledge, —harsh, bloody, cruel, inexorable.[2]

The seminarians made several demands for adjustments in curriculum as well as for elimination of some school rules which they regarded as non-applicable to adults. The school authorities were willing to make some concessions but were not willing to go far enough, or move fast enough, to suit the veterans. As a result, the students of both Osnabrück seminars held a meeting to discuss a course of future action. The principal spokesman for the Catholic seminar was Remarque and the spokesman for the Evangelical seminar was Rabe. It was decided to send Rabe and Remarque to Hannover to discuss the general situation with the provincial school council and to seek clarification concerning several curricular issues.

The council agreed to four of the specific demands presented by Remarque and Rabe. They agreed to recognize the soldiers' council and also agreed that Director Wess had to accept the former soldiers into his institution. The beginning of the term was set for the following week. It was also finally agreed that two afternoons of each week would be free time. Although a fairly successful beginning had been made there was still no decision regarding the key issue of the length of the program. Rabe said that Geheimrat (Privy Councillor) Oeltjen hid behind the fact that there were no guidelines in this situation. That was certainly true. However, bureaucratic caution was not to win the day in this instance. Rabe and Remarque were not satisfied with partial victories and decided to press their advantage by going to Berlin to seek out higher authority.

In Berlin they were able to get a prompt hearing from Minister of Education Hoffmann. This meeting was a complete success. Hoffmann set specific guidelines for the duration of the special teachers' training program to accommodate the veterans. Other concessions so altered the curriculum that the final "training" received was of doubtful value in some instances.

Remarque's success in negotiations must have been respected by his fellow students because after returning from Berlin in January of 1919 he served as the chairman of the Association of Seminarians for the Hannover district. He continued in that capacity until he accepted his first teaching assignment in the small village of Lohne.

The first year of his return to civilian life was a very good one for Remarque. He had achieved a respected status among his peers. There was time to devote himself to his beloved writing and also time to socialize. He treasured the quiet hours of piano playing or writing in his small room on Hakenstrasse but at heart he was a very gregarious person who needed to be with people and to enjoy their respect. Remarque was always proud and ambitious with a keen eye for what was required to be regarded as successful. It was apparent to all his acquaintances that he regarded dressing well as a basic requirement. Remarque was often a picture of studied elegance on the streets of Osnabrück and in favorite haunts such as the Cafe Germania. His attitude was that in order to get ahead in life one must place great emphasis on one's clothing. This view, certainly not one of his most profound, did not advocate a course of action which was contrary to his nature. Remarque had a life-long love of fashionable clothes. The flamboyance in his attire during this period was modified through the later years of increasing affluence into an understated, conservative elegance.

Remarque played to the hilt the role of bon vivant and cavalier. When it was time to organize and arrange the most important social event of the seminarian's year, the "Rosenfest" (the rose party or ball), he was the only logical choice for the office. He carried out the responsibilities of the job with his usual verve and enthusiasm and the ball was a complete success. The event was held in June 1919. The rose motif was carried out in the table decorations, the ladies' bouquets, the rose boutonnieres, and even the rose scent sprayed in the hall. Remarque's eloquence was at its best as he extolled the beauties of women and roses. As if he had to make up for the time his army service had taken him away from the arts and music, he now became involved in as many activities as he could manage. He also resumed giving piano lessons in order to be able to afford a higher standard of living. Theatrical and musical performances in Osnabrück often found him in attendance. Remarque also occasionally contributed theatre, art, and music criticism to the local newspapers. Even at this relatively early age he possessed an impressive fund of general knowledge to which his inquisitive nature and avid reading made continued contributions. He also developed an active interest in painting at this time. Unfortunately none of his paintings has surfaced although he gave some of them to friends.

During 1919 Remarque continued publishing his creative efforts in the Dresden periodical *Die Schönheit*. Four of his writings are known to have appeared at this time: "Ingeborg", subtitled "Ein Erwachen" (an awakening); a poem "Abschied" (parting, departure); a one-page prose description of a romantic encounter at a masked ball called "Schöne Fremde" (beautiful stranger); and a short sketch entitled "Die Stunde der Erlösung" (the hour of release). The three prose works have the same overly sentimental, romantic quality of the 1918 writings. Translated excerpts from "Ingeborg" will give the flavor of this one-page effort.

> "Roses—
>
> Yellow and red—
> And so fragrant(ly)
> Roses bloomed
>
> And Ingeborg, the beautiful daughter of the king, slipped from the charge of her attendants and ladies out into the garden which was wet with dew. —A small bird twittered: 'Ingeborg, Ingeborg, when the rose blooms, your longing will be fulfilled'. And Ingeborg inclined her lips to a wonderfull rosebud, which stood apart from the others, kissed it again and again and said: 'Unfold, oh rosebud, unfold oh heart'. The bird of longing twittered in accompaniment and Ingeborg was full of sweet thoughts.
>
> More and more roses came into blossom in the garden.
> Yellow and red—
> So heavy with fragrance!
>
> Day after day Ingeborg kissed the rosebud, it became ever more full and more beautiful, morning after morning the bird of longing sang, heavier and heavier became Ingeborg's heart and more filled with longing.
>
> And in a blue summer night a blissful light filled Ingeborg's dream, and a clear voice spoke: Come!"[3]

It is difficult, if not impossible, for Remarque enthusiasts to relate this juvenilia to the post-1929 novelist. It should be remembered, however, that the author of the later realistic novels never ceased to be a romantic. Remarque was an excellent example of the theory that every apparent cynic is at heart an idealist.

Some idea of the content of his poem "Abschied" can be had from the following unrhymed rendering which is presented with apologies to the muses and to Remarque's henceforth unquiet poetic spirit.

"Parting

"Ich leave. (I) want to seek forgetfulness
and wander to the end of the world—
What does crying help—what does swearing—
I wish you every happiness with the other
Yet know (this): If on a starry night
You awaken suddenly; —your pillows wet from weeping—
You don't know, why you awaken so suddenly—
And everything seems strange and puzzling—
If you stare with wide eyes into the darkness
and reflect, —and don't fall asleep again
and hope for (something) long forgotten, long dead:
Then you will be mine![4]

In the summer of 1919 Remarque and his classmates had to face the normally rigorous final examinations before being certified to teach. Fortunately for them the concessions they had won from school authorities had so attenuated the examination that passing was almost assured. Whether the relaxed requirements were equally beneficial to their future students is highly unlikely.

Instructions have arrived requiring that returned men shall be treated with indulgence in the examination. They are to be allowed to submit subjects in which they are to be examined.

Unfortunately the subjects in which we are specially interested do not figure in the syllabus, so we simplify matters after our own fashion. Every man is to submit two questions in each subject and to undertake to be able to answer them.- - -

Willy is uncommonly fastidious. He turns over and over the pages of his history book, and only after long searching up and down does he plump at last for the two questions following: "When was the battle of Zama?" and "When was the reign of Otto the Lazy?"

Westerholt and Albert take the lists of questions and subjects to the several masters. They go first to the principal, who eyes them with some apprehension; he has not been led to expect any good at our

> hands. He studies the lists and then lays them aside with a gesture of disgust.
>
> "But, Gentlemen, the Minister requires that you submit such fields as you may be specially interested in; that is to say, certain definite large sections from each course of study. But what you offer here is no more than bare, simple questions."
>
> "The fields of our interest are no greater," answers Albert.
>
> "But then don't we make up for it by knowing them so very tres bon?" adds Westerholt.
>
> The principal hands the lists back. "No, I cannot agree to that. It would merely be to make a farce of the whole examination."
>
> "Well, isn't it so, anyway!" retorts Westerholt, beaming.
>
> The principal shrugs his shoulders, but eventually accepts the lists.[5]

Remarque passed his final examination on June 25, 1919. He had elected lyric poetry as his area of special interest and discussed Herder's folk song collection and some aspects of Goethe's work. He also interpreted Goethe's poem "Heidenröslein". All in all, it was not a particularly arduous examination. His teacher certification was made official on August 1, 1919. The grades he received for his academic performance were not distinguished by their excellence. In drawing and religion he was given a mark of "gut" (good). However, all of the other marks were merely "genügend" (satisfactory).

With official permission to teach in a "Volksschule" (elementary school) came the worry about receiving a teaching assignment. The veterans, who were now novice teachers, had done very little to endear themselves to school authorities. Consequently, it was very unlikely that those authorities would take particular pains to change the usual policy of assigning new teachers to the least desirable positions. In most cases this meant assignment to a job in a remote village. And even at that there were not enough teaching positions to go around.

5

The Reluctant Teacher

Remarque was fortunate enough to be given an immediate assignment even though it was only as a temporary substitute for a veteran teacher who was still being held by the French as a military prisoner. The school was located at Lohne, in the administrative district of Lingen, northwest of Osnabrück. Lohne was a very remote hamlet in the marshy land near the Dutch border. If it were a military post Lohne would have been considered a hardship assignment. At that time three teachers taught more than two hundred students on a shift basis in a two-room school. The school accommodated four grade levels. Remarque was well-liked by his students and members of the community. He carried out his teaching responsibilities efficiently and well and in general was a welcome addition to the isolated little village. Remarque was employed in Lohne from the beginning of August until March 31, 1920. The teacher he had replaced, a man named Wulfern, returned and Remarque was no longer needed.

Hanns-Gerd Rabe reports that in December of 1919 it was intimated to the city authorities in Osnabrück that Remarque had participated in Spartacist activities during the time he was a student in the Lehrerseminar.[1] Remarque's old adversary Director Wess reported that the faculty of the Lehrerseminar considered Remarque a Spartacist on the basis of remarks he had made during his training. It seems likely, however, that these vague accusations were made on the basis of personal pique as a result of Remarque's activities as a student leader. It seems equally likely that given Remarque's outspoken, iconoclastic nature there would be no shortage of material which could be used against him, particularly if taken out of context. However unfounded the accusations may have been, it was necessary for Remarque to make an official statement in the matter to school inspector Egert in Lingen. In his denial Remarque stated: "I have participated in no Spartacist activity and I must request proof for this participation."[2] His denial of involvement was obviously not completely acceptable to the authorities in Osnabrück who went on record as expressing extreme disapproval of his conduct. Remarque's powerful enemies had won the day even though their victory was in the form of a reprimand without really serious effect.

After Wulfern resumed his teaching duties in Lohne, Remarque returned to Osnabrück. Fortunately his period of unemployment was very brief. On May 4, 1920 he began another teaching stint. This time he was hired to serve as a temporary replacement for an ill teacher named Nieberg in the small village of Klein-Berssen in the poverty-ridden Hümmling area. If possible, this assignment was even more depressing than Lohne had been.

It would not be difficult to fix blame for bad teaching, or give credit for good teaching, in the new situation because he was the only teacher for a range of eight grades meeting in one classroom. There was also very little opportunity to escape the school atmosphere because Remarque also occupied the teacher's quarters in the school. At least in Lohne he had boarded and roomed with a local family.

In Klein-Berssen the school was under the shadow of the church in more ways than one. It was not only close in location but also under the domination of the strong-willed resident Roman Catholic priest Father Brand.

Remarque's brief tenure in Klein-Berssen was marked by unpleasantness and controversy. From the beginning Brand made it is clear that he expected the teacher and the school to be under the complete control of the Church. Remarque made it equally clear that he expected to control the running of the school. Neither of the men was hesitant about expressing his opinion and a vitriolic exchange of recriminations resulted. The situation finally deteriorated to the point that it was necessary for an investigative committee to look into the matter. They were unable to make a definite decision and the impossible situation remained unresolved until the regular teacher Nieberg, whom Remarque was replacing, returned to claim the position. It remains uncertain whether Nieberg had really recuperated from his illness when he returned or whether his return was hastened by Brand and/or the school authorities. Brand's relationship with Nieberg had not been free of conflict but it appears certain that Brand preferred him to Remarque.

It also seems certain that when Remarque's professional responsibilities in Klein-Berssen ended on July 31, 1920 his long-felt unhappiness with teaching had intensified to the point that almost any other occupation seemed as attractive. His dissatisfaction is certainly understandable. The only teaching opportunities open to him were positions as a substitute in remote and unattractive areas with almost no possibility of involvement in the cultural activities which were so important to him. Accusations had also been made against him which he had not been given a fair chance to rebut. However, the most important factor in producing his disillusionment was the acrimonious relationship with Brand. When Remarque left Klein-Berssen it is likely that he did so with bitterness in his heart and a song on his lips.

Upon his return to Osnabrück he reluctantly agreed to accept what was to be his last teaching position. Once again it was a substitute assignment for an ill teacher. But this time there was no complaint about the school's location because the job was at Nahne on the outskirts of Osnabrück. He had asked to be considered for a position near home. Nahne was an island of tranquility in comparison with Klein-Berssen and Remarque was able to enjoy all the attractions of his hometown. The job, however, lasted only from August 20 to November 20, 1920. Shortly after his release from the Nahne assignment he requested of the school authorities in Osnabrück that he not be considered for any further teaching assignments. On December 12 he received their written agreement to his request. A short time later, on December 17, he received from the school authorities a less welcome communication. This was a reprimand given because of the overall tone used by Remarque in his correspondence with school officials during the Brand controversy. A disciplinary code dating from 1852 served as the basis for the reprimand. This was indeed the last straw for Remarque. As a postscript to his short-lived and ill-fated teaching career it should be noted that in 1922 Osnabrück authorities wanted him to return to teaching. However, at that time he was employed in Hannover by the Continental Rubber Company. On November 16 he wrote a letter to school officials in Osnabrück in which he declined their offer and expanded upon his position and responsibilities with Continental. It is obvious that he relished the opportunity to let them know, by implication, that his career had transcended the possibility of accepting job offers from local school boards.

Remarque's rejection of teaching as a profession had been decided by him even before his abortive career began. He never really wanted to be a teacher and made the choice originally only because he wanted to please his parents and because nothing better offered itself. The nature of the teaching positions offered him and the Brand controversy were also decisive factors. However, if one judges by the evidence in *Der Weg zurück* the truly persuasive reason might be the teacher's disillusionment as a result of his war experiences.

In the book the young teacher Ernst Birkholz expresses himself on the validity of what he has to teach his young charges in a manner which is often overly melodramatic. The following quotation is a typical example of the way in which he "preaches" about his strongly-felt beliefs.

> "Morning comes. I go to my class. There sit the little ones with folded arms. In their eyes is still all the shy astonishment of the childish years. They look up at me so trustingly, so believingly—and suddenly I get a spasm over the heart.
>
> Here I stand before you, one of the hundreds of thousands of bankrupt men in whom the war destroyed every belief and almost every strength. Here I stand before you, and see how much more alive,

how much more rooted in life you are than I. Here I stand and must now be your teacher and guide. What should I teach you? Should I tell you that in twenty years you will be dried-up and crippled, maimed in your freest impulses, all pressed mercilessly into the selfsame mould? Should I tell you that all learning, all culture, all science is nothing but hideous mockery, so long as mankind makes war in the name of God and humanity with gas, iron, explosive and fire? What should I teach you then, you little creatures who alone have remained unspotted by the terrible years?

What am I able to teach you then? Should I tell you how to pull the string of a hand grenade, how best to throw it at a human being? Should I show you how to stab a man with a bayonet, how to fell him with a club, how to slaughter him with a spade? - - - Should I describe to you how brains look when they scatter about? What crushed bones are like—and intestines when they pour out? Should I mimic how a man with a stomach wound will groan, how one with a lung wound gurgles and one with a head wound whistles? More I do not know. More I have not learned. - - -

Should I explain to you that the books you hold in your hands are but nets with which men design to snare your simple souls, to entangle you in the undergrowth of fine phrases, and in the barbed wire of falsified ideas?

I stand here before you, a polluted, a guilty man and can only implore you ever to remain as you are, never to suffer the bright light of your childhood to be misused as a blow flame of hate. About your brows still blows the breath of innocence. How then should I presume to teach you? Behind me, still pursuing, are the bloody years. - - How then can I venture among you? Must I not first become a man again myself?"[3]

It appears very unlikely that Remarque identified with young Ernst Birkholz to the extent that he had to "become a man again" before he could presume to teach. The really compelling reason for turning away from teaching was his overriding interest in a literary career.

6

The Hand-to-Mouth Years

Even though Remarque's pedagogical career had come to a close, his literary career was advancing. Nineteen twenty had been a particularly good year for him in this respect. Although the monetary return from his published pieces was so small as to be almost non-existent, the satisfaction he got from seeing them in print was encouragement indeed. The major publication of course was the first novel *Die Traumbude* which depicted the romantic idealists of the Hörstemeier Circle. Following this, an early poem, "Abendlied" (Evening Song), was published in a local paper, the *Osnabrücker Tageblatt*. Other poems, "Cis moll" (C Sharp Minor) and "Nocturne", appeared in *Die Schönheit* and *Jugend* respectively. Although the titles of the last two poems are indicative of his musical interests, they are without apparent significance because the poems are love poems. A much more interesting publication was an essay, "Natur und Kunstwerk" (Nature and Work(s) of Art), which appeared in *Die Schönheit*. In this piece Remarque elaborated on his belief that a work of art has to transcend mere imitation of nature.

In 1921 Remarque had "Flieder" (Lilacs) published in *Die Schönheit*. This is the only work he is known to have published in that year. It was a time in which he was growing increasingly apprehensive concerning his prospects for literary success. It is known that Remarque sent poems to the Austrian writer Stefan Zweig for his critical judgment. The letter which accompanied the poems had a tone of desperation as Remarque implored Zweig "remember that this is a matter of life and death for me."[1] Remarque received a gracious response but apparently nothing more concrete at that time. Eight years later, after the success of *Im Westen nichts Neues*, he had occasion to call on Zweig's help in making arrangements for the translation of the novel into French. Zweig was very helpful and Remarque wrote to express his appreciation.

The insecurity felt by Remarque in his literary career in 1921 was in part also a reflection of the uncertainty of his economic situation. It was the worst possible time for him to assert his independence by giving up teaching. Inflation in Germany was in full swing with the attendant loss of the Mark's purchasing power. Unemployment was widespread and Remarque brought few special skills to the job market. For a while he eked out a marginal existence by peddling cloth out of a suitcase. He also occasionally contributed art, theatre, and music reviews to the *Osnabrücker Landeszeitung*. The income, if any, from this source was certainly negligible.

In the 1921–22 period his musical talent enabled him to obtain an interesting, and more rewarding part-time job. On Sundays he played the organ for religious services at the Michaelis Chapel of the state mental institution. The "Landeskrankenhaus" (state hospital) then as now was located just outside of Osnabrück on the gently rising hills of the Gertrudenberg. In exchange for his musical contributions Remarque received a very small amount of money and, more importantly, a good Sunday meal with wine. As a bonus there was the good company and friendship of his dinner companion Father Biedenieck. In 1956 Remarque published a novel *Der schwarze Obelisk* (*The Black Obelisk*) in which he goes into this relationship at some length. In the novel the priest's name is changed slightly to Bodendieck. *Der schwarze Obelisk* is in many ways the most directly autobiographical of his novels. This is certainly true in what we learn of Remarque's postwar life in Osnabrück. The economic difficulties of life in Germany during the inflation period may have been hard to cope with but they did provide a rich source of novelistic material.

The novel's title alludes to the most expensive item in the inventory of the Kroll stone-cutting and grave stone company.

The Remarque protagonist, named Ludwig Bodmer, is employed by Kroll Brothers as a salesman and factotum. The fictional "Kroll Brothers" actually represent the Vogt Brothers, a stone-cutting and grave stone company located at Süsterstrasse 2 in Osnabrück by whom Remarque was employed in 1922. This was the most satisfying and lucrative job he held before he left his hometown. Even with the uncertainties and near privation of the time it was a period to which Remarque obviously looked back with much fondness. The rollicking, humorous, and often bawdy novel is partly a nostalgic tribute to the way things were and partly to the way they should have been if life were always like an interesting novel. The work captures perfectly the gallows humor which helped Remarque to survive this difficult time and which sustained him all his life.

Specific information about Remarque's relationships with women at this time is almost impossible to obtain. One enigmatic relationship finds fascinating expression in *Der schwarze Obelisk*. On one of his trips to the insane asylum he met a lovely girl whom he called in the novel Genevieve. Genevieve was a schizophrenic who could move abruptly from one personality to another. When he saw her Ludwig Bodmer (Remarque) never knew whether he would encounter Isabelle, the appealing personality to whom he was strongly attracted, or Jennie, distrustful, unpleasant, and sometimes lewd. Ludwig eventually fell in love with Isabelle who perceived the world in a fresh and delightful way. Unfortunately when her doctor succeeded in curing Genevieve's schizophrenia he, by necessity, also exorcised the charming Isabelle. All that remained was the pleasantly innocuous Genevieve to whom Ludwig no longer meant anything. The reader is intrigued by the mercurial personality of Isabelle and impressed by Ludwig's obvious affection and concern for her. It is frustrating that nothing can be discovered concerning the identity of this fascinating girl who was obviously so important to Remarque. Before he wrote *Der schwarze Obelisk* he had thought seriously about doing a novel dealing solely with Genevieve. However, he thought such a treatment would be too static without sufficient interest to sustain an entire novel. He therefore decided to incorporate this haunting love story in his novel about the early part of his life.[2]

In his retrospective view of life in the Osnabrück of 1923 Remarque had a lot of fun at the expense of local poetic types. The 59-year old successful author obviously had a much more relaxed attitude about things creative than did the young man who wrote so beseechingly to Stefan Zweig for assistance. It will be seen on closer examination, however, that while fun is made of the poetic efforts and posturings of the unintentionally comedic members of the "Werdenbrück Poets' Club" the Remarque character Bodmer escapes relatively unscathed. It is apparent though that Bodmer gives himself no airs in regard to his own literary efforts.

> On the table lies a yellow portfolio with the poems I have pecked out in triplicate on the Erike typewriter. From time to time I send a few of these to the newspapers. They either come back or there is no answer; then I peck out new copies and try again. I have only twice succeeded in publishing anything in our local newspaper, and then, to be sure, with Georg's help, for he knows the editor. Nevertheless, that was enough for me to be made a member of the Werdenbrück Poets' Club, which meets each week at Eduard Knobloch's in the Old German Room.- - -[3]
>
> I push the poems aside. They suddenly seem to me flat and childish, typical of the attempts almost every young man makes at one time or another. I began to write during the war, but then it made some sense—for minutes at a time it took me away from what I was seeing. It was like a little hut of protest and of belief that something else existed beyond destruction and death. But that was a long time ago; today I know that there exists a great deal more besides and I even know that both can exist simultaneously. I no longer need my poems for that; in the books on my shelf it has all been said much better and more convincingly. But what would become of us if that were a reason for giving something up? Where should we all be? So I go on writing, though what I write often seems gray and wooden in comparison with the evening sky which is now growing spacious and apple green above the roofs while twilight fills the streets with a drift of violet-colored ashes.[4]

At the conclusion of *Der schwarze Obelisk* Ludwig Bodmer departed Osnabrück at inflation's end for a job on a Berlin newspaper. In Remarque's own case the Berlin employment was preceded by three years in Hannover.

7

The Young "Conti" Editor in Hannover

While carrying out a variety of jobs for Vogt Brothers in 1922 Remarque made contacts at the Continental Rubber Company in Hannover. As a result of these contacts he was encouraged to apply for employment on the company magazine *Echo Continental*. On the strength of his ideas, and the sample work he submitted, Continental offered him a position as editor and publicity manager. Remarque wasted no time in accepting this long-awaited opportunity. In October of 1922 he made the move to Hannover where he took up residence at Nikolaistrasse 11. With this move he put Osnabrück behind him. He was never to reside there again for an extended period although he did return for visits and once even to find seclusion for work on a novel.

It is impossible to obtain complete information concerning his work for *Echo Continental* because allied bombing raids during the second world war, and the fires resulting from those bombings, destroyed the Continental archives which contained company records and copies of *Echo Continental*. Fortunately the company was able to buy some copies of the magazine from private owners which enabled them to make a start at rebuilding the archives. Among the acquisitions were copies of 1923 and 1924 issues for which Remarque was editor and contributor.

In addition to carrying out his editorial responsibilities for *Echo Continental* Remarque had new opportunities to make use of his poetic talent. However, the product of his poetic efforts in the commercial interests of the Continental Rubber Company was entirely different from the sentimental poetry he had hitherto published.

In 1923 he initiated two cartoon strips in the *Echo Continental*. The first of these was a six-picture-panel cartoon depicting specific adventures of the "Contibuben" (the Conti-nental rascals). Their comic misdeeds appear to have been patterned after the Max and Moritz characters. Their misadventures, however, were short-lived because this cartoon appeared only twice. The first appearance, labeled "Der Contibuben erster Streich" ("The first prank of the Conti-rascals") dealt with the boys' use of a cylinder of compressed air to inflate not only tires but a dog which then balloons up and floats around until it gradually deflates and returns to earth. The second and final episode deals with the boys' wild ride in a sport roadster during which a pile of four tires secured to the back of the careening car comes loose and causes havoc among nearby pedestrians. The policeman Krause at the scene has to make a judgment regarding the damage done. However, he arrives at the decision that: "This is no accident, and no life has been lost, because the two boys are driving on "Conticords"[1] (Continental Cord Tires). Although the lines of doggerel verse which serve as captions for the drawings are often amusing and sometimes cleverly done, on the whole it is a rather lame effort. The credit indication for the cartoons is "E.M.R." in the lower righthand corner. It is apparent from these initials that Remarque had by this time adopted "Maria" as a middle name. This must have come with the move to Hannover because there is no evidence of the name prior to this time.

A second cartoon series which began after the aborted "Contibuben" venture proved to be very popular with *Echo Continental's* readers. Once again Remarque supplied the same type of verse. This time he appeared to warm a bit more to the task and produced some delightful, and occasionally outrageous, verse. The subject of the cartoon series was Kapitän (Captain) Hein Priemke, a crusty old sea captain who soon captured the affection of the readers and became a familiar symbol of Continental Rubber. In each issue the strip worked in a commercial message for a different item manufactured by Continental Rubber. The products mentioned included inflatable rubber boats, water hoses, tennis balls, rubber squeeze bulbs for spray atomizers, automobile tires, bicycle tires, coats, and bathing caps. The blatantly commercial purpose of the cartoons is not offensive, however, because of the nonsensical fun of Captain Priemke's adventure.

A good example of the skillful way in which Remarque combines the sales pitch with humour is Captain Priemke's "fourth adventure". In this cartoon Priemke considers marriage with a spinster named Friederike who is almost as corpulent as he. Before they become engaged she suggests that they can test their love and she can give him her answer in the seclusion of their retreat. While at the resort they go swimming together. A large wave strikes them and Priemke is horrified to see floating on the water a wig which, a moment before, had been on the now bald head of Friederike. A prose translation of the verse will suffice to capture the meaning, but unfortunately not the charm, of the last twelve lines as Hein Priemke makes his personal decision and also delivers the Continental message.

> "Then Hein cries out in wild horror
> 'Friederike, it is all over!'
> Then he swore to himself upon the spot:
> You will remain a bachelor forever!
> Just think: if the old frump
> Had had a Conti bathing cap,
> This sort of thing would never
> Have happened to her.
> And I would have been conned!
> Conti bathing caps stay in place whether
> The wind is blowing from the East, North, or West—
> 'Girls, if you want a man to believe,
> Wear Conti-caps while swimming!' "[2]

Six of Priemke's adventures were published in 1923 and ten in 1924. Curiously, the first adventure was labeled the second.

The reason for this is unknown. If the first adventure ever existed it was never published in *Echo Continental*. In Priemke's last adventure, labeled as such, he returns with his Melanesian friend Okuhahayn, a cannibal chief who appeared in 14 of the series, to Okuhahayn's island home to open a dealership for Continental tires. When Okuhahayn and Priemke are last seen business is flourishing because of the high quality of Continental products and service. The first basic principle of their business is "Immerfort der Conti treu!" (Eternally faithful to Conti!).

The first article Remarque wrote for *Echo Continental* in 1923 was entitled "Wenn der Frühling in die Lande zieht—" ("When Spring Comes to the Country"). After the introductory sentences "A beautiful lady on a beautiful spring day received two beautiful letters. One of them read as follows:"[3] the article continued with a letter from a bicyclist extolling the pleasures of bicycle riding in the wonderful spring weather and enumerating its advantages over automobiles for certain kinds of nature outings. Strangely enough, the name of Continental bicycle tires soon finds its way into the "letter". The second part of the article, the second "letter", makes its predictable points about the advantages and joys of automobile travel, naturally on Continental tires.

A more interesting 1923 prose effort, this time signed "que" and not "E.M.R.", is a fairly short, three-column essay entitled "Reklame und Händler" ("Advertising and Dealers"). In this piece the 25-year old editor, and newly-fledged publicist, sets out to instruct Continental dealers and other readers concerning the advantages gained by dealers and the public from advertising. A translation of the first paragraph will suffice to show the basic content.

"Already repeatedly proof has been provided for the fact that an article is not made more expensive because of advertising but on the contrary is made cheaper. The lay opinion that the advertising costs are added to the production costs and thus make the article more expensive is correct only in the supposition and not in actuality. Goal-oriented advertising always has as a result increased demand and, because of that, increased sales. In this way business costs are distributed to a greater number and manufacturing costs are reduced."[4]

It can only be speculated as to why Remarque felt the necessity to include such editorial comment. The most likely explanation appears to be that he had reason to believe that dealers of Continental products needed reassurance the large company advertising ventures, and *Echo Continental* for that matter, were worth the money expended. There is no indication as to whether Remarque's rather simplistic economic theories served as more than a space filler. His article is, however, strong evidence that Remarque did not lack confidence in expressing his views. He was obviously also protecting his own economic interests. It should be remembered that Remarque was in charge of advertising and publicity in addition to his editorial duties. The magazine gives the reader an idea of the scope of those duties with its succinct statement "Verantwortlich für den gesamten Inhalt: Erich Maria Remarque ("responsible for the entire content: Erich Maria Remarque").

The final 1923 advertising essay he wrote was a two-page piece called "Sport Ferien" ("Sports Vacation"). With a very light, often lyrical, touch he mentions various vacation pursuits ranging from cycling to boating. At the appropriate places the reader will once again see, printed in bold type, the names of various Continental products, the use of which would make the described vacation pursuits safer and/or more pleasureable. This essay was signed "que".

The years in Hannover were good ones for Remarque. After putting behind him the somewhat provincial atmosphere of Osnabrück his ambitious nature thrived on the new responsibilities. He was also pleased with the diversity of cultural interests offered by Hannover. However, cultural diversions were not the only interests which made life interesting for him. Remarque was a very popular man among the ladies. His blonde good looks, combined with an attitude which could be intriguingly aloof and solitary or boyishly charming and gregarious, made him quite appealing to women.

Although the circumstances of their meeting are uncertain, it was in Hannover that Remarque met, and became attracted to, Jutta Ilse Ingeborg Ellen Zambona who was later to become his wife. She was a divorcée who had reportedly been married to an industrialist named Winkelhoff.

His personal literary efforts almost came to a standstill during the Hannover period. The only thing he is known to have had published in a journal other than *Echo Continental* was a poem "Einer Frau" ("To a Woman") which appeared in *Die Schönheit* in 1923. "Einer Frau" has further significance in that it was the last thing he had published in *Die Schönheit* and also the last known poem he had published. From this date he apparently reserved his love poems for his lady of the moment. It is a shame for the Remarque literary legacy because a more mature Remarque, with more to offer than the youthful romantic lyricist, might have given an extra dimension to his legacy of starkly realistic narrative fiction.

Remarque took advantage of every opportunity for travel which his job required or which he could possibly justify. He had always loved to travel and now had the perfect excuse to combine his professional concerns for the promotion of Continental products with pleasurable trips to European automobile races, sporting events, and resorts. Accounts as to where his travels took him vary somewhat but there is agreement that while he worked for Continental he traveled in Italy, France, Switzerland, the Balkans, and Turkey.

There is no doubt, however, concerning Remarque's style of travel. He was a man who believed in going first class whenever circumstances permitted. Moreover, he always managed to do it with style and flair. Remarque, the consummate man of the world, established his credentials early, particularly because he was traveling on his employer's money.

Remarque worked for Continental until the beginning of 1925. By this time he was recognized as a capable and imaginative editor. With the knowledge he had gained in Hannover, and with the contacts he had made elsewhere, he was ready for a career move. It is very likely that his relationship with Jutta Zambona, and her wishes in the matter, played a significant role in his decision to leave Hannover for Berlin. However, Berlin itself, the most vital and exciting German city of the time, was the magnet. To Remarque real success had to be achieved in Berlin. And Remarque was eager for success and recognition.

Although Remarque's parting from Continental appears to have been amicable, some question is raised by a later event which would seem to reflect doubt on that amicability. In October, 1971 the Continental Rubber Company celebrated its 100th anniversary and asked Remarque to write a short greeting in honor of the occasion. Instead of the expected agreement, the company was surprised to receive a rather curt refusal of the invitation. Remarque commented that this period of time was not one of those upon which he looked back fondly. On the face of it, his refusal seems rather peevish and petty. However valid his reasons may have been, former editor Remarque had unfortunately gotten away from his own slogan which he wrote for Captain Priemke 47 years earlier: "Eternally faithful to Conti".

8

Up the Ladder of Success in Berlin

In 1925 Remarque became picture editor of the Scherl Publishing House's weekly magazine *Sport im Bild* (*Sport(s) in Picture(s)*). In many ways the work was almost a continuation of what he had done in Hannover. He was not huckstering products but he was dealing with sports and sports personalities and many of these were persons he had known at Continental.

One of the most interesting was Rudolf Caracciola, the German and European racing car champion whom Remarque greatly admired. Remarque himself was not only a racing car buff but a very capable driver who loved the excitement of high-speed competition. He was more than just a talented amateur for he had logged a great number of hours test driving cars equipped with Continental tires under all sorts of weather conditions and terrain. This activity was frequently much more to his liking than editorial chores. So when Remarque and Caracciola set off on one of their racing car jaunts Remarque was impressed but not overawed by the driving skills of his illustrious companion. He and Caracciola hit it off famously with a mutual appreciation and friendship which continued until Caracciola's death in 1959.

Remarque was in his element in Berlin. The brash vitality of the city and its wide range of intellectual, cultural, and sensual activities were tremendously appealing and stimulating for him. It was an exciting city and an exciting time. Berlin attracted many of the most talented people in all fields from all of Germany and Central Europe. Berlin was where important things were happening. Success in Berlin was seen as true success. For the first time in his life Remarque felt that he was in a place and situation in which he could achieve real success. It only remained to find the vehicle for that success.

When Remarque joined the ranks of the Berlin journalists he fitted in perfectly with that aggressive and cliquish group. The camaraderie and the socializing were pleasant fringe benefits of the job. Long "editorial" conferences at favorite Berlin cafes were the usual practice. The Cafe Jädicke on Kochstrasse was one of the haunts of editors from the Ullstein and Scherl publishing houses. More popular were "Das Romanische Cafe" on Tauentzienstrasse and Viktor Schwannecke's Cafe on Rankestrasse. "Das Romanische Cafe" was rather staid whereas Schwannecke's establishment had a pronounced theatrical flavor in keeping with Viktor Schwannecke's own theatrical past. Remarque not only patronized those clubs but also a number of other favorites, among them the "Film Club."

It is difficult to determine whether Remarque's lifelong fondness for drinking establishments was due principally to his love of drinking or his desire for conviviality. Perhaps it is not necessary to make a decision because both of those loves were essential for him. During the early days in Berlin there was also a third reason. The young and ambitious Remarque was hungry to be a part of everything and eager to make as many contacts as possible. In his view, the clubs, cafes, and bars of Berlin were excellent places not only for the pursuit of pleasure but also to become known by people who might further his ambitions.

Remarque was very much a young man in a hurry. Because of that fact he occasionally did things which in retrospect appear bizarre. Perhaps the most bizarre occurred rather early in his Berlin career and brings to mind the controversy regarding Remarque's uniform and military decorations in Osnabrück after the war. With the first sizeable amount of money he was able to accumulate, 500 marks, he made a financial agreement with an impoverished Rittmeister (Cavalry Captain), a certain Freiherr (Baron) von Buchwald, to be adopted by him. The only known advantage Remarque gained from this pitiful transaction was the right to add to his calling cards the distinctive five-pronged, pearl-tipped, crown indicative of nobility before 1800. After 1800 seven pearl-tipped prongs were used. For Freiherr von Buchwald the business agreement may not have been quite as demeaning as it appears. The chances are good that his own title may have been acquired originally by an exchange of money and/or the recognition of commercial success which translated into family elevation to the lowest rank of the nobility. It is, however, a sad commentary on the state of the former nobility, and the venality of the times, that such a bargain could be struck. With his new, if spurious, credentials Remarque, monocle in place, was a striking figure in the lower reaches of Berlin society. He maintained this role until after the appearance of *Im Westen nichts Neues*. Even at that time Remarque was still registered at the police station in Berlin-Wilmersdorf as "Ehemann (married man) Erich Freiherr von Buchwald gen. (named) Remark."[1] Remarque's use of the title appears to have ended when he achieved real success and was less dependent on posturing for his ego satisfaction.

The highly visible Remarque who delighted in, and required, the pleasures of cafe and cabaret society should not be allowed to obscure the serious, intensely private Remarque. This Remarque, beneath the veneer of cynicism of the often disillusioned romantic, was a man of deeply-held convictions for whom close personal relationships were very important.

His most important relationship in the Berlin period was with Jutta Ilse (Jeanne) Zambona who had come to Berlin with him from Hannover where they had met. They shared the same address in the Berlin suburb of Charlottenburg, Kaiserdamm 114, at the time of their marriage. On October 14, 1925 they appeared before the magistrate Kossarann at the Charlottenburg registry to request that a civil marriage be performed. They were accompanied by two friends who served as witnesses, Werner Hemminghaus and Viktor Greiner. Hemminghaus, who was 37 years old, was a merchant in Hannover. Greiner was a civil servant in Charlottenburg. The short wedding ceremony was disposed of expeditiously and efficiently by the magistrate under the authority of the civil code. It is characteristic of Remarque that the important events in his life were carried out with dispatch whereas trivialities could be elevated to ceremonial occasions. In the case of the marriage, however, personal taste may not have entered into the matter. Because of Remarque's negative attitude toward the Roman Catholic Church he would have had no interest in a church wedding. And certainly the fact that Jeanne was a divorcée would have ruled out a religious ceremony. The simplicity of the ceremony did not really matter. It was simply a confirmation of the love they had for each other.

In the early days their life together was financially very difficult, but very happy. Jeanne had given up a financially secure existence with her industrialist husband Winkelhoff apparently because of her love for Remarque. However, "Johannes", Remarque's pet name for her, and Erich both regarded those early financial deprivations as temporary. The Remarques were attractive people who had many friends, shared the same basic outlook on life, and had a resilience which allowed them to cope with adversity. Because of the contacts offered by Remarque's journalistic position, and with the new direction his own writing was taking, there was much reason to hope for improvement in regard to the material things which were very important to both of them. Berlin, then as now, was a city in which everything was available for a price. It was a delightful place for the affluent but it was a hard place to survive for those less fortunate. Fortunately the Remarques were adaptable.

"Jeanne" Remarque was born Jutta Ilse Ellen Ingeborg Zambona in Hildesheim, Germany on August 28, 1901. She was the daughter of Heinrich Emil Zambona and Antonie Ida Wilhelmine Zambona, née Werges. Jeanne had a full sister Edith and a half sister Hertha. Their family background was Italian and Danish. Jeanne did not speak Danish although she was fluent in German, French, English, and Italian.

Jeanne was a very attractive woman. She had a fair complexion, brown eyes, and reddish-blonde hair. At five feet seven inches, with a weight of 115 pounds, she was fashionably slender. With her good looks, poise, and charm she was striking confirmation of Remarque's good taste in women.

Remarque at this time had established a record as a successful ladies' man. Not only could he be charming but he was relentless in pursuit. Women were intrigued by the handsome blonde and blue-eyed young man who could be, by turns, flirtatious, intellectual, quiet and introspective, or the life of the party. Later, in more affluent times, Remarque had the justified reputation of being an ardent collector of beautiful things, particularly beautiful women. It was always a point of pride with him to be seen only with attractive female companions. In the early days, before the great commercial success of *Im Westen nichts Neues*, there was no reason for suspicion that those female companions were with him for any reason except the enjoyment they had from the relationship.

Although Remarque was no admirer of the institution of matrimony, there can be no doubt that he entered into this first marriage with the enthusiasm of a man really in love. Anyone who has read Remarque's novel *Drei Kameraden* (*Three Comrades*) and is aware that Jeanne was the model for Patricia Hollmann, the female love interest in that most moving of all the Remarque stories, will have no doubt as to the sincerity and depth of that love. Just as with Pat Hollmann, Jeanne had contracted tuberculosis as a result of wartime deprivations. However, in Jeanne's case there was not the same premature tragic death. Pat and Jeanne both typified Remarque's feminine ideal: an attractive, understanding woman who could be both lover and comrade.

The Remarques became increasingly active socially as their financial circumstances permitted and their circle of acquaintances increased. They particularly liked to attend balls and large gala affairs such as the one in Berlin mentioned in *Die Literatur*. This translation of a part of the article describes one of Jeanne Remarque's social triumphs. "The judges of the nightly beauty competition unanimously awarded the first prize to the charming Mrs. Remarque who was the center of attention in a particularly striking backless dress."[2] Remarque must have been pleased because he was very proud of his beautiful wife and liked to show her off.

Although he enjoyed having a high social visibility he never lost sight of the fact that the success for which he was so eager would have to be achieved from his writing. Unfortunately now it was often difficult for him to find the time for his own writing projects. There were no more published romantic poems which were much in evidence in the Osnabrück days. It is likely that he continued writing poetry for his own enjoyment but it was not made available to the public.

A light-hearted prose effort published in *Sport im Bild* in 1927 was more a reflection of his life style than evidence of the serious writer he was to become. The essay *Hymne auf den Cocktail* (Hymn to the Cocktail), formerly entitled *Über das Mixen kostbare Schnäpse* (Concerning the Mixing of Precious Drinks), was a highly descriptive paean of praise of alcohol. In the essay Remarque showed the first literary evidence of his knowledge of bibulous matters which was later to expand with increasing affluence and enthusiastic practice into that of a true connoisseur. Unfortunately he also showed a style which was reminiscent of such earlier efforts as "Ingeborg". Remarque began with a descriptive attempt to establish a mood. "The half light made shimmering rubies, opals, and topazes of the bottles containing the liqueurs. It was captured in the cut of the glasses (and changed) into silvery accents and was swallowed up in the twilight of the corners as in thick carpets. The ladies had the colors of slender flamingos. Lavalette smiled: Opium is a good drug; it tranquillizes and reveals the meaning of things. But one can only smoke it in Saigon and Canton. Everywhere else it is adulterated. Morphine is a matter of tasteless despair and cocaine is an intoxicant for life's dilettantes. They act too abruptly for one to be able to associate style with them. Therefore there remains only the mixing of liqueurs in order, with tact, to make the sensation of an hour more intense. Wine makes the poets speak."

Remarque also waxed increasingly poetic as he went from

general comments to specific information regarding the niceties of blending ingredients to achieve the perfect mixed drink in various categories. In his description the procedure at times had overtones of a ritualistic or even mystical experience.

The sybaritic subject and the foolish pretensiousness of this pot-boiler by the twenty-nine year old author combined to produce a work which later critics of Remarque could scornfully point to as evidence of moral decadence.

Remarque's next published work, also in *Sport im Bild*, was a serialized "automobile novel" which ran for the last three issues of 1927 and the first four issues of 1928. The story, entitled *Station am Horizont* (Station on the Horizon), was quite popular and drew heavily upon his experiences from the period of his employment for Continental Rubber. The work was a literary light-weight and was accurately described by one of Remarque's friends, Christian Krüger, as an "unpretentious novel with first-class radiators and beautiful women".[3] The story was not published in book form.

Fortunately for his personal fortunes, as well as for his place in literary history, his writing at this point was about to take a new more realistic direction. With the new realism came greater authority and credibility and, ultimately, ready acceptance by a world-wide readership. Remarque's writings gained lasting fame only after he moved away from the escapism of the twenties by turning to a starkly realistic style based on past wartime experiences.

9

The Spokesman of a Generation

In the autumn of 1927 Remarque began the actual writing of a story about the war which had been in the back of his mind since his hospital convalescence at Duisburg. The work originally took shape without any definite expectation that it might have commercial prospects. It was simply a book that he felt compelled to write. Remarque was certainly not breaking any new literary ground by choosing the war as a subject. In Germany Ludwig Renn, Arnold Zweig, and other lesser lights, had already enjoyed moderate success with their books about the "Great War."

In a matter of five weeks Remarque completed the episodic novel which was to become the classic war novel with a message transcending national borders. He was fond of saying that the novel wrote itself. If so, the novel was evidently not subject to the same number of revisions as his subsequent works.

For his war novel Remarque, with characteristic irony, chose the title *Im Westen nichts Neues* (*All Quiet on the Western Front*). The phrase had been a standard German army war communique form. The irony is in the fact that there was nothing significant to report on that October day in 1918 when Remarque's protagonist Paul Bäumer met his death. Paul was one of the last survivors in the class of Gymnasium students who had gone into army service together.

When Remarque wrote his war novel he drew not only on his own experiences but also on those of other comrades and war veterans with whom he had discussed the stupidity and horror of the war. Paul Bäumer's first-person narrative, therefore, transcended Remarque's personal story and Bäumer became a kind of "Everyman" protagonist who spoke for all of the young soldiers of his generation.

Remarque's brief introductory statement for the novel made it clear that he was speaking for more than himself:

"This book is to be neither an accusation nor a confession, and least of all an adventure, for death is not an adventure to those who stand face to face with it. It will try simply to tell of a generation of men who, even though they may have escaped its shells, were destroyed by the war."[1]

In a September 22, 1929 interview with Cyrus Brooks of the *New York Times* he discussed his personal experiences and the growing need he had to express those things he had seen during the war:

> "Coming back to Germany after the war was a terrible experience for every one of us. After the strain and hardships of horror of the war we returned to find the country in a state of disintegration, everywhere hunger, depression and bereavement. My own homecoming was overshadowed by the loss of my mother, which was a great blow to me. I had entered the army as a mere boy and was not one of the few lucky ones with a job to come back to, so I had to turn my hand to whatever offered—school teacher, handworker, journalist. I could not settle down to anything, there was a continual restlessness and dissatisfaction that drove me from one job to another." - - - - -
>
> "The truth was, there was something on my mind—the weight of horror and suffering I had seen during the war years. It was still there, unexpressed and chaotic, robbing one of peace of mind, making it impossible to settle down to the ordinary avocations of civilian life. At last—I was on the editorial staff of a Berlin illustrated weekly at the time—I realized that I had to get these things straight in my own mind, to get them into focus once for all.
>
> "The idea of my book came as a sort of safety valve. I came home one night from my work and started to write it. For obvious reasons I adopted the fiction form, but what I put down was the truth. I was not writing for any wide audience; my object was to see clearly the experiences I had been through and therefore I wrote with the utmost simplicity and integrity as though I were telling the story to an intimate friend. I avoided all panegyric and let the terrible facts speak for themselves."[2]

Although the writing had been relatively easy, the task of finding a publisher was considerably more formidable. Remarque, with his usual self-assurance, decided to submit his manuscript to the Samuel Fischer Verlag, one of Germany's most prestigous publishing houses. The Fischer Verlag, in a monumental error of judgement, decided not to publish the manuscript. The reason given was that the public was no longer interested in reading stories about the war. Disappointed but undaunted, Remarque next submitted his manuscript to Ullstein's Propyläen Verlag. Ullstein's acceptance produced a financial bonanza for them.

It had been generally thought that Max Krell, a former head reader for Ullstein, had been responsible for the wise decision to publish *Im Westen nichts Neues*. When Krell died in 1962, and obituaries credited him with this decision, a statement of disclaimer and clarification was made by Heinz Ullstein, the Ullstein firm's business manager. Ullstein pointed out that the person responsible for deciding whether or not to publish a book at that time had been Paul Wiegler not Max Krell. When Remarque submitted the manuscript it was first read by Fritz Ross who enthusiastically recommended to Wiegler that the work be published.

After Wiegler's concurrence it was decided to allow the book to appear first in newspaper serial form in order to build public interest in the prospective book. *Die Vossische Zeitung* ran installments of the story from November 10 to December 9, 1928. These installments proved to be very successful in stimulating reader interest. Remarque's story accounted for the first complete sell-out in the paper's history. Printing of the book began January 31, 1929. By the end of 1929 it had been translated into twelve languages and had sold more than a million and a half copies. It remains one of the greatest commercial successes among German books. At the time of Remarque's death in 1970, 30 to 40 million copies had been sold worldwide.

The initial astonishing success, however, was a very mixed blessing for Remarque. On the positive side, it represented the commercial success and literary recognition that he had always wanted. The lavish praise of such literary luminaries as H. G. Wells, Walther von Molo, William Allen White, Heywood Broun, Christopher Morley, and H. L. Mencken was very heady for the young writer. As a more practical consideration it also meant that anything he wrote for the rest of his life would have a publisher eagerly waiting.

The negative aspects of his newly acquired fame, however, were perplexing and difficult to cope with. In a September 22, 1929 interview with Cyrus Brooks he said: "As for what they call fame, I don't want it. It comes between a man and reality. As soon as you become a celebrity you lose touch with humanity, with life. That is why I live so quietly and keep out of the limelight. I must keep in touch, otherwise I can not write simply and directly for the minds and hearts of ordinary men and women. I want to have a little place in the country and breed dogs."[3]

It was, however, obviously impossible for Remarque to have his wish to avoid the limelight. Beseiged with requests for interviews, lectures, and various types of commercial commitments, Remarque, who had even lost the name plate on his door to souvenir hunters, decided to leave Berlin. He sought to gain a much needed perspective on his situation by taking an extensive driving tour of France. It is interesting to note that during this trip he always registered at inns and hotels under a pseudonym and gave his occupation as "dog breeder".

One of the worst aspects of celebrity status for Remarque was the strain it had put on his friendships. This was particularly bitter for the man who said in *Im Westen nichts Neues* in summarizing the effect of the war on his generation: "But by far the most important was that it awakened in us a strong, practical sense of *esprit de corps*, which in the field developed into the finest thing that arose out of the war—comradeship."[4]

In a 1930 interview with the author Friedrich Hirth, Remarque spoke at some length about the change in some of his friends. During the conversation he said: "What actually happened? Before my 'success' my friends used to greet me joyfully, but now if I announce that I am going to visit them I no longer find myself in the cordial intimacy of long ago—they receive me flanked with a group of unknown people to whom I seem like some curious animal. —Formerly when I returned from a six months' journey, all my friends were glad and gave me a party. Today their sensitivity has no bounds and if I neglect one or another of them, he treats me contemptuously."[5]

As vexing as these changes in his personal relationships were to Remarque, they were later to seem less important in comparison with the abuse he suffered as a result of the vitriolic attacks on him and on his book.

Although Remarque wrote that his novel was not an accusation, it is immediately clear that it is replete with accusations against various targets. Those targets are the groups regarded by him as being responsible for the senseless slaughter of his comrades and for the wretched plight of his country as a result of the war. The indictments, directly or by implication, were made against incompetent military and governmental leadership, war profiteers, and the misguided, chauvinistic teachers who deceived Remarque and his classmates regarding the true nature of the war.

However, at no time did Remarque ever deprecate the German soldier or the soldier-enemy he faced. Remarque's interpretation of comradeship was broad enough to encompass even those men who were his enemies on the battlefield because he realized that they were as much the pawns of their own government's policies as he and his comrades were of the German government.

Because Remarque's popular book had generated such an enthusiastic response from German readers it was immediately seen by ultra-nationalists as a serious threat. The National Socialist Party was violently opposed to the book's anti-war, anti-militarism message. They regarded it as a defeatist document diametrically opposite in tone and content to the propaganda image of the German soldier which they wished to promote.

Almost immediately desperate efforts were made to discredit the book by impeaching the credentials of its author. Groups which had their own reasons for hostility began to spread a number of rumors. One of the stories, which still surfaces occasionally, was that Remarque's real name was Kramer and that he was Jewish. It was also said that he was really 55 years old and had never been at the front. Another rumor claimed that he had reworked the diary of a fallen comrade to produce *Im Westen nichts Neues*. These stories were essentially acts of desperation which did very little to impede the book's progress or lessen its impact. It was true, however, that Remarque's combat experiences were not as impressive as those of his protagonist Paul Bäumer. His credentials, although limited, were nevertheless valid.

The attacks on him persisted. In September, 1929, The German Officers' League, on the basis of a report that Remarque might be awarded the Nobel Prize for literature, wrote to the Nobel Prize Committee to protest in advance any such course of action. Although Remarque was never awarded the Nobel Prize it appears unlikely that the German protest was the sole reason.

Among the most literate and imaginative of Remarque's individual critics was Dr. Salomo Friedländer who, in 1929, wrote a book entitled *Hat Remarque wirklich gelebt?* (*Did Remarque Really Live?*) This effort was written under his pseudonym "Mynona", a reversal of "anonym" which translates as "anonymous". By selectively quoting persons who had known Remarque, and by using material out of context, he managed to present a distorted view of Remarque and his work which still bedevils Remarque's memory. Friedländer, however, apparently was motivated less by pure malice than by a desire to maintain his position as a popular satirist and devil's advocate. He was able skillfully to exploit much of the ambiguity surrounding the new celebrity.

Other treatments were far more vitriolic. In retrospect it is somewhat difficult to understand how this book, whose message is now almost universally acceptable, could cause such bitter controversy. However, the book's success left dozens of published attacks in its wake. Among the most interesting were Wilhelm Müller-Scheld's 1929 essay *"Im Westen nichts Neues,* eine Täuschung" (*"All Quiet on the Western Front*: a Deception"), Gottfried Nickel's *"Im Westen nichts Neues,* und sein wahrer Sinn; eine Betrachtung über den Pazifismus und Antwort an Remarque" ("All Quiet on the Western Front, and its true meaning; a consideration of pacifism and answer to Remarque"), also written in 1929, and, finally, Peter Kropp's 1930 interesting, but shorter, essay "Endlich Klarheit über Remarque und sein Buch" *Im Westen nichts Neues*" ("Clarity at last Concerning Remarque and his Book: *All Quiet on the Westen Front*").

Just when it seemed that Remarque's critics had exhausted almost every possibility for abuse, as well as general silliness, the literary periodical *Die Literatur* reported contributions pro and con in the "screaming horse" controversy. The controversy developed when issue was taken with Remarque's description of horses screaming in pain as a result of war injuries. His critics said horses did not scream. The last word, however, was had by a Czech veterinarian, a Dr. E. Januschke, who reported: "In response to my inquiry, several of my veterinarian colleagues, who served in the war as veterinarians or as frontline officers, have told me that they have often heard severely wounded horses scream frightfully."[6]

Among those German authors who had already written books dealing with the war, only one, Arnold Zweig, who had written *Der Streit um den Sergeanten Grischa* in 1927, had his nose put seriously out of joint by Remarque's overwhelming success. Harry Kessler in his book, *In the Twenties*, makes some revealing comments about Zweig's reactions. In Kessler's journal entry for Friday, August 30, 1929 he indicated that "Zweig has accused him (Remarque) of being slappdash, but Zweig's artistry comes between his book and the reader, whereas he (Remarque) is only concerned to get close to the reader."[7] Kessler presents Zweig in a very unflattering light later in the same entry.

"Dinner at the Hugo Simons. Arnold Zweig was there and, pretending to present bouquets, was venomous about Remarque. As if someone had attacked the latter, though everyone was singing his praises, he said, 'No, no it's a good book', the word 'good' being pronounced with condescension. 'Remarque is a "good" amateur and he could even have turned his book into a great novel. His amateurism lies precisely in having failed to see the angle from which he should have tackled his subject. He lit on it, but passed it blindly by. There, where he describes the farmer's lad who can't stand the war any more when he sees the trees in blossom and thereupon runs away. That is where I would have started the story and centered everything else around this boy. Then it would have become a great book.' Altogether Zweig was at pains throughout the evening to prove himself maliciously witty. As he has only the malice and not the wit, the upshot was merely excessively tedious literary tittle-tattle."[8]

Rudolf Binding, another German author who wrote about the war on the basis of his personal experience, also had some reservations about Remarque. Binding had served in combat and as a cavalry officer. His literary treatment of the war gave it a nobility and glory that Remarque's book obviously did not. Binding had the outlook characteristic of the officer corps. Although Remarque's approach was not compatible with his own views, Binding did not really question the overall accuracy of the events depicted. However, he appears to have been quite disturbed by the fact that a man who wrote such trivia items as "Über das Mixen kostbarer Schnäpse" for publisher Paul Steegemann's "snob journal"[9] *Störtebeker* would have the audacity to approach a subject as sacrosanct as the war was for Binding. Binding also was on the side of those Remarque critics who maintained that wounded horses do not scream. Because of Binding's extensive experiences with horses as a cavalry officer, horse breeder, race rider, and para-professional veterinarian, his opinion has to be carefully considered. As reported in *Der Spiegel*, Binding stated: "Wounded horses do not scream. With almost closed mouths they moan very dully, and barely audibly, through their noses".[10] Debate on this relatively minor point finally ran its course. It ended with each faction still convinced of the correctness of its original view.

The hostility, or opposition, of writers such as Zweig and Binding, as well as niggling technical criticism, had no perceptible impact on the German reading public which was eager to obtain copies of the new literary sensation. Sales of up to 15,000 per day kept seven printing and binding establishments going full-time.

10

Coping with Success

Remarque's sudden success was a bitter-sweet experience. He was prepared neither for the rewards nor for the abuse. The sudden arrival of fame and fortune was a severe test of his character. It was a test which he passed with high marks. It was also an indication of his judgment and strength of character that he decided not to respond to any of the completely unfair and scurrilous attacks on him. He was wise enough to realize that nothing was to be gained, or the slanders corrected, by replying to his critics. Consequently he chose the way of silence. For several months he gave no interviews worthy of the name.

The Living Age for June, 1931 ran an article concerning a rather novel telephone interview with Remarque. The author, W. Duesberg, a neighbor who lived quite near Remarque's Berlin apartment at 5 Wittelsbacherstrasse, dropped in on him one day and sought an interview. Duesburg, who was apparently insensitive to Remarque's discomfort at his visit, reported that Remarque said: "You know, it troubles me to have you here. Let's talk on the telephone and I shall feel much freer." Duesburg continued: "I returned to my house and called Oliva 54-51, and Remarque, who is usually cold and reserved and speaks with lowered eyes, surrendered completely. The telephone gives him courage, for Remarque is incapable of the evasions necessary when callers become too insistent, and a telephone conversation can be ended by simply hanging up the receiver."[1]

Duesburg went on to elicit comments from Remarque concerning his past work experiences. When he stated that Remarque should have a high opinion of himself because of his success, Remarque is quoted as replying:

> "By no means. And I beg you not to believe that I say this from false modesty. I have done nothing unusual. Other war novels are much better than mine, and I should be very happy if, when people saw me, instead of saying, 'Look, there goes Remarque, the author of the famous book,' they would say, 'There's a nice fellow.' My success is due to luck. I do not consider myself in any way an exceptional or superior being. My friends say, 'You're crazy. You ought to thank God for having been so successful.' I can't understand them, and neither do I feel obliged to wear a jubilant expression. Perhaps it will come some day, but at present I am not at all satisfied with myself. . . . When people ask me for interviews I refuse and I shall always do so. In order to talk to others it is necessary to have something to teach them. One thing, however, has given me great pleasure and that is the letters that I have received from everywhere during the last two years. Some of them were very moving. The anonymous ones were the most sincere. I have not been able to open them all and that has made me feel very remorseful. Often I pick up a few at haphazard and answer them. I have also received reliquaries, images of saints from Mexico."[2]

When asked about his plans for the future Remarque indicated that he wanted to "acquire the experience that I lack, and above all, a knowledge of men."[3] More interestingly, Duesburg quoted him as saying: "Perhaps I shall also conquer this terrible timidity that others take for hostility or vanity. For instance, this conversation that we are now holding will make me nervous for two days. Forgive me, but I am really very depressed."[4]

Assuming that Remarque was accurately quoted by Duesburg, his comments about his timidity sound exaggerated enough to have been a put-on of the aggressive Duesburg. It is true, however, that Remarque was by inclination essentially a very private, introspective person. It was certainly true that he favored telephone conversations when dealing with persons not well-known to him because it was easy to terminate such conversations. It is also true that whatever part his shyness or timidity played in his decision not to answer criticism, his enemies chose to regard that silence as further evidence of snobbishness. The irony in their criticism lies in the fact that, in many ways, his great success caused him to be less snobbish.

In addition to refraining from answering criticism he also avoided reading reviews of his novel. Soon after the success of *Im Westen nichts Neues* appeared certain, Remarque took refuge in the Swiss resort of Davos for a vacation. Subsequently Remarque established a pattern of trips to Davos because of Jeanne's health. While he was vacationing in Davos, his publisher Ullstein wrote that all the criticisms of the book were being collected and would be sent to him. Remarque asked them not to do that. A 1930 article by Frederic Lefevre quoted him as saying in regard to those reviews:

> "I was afraid that if I read them at the beginning of my career they would make me proud or uncertain, and that in either case they would throw me off my track.
>
> I have never read a single criticism of my book, any more than I have ever granted a single interview. I am unable to understand why people keep wanting to get statements from me, since the best revelation of my soul is in my book, that book which, as far as I am concerned, has but one advantage—that it made me independent."[5]

In the long run the bothersome and difficult aspects of fame were outweighed by the wonderful awareness that he had achieved financial independence. The first tangible proof of the drastic change in his personal financial fortune came in the form of the payment of 10,000 Marks which he received for the serial publication of his novel in *Die Vossische Zeitung*. The terms of his first contract with Ullstein provided that he was to receive 1,000 Marks a month for a guaranteed period of 24 months. There was also a provision that he was to bear some of the costs of any losses to Ullstein in the publishing of the book. That provision became purely academic when book sales soared.

One thousand copies of the book were printed in Braille and were given free of charge to veterans who had lost their sight as a result of war injuries. It is not known whether Remarque or an Ullstein executive suggested this action. Whoever made the suggestion may have been given the idea by the outpouring of letters from veterans praising the book for its authenticity.

Prior to the publication of *Im Westen nichts Neues* the Ullstein Verlag ran a teaser campaign of advertising with signs pasted on the advertising columns of Berlin. There was a series of four different bold-faced signs. The first week the signs said "Er kommt" ("It is coming"), the second week "Der grosse Kriegsroman" ("The great war novel"), the third week "Im Westen nichts Neues", and the fourth week "Von Erich Maria Remarque" ("By Erich Maria Remarque").[6]

In some of the Ullstein publicity releases for the book Remarque was referred to as a former Lieutenant. Once again the perplexing question is raised. Was Remarque the source of the information or was it carry-over misinformation from another source? In view of the fact that the usual practice would have been to have the author supply, or at least approve, the information, Remarque was very likely responsible for his retroactive "promotion".

In an attempt to tone down any possible negative public reaction to Remarque as a "snob", Ullstein asked him to quit wearing the monocle. He reluctantly agreed. However, the monocle later reappeared occasionally even after he moved to the United States.

Der Spiegel reported that after the book had become an immediate success Paul Steegemann, the publisher of Remarque's earlier "snob" publication "Über das Mixen kostbarer Schnäpse", wrote to Ullstein that he was considering bringing out that essay again. Ullstein got the message and reportedly paid him a compensatory sum for agreeing not to publish.[7]

It was also at this time that Ullstein carried out for their star author a wish which he had cherished since two years after the publication of *Die Traumbude* in 1920. They bought up from Die Schönheit Verlag in Dresden all the copies of that book which they still had in stock. Remarque was delighted by the action which in effect allowed him to wipe almost clean his literary slate and begin with *Im Westen nichts Neues*. Remarque was quoted as saying that *Die Traumbude* would have been cause for suicide if he had not written anything better.[8] Although the continued existence of his first novel might have been the cause of some literary embarrassment, Remarque was soon able to rest easy because Ullstein did a thorough job. Copies of the book are almost impossible to find today.

Im Westen nichts Neues was translated into all of the major languages of the world in a relatively short time. In general the arrangements went smoothly and the translations were good to competent. There were exceptions, however. Perhaps the most amusing, and certainly the most outrageous, translation of his novel was the result of a pirated version in India which underwent several revisions of the first, hopelessly bad, translation. At the end, the finished product no longer bore any resemblance to Remarque's story. It had become a drama of jealousy involving a forester and a poacher.

Pirated editions sprang up in several places. In most cases little could be done. Russia was the worst offender. From 1929 to 1970 Remarque's books were published more than thirty times within the Soviet Union without any royalties being paid. Fortunately for Remarque, these losses of income, as large as they were, were relatively painless in view of his royalty bonanza from non-pirated editions.

11

The Filming of "All Quiet on the Western Front"

The phenomenal success of Remarque's novel, as well as the controversy surrounding it, made it inevitable that Hollywood producers would wish to acquire screen rights to this valuable property. Carl Laemmle, the German-born president of Universal Pictures, wasted no time in going to Germany and purchasing from Ullstein the film rights to the novel. In his first statement after signing the agreement he promised to preserve the unique quality of the book and transfer it to the screen unchanged.

Laemmle met with Remarque on August 10, 1929 in Berlin and was very much impressed by him. During their talk Laemmle proposed that Remarque do the screen play and even play the role of Paul Bäumer if he were interested. Remarque declined the suggestion on the grounds that he was not an actor and because he wanted to get started on his next novel, *Der Weg zurück*.

Laemmle was determined that Universal Pictures' film version of *Im Westen nichts Neues* should be as great a classic as the book. He was astute enough to realize that the unique quality of the book should be transferred to the screen with a minimum of tampering. His son Carl Laemmle, Jr., was to be producer in this enterprise and Lewis Milestone the director. Two celebrated authors were engaged to do the screen adaptation and to write the dialogue. Maxwell Anderson, who had been co-author of the stage play, "What Price Glory?", and George

Abbot, co-author of "Broadway", both wrote dialogue. Anderson did the adaptation and Abbott wrote the screen story.

The role of Paul Bäumer, which was undoubtedly the best male role of the year, went to 20-year-old Lew Ayres. Ayres' prior movie experience consisted of a bit part in one picture and a role as Greta Garbo's young lover in "The Kiss". Ayres requested a test for the Bäumer role and was told two days after the test that the part was his. Other key roles were filled by Louis Wolheim as Katczinsky, John Wray as Himmelstoss, George "Slim" Summerville as Tjaden, Raymond Griffith as Gerard Duval, Ben Alexander as Kemmerich, and William Bakewell as Albert.

In order to simulate the scope of the action described in the book, Universal built a large military camp on the 930 acre Irvine Ranch in Southern California. Twenty acres were dynamited to make an authentic-looking No-Man's land and a network of trenches was constructed under the direction of military veterans. In fact, there were 2,000 film soldiers, largely ex-service men of several countries, who lived under military regulations during the filming.[1]

Battle realism was achieved by the use of more than 20,000 pounds of black powder and tons of dynamite. Six thousand land mines were planted and detonated. Twelve flame throwers were used, as well as twenty German howitzers which had been captured by the American Army. Universal borrowed the howitzers from American Legion Posts which had them displayed as war trophies.

A French village which covered ten acres was built in order to be destroyed in one of the movie's bombardment scenes. A canal, a half mile in length, was dug for the scenes in which Paul and his comrades had a rendezvous with the French girls.

The barracks training scenes were shot at Universal City using exterior sets which were some of the largest ever built up to that time.

The battle scenes shot at the Irvine Ranch involved two thousand men and extended over half a mile. They presented the greatest problem for director Lewis Milestone. Six assistant directors rehearsed the big scenes with the aid of telephones, sirens, pistol shots, and whistles. Former army sergeants were put in charge of individual groups and rehearsed many of the scenes a dozen times before the shooting. An attempt was made to keep use of the megaphone to a minimum. A 280 ton crane, which carried cameras and sound equipment, was used to achieve maximum realism by getting as close as possible to the action.

The critical response to the film was overwhelmingly favorable. Lewis Milestone and Lew Ayres, both relatively unknown, became world-famous almost overnight. Milestone received an Oscar for his direction of the film and there were three other Oscars for writing. The movie also received *Photoplay Magazine's* Gold Medal Award for Best Movie of the Year.

The movie played in many of the major cities of the world to large and responsive crowds. Only in Berlin, the city in which the book was written, was there difficulty during the showing of the film. The trouble began the evening of December 5, 1930. The five o'clock performance had just begun in the Mozartsaal on Nollendorfplatz with hundreds of viewers in attendance when Goebbels' thugs struck. Their intention of producing chaos at the showing was carried out successfully. Young toughs ran through the theatre bellowing "Germany Awake". White mice were released, stench bombs set off, and beer bottles were hurled into the crowd. The inevitable panic ensued. With the help of the police the theatre was finally cleared although the remaining performances for the evening had to be cancelled.

In the wake of the resultant nationwide controversy the film was banned a few weeks later by the authorities "for reasons of the maintenance of safety and public order". Copies of the film were later burned along with Remarque's books at the Berlin book burnings.

"All Quiet on the Western Front" was re-issued in the United States in 1939. This time the film had a pictorial prologue and epilogue. The voice of the narrator broke into the film approximately a dozen times. Unfortunately the editorial tampering with the film, which was done to capitalize on the anti-German spirit of the times, detracted from the film's integrity and impact.

The Germans did not get another opportunity to see the movie until 1952. The first showing took place April 25, 1952 in Berlin. Ullstein also re-issued the book at this time.

12

Enjoying the Good Life

The sudden prosperity produced by his income from the book allowed Remarque the opportunity to adopt the life-style he had formerly only seen others enjoying. He could now really enter the world of affluence he had vicariously experienced in his journalistic assignments and forays into cafe society. Success had been so long in coming that he was determined to make the most of it.

In a 1946 interview with Robert Van Gelder in New York Remarque provided an interesting commentary on the manner in which he chose to deal with his sudden good fortune.

"My father told me,. . . . my father, a good man, told me 'Erich, never lose your ignorance, you can not replace it but you always can become refined.' I have longed . . . for a normal simple life. My friends say, 'Erich, you are so at ease; you know how to accept what comes', which is, of course, not true, though I try to make it seem true, as who does not? Naturally, I make the best of my life, following certain rules. . . . As an example, after I wrote 'All Quiet'—well, you know how fantastic that was. A success—clippings this high in my publisher's office—and for me a completely unexpected success. There are two ways of accepting such fantastic success, such luck. One way is to hoard the windfall, to use it to build on, to use it as a means to bring in yet more money, to base security on it. The other way is to waste it. Of course, that is what I did.

That is what a windfall is for. When it comes one should meet it happily and happily toss it about. What kind of person wants to put out luck at interest? . . . If you met a beautiful woman, a charming girl, the girl you had dreamed about as you sat in bars and walked in the streets and hoped all your life that some day you might meet—what would you do with such a girl? Would you say, 'Come, come home with me and cook my meals?' Oh, no, oh, no, not if you could get some one else to cook, not if you could take her to a fine restaurant, with good service, good wines, good coffee. Neither do you ask luck to cook for you, to supply your daily bread. You waste your luck, you toss it about. There is an old story that life is like a woman, loving a waster and despising a provider. Perhaps it is so."[1]

One of the first things he did with the royalties from his book was to make himself a present of a Lancia Lambda roadster. He had cherished a hope of owning a Lancia since the time he went on writing assignments for the Continental Rubber Company. In the course of those assignments, and because of his friendships with race car drivers, mechanics, and other automotive experts, he became very knowledgeable about cars. Much of his knowledge came from friends on the Mercedes racing team and particularly from the European racing champion, Rudolf Caracciola, who was a special friend. Griffith Borgeson in "Road and Track" quoted Remarque as saying in a 1963 conversation that Caracciola "taught me to handle a spur-cut gearbox properly and how to handle a good car at speed. In the Dilambda I used to love to take on big, supercharged Mercedes on any twisting course and leave them behind. The Lancia's front suspension and roadability were formidable things."[2] Borgeson further reported that Remarque wanted a more powerful car in 1931 and "bought the Dilambda chasis from the Lancia agent in Berlin and commissioned the Cabriolet body to be built by the coachbuilding firm of Voll and Rohrbeck there."[3]

Remarque had a talent for driving which his friends helped him to develop. With his competitive nature and his love of speed and risk-taking he had all the tools to be a very good driver. In addition he enjoyed taking a fast car through its paces on a track or on the road. He particularly enjoyed passing other fast cars on the highway. Cyrus Brooks of *The New York Times* reported a first-hand example of this which he observed during a 1929 interview with Remarque in Berlin. He and Remarque were driving westward down Bismarckstrasse out of Berlin at the time.

> "Nearly abreast of the Funkturm, the Berlin version of the Eiffel Tower, we turned sharp to the left and brought up at the entrance to Herr Stinne's private motoring track, on which for a small fee the speed man can try the paces of his car. In front was a big racer containing two boys in berets.
>
> 'We'll see how they can drive', said Herr Remarque with a mischievous flash of his teeth.
>
> The racer was speeding away in front of us when Remarque opened the throttle of his car and she roared like a bomber airplane taking off. The speedometer needle spun round, 100, 120, 130 kilometers, and remained glued to the end of the dial. Inside of two minutes the boys with the berets were behind us. On Herr Remarque's face was a happy, intent smile. He is a devotee of speed."[4]

It was inevitable that the "devotee of speed" would have his share of accidents despite his skill. In early January of 1930 he drove some friends out to the Avus race track in Berlin. The Bugatti he was driving was going too fast for track conditions when it slid along the wet asphalt and flipped over. Fortunately no one was seriously injured. His friends were shaken up and he injured his nose and right leg. The next reported accident took place July 10, 1931 in the Netherlands in the town of Leyden. There his car knocked over a lamppost. The car was heavily damaged but Remarque's injuries were minor. He paid the equivalent of $48.00 in damages and, to show his appreciation to the Dutch police for their assistance, gave them copies of *Im Westen nichts Neues*. Presumably he carried complimentary copies to smooth his way through minor difficulties.

Remarque's sudden celebrity status made him the darling of cafe society. His presence was much in demand at parties and literary salons. In many ways, however, he was less active socially than he had been before the success of the book. However, he particularly liked to frequent the literary salon of his friend Betty Stern at her home at 16 Barbarossastrasse. Mrs. Stern presided over her salon until she left Berlin to go into exile ahead of the Nazi take-over. Remarque portrayed Mrs. Stern very sympathetically as "Betty Stein" in his last novel *Schatten im Paradies* (*Shadows in Paradise*).

His fame inevitably brought with it the attentions of many desirable women who were greatly attracted to the handsome, 31 year-old Remarque. The fact that he was married did not deter him from taking advantage of many attractive opportunities for "extra-curricular" romance.

It is not possible to determine whether it was because of these affairs, or because of the sudden, radical change in their lives, but Jeanne and Erich were divorced as unceremoniously as they were married. Their divorce was granted in January, 1929. However, it was not generally known until April because Jeanne continued to live at their residence.

Perhaps, given Remarque's nature, the divorce was inevitable. It was, in any case, a very traumatic experience. Nevertheless it was confirmation of Remarque's need to be a free agent. This despite the fact that his love for Jeanne appears to have been the most sincere romantic love of his life. Any reader of his novel *Drei Kameraden* (*Three Comrades*), in which the love interest, Patricia Hollmann, was modeled after Jeanne, has no doubt as to the depth and sincerity of that love.

Undoubtedly much of the blame for the breakup must be attributed to Remarque's independence and need for privacy. He always liked to compartmentalize his loves and friendships in order to ensure himself a time and place for solitude and introspection. This desire led to his later practice of having apartments or hotel suites apart from those of his love interests or his wife. Even though they might be adjoining apartments, or one floor above or below, they were separate enough to make the emotional commitment slightly less than total. Remarque always appeared to be saying: "Although I like you, each of us must maintain his identity."

Even though some of his personal relationships suffered because of his celebrity status and financial success, the new wealth enabled him to acquire a splendid home in Switzerland. Remarque bought the house in 1931 from a man named Meier who had bought it from Hermann Rüdisühli, a Swiss landscape painter. Rüdisühli had bought it from another painter, Arnold Böcklin.

The beautifully situated villa, formerly known as "Casa Monte Tabor" now called "Casa Remarque", offers a spectacular view of lake Maggiore and the surrounding mountains. Located a short distance up the winding road which rises up from the picturesque lake town of Ascona, the villa appears undistinguished when seen from the road. However, the beauty of the terraced side overlooking the lake makes it easy to understand why two painters chose it for their home. Remarque prized it not only for its idylic beauty but also for the privacy it afforded him. It was a sanctuary which he enjoyed and treasured until the end of his life.

13

The Second Book and Film

A combination of pressure from his publisher and his readers, as well as a need to prove to himself and others that he was not just a "one book author", made the writing of a second book inevitable. The challenge of writing another book would also help to distract him from the marital difficulties he was having with Jeanne.

In October of 1929 he placed an anonymous advertisement in an Osnabrück newspaper requesting a quiet apartment. The ad was answered by Frau Maria Hoberg who lived on Johannisstrasse. In November, Remarque and Rudolf Vogt, from the Vogt Brothers' firm for which he formerly worked, came to see Frau Hoberg and inspect the apartment. Remarque was very pleased with his quarters and with the Hobergs. He was particularly pleased to have the anonymity of an Osnabrück sanctuary for his writing.

For a month he remained at the Hobergs working with remarkable persistence on his novel which was not progressing well at all. In contrast with *Im Westen nichts Neues* this was obviously not to be a novel which "wrote itself". After breakfast each day with his landlady he worked until dinner, which he frequently took with his friends the Vogts. In general his working conditions in this temporary, self-imposed exile were as pleasant as he could have wished. However, he fretted over the slow progress of his work and, particularly, the long absence from Jeanne. The marriage even then was in serious trouble. The Osnabrück sojourn was, in effect, a trial separation as well as a period of intense literary activity. Essentially, however, it was an attempt to find solitude by a harried man who realized that he could no longer work in Berlin because of the demands placed upon him.

His second novel was entitled *Der Weg zurück* (*The Road Back*) and in it, as Remarque said in an interview with Wythe Williams in October of 1929, ". . . I describe the way back to life, how a young man like myself—and Paul Bäumer—experienced war as a youth, who still carries its scars and who was then grabbed up by the chaos of the postwar period, (and) finally finds his way into life's harmonies."[1]

In this sequel to *Im Westen nichts Neues* Remarque, having killed off Paul Bäumer, the Remarque-protagonist of the first novel, takes the new protagonist Ernst Birkholz, and his comrades from the final days of combat at the front through the long journey back home to cope with the uncertainties and disillusionments of civilian life. The readjustment to civilian life is a very painful one for Remarque's characters as it was for Remarque. Qualities such as fidelity, bravery, and decency which were highly esteemed by the veterans often appear to be in short supply in a civilian world which neither welcomes the veterans nor understands and appreciates the experiences they have had. Peace claims a price from them which, although different in kind, is almost as great as that exacted by the war. Those men regarded as the finest and best by their comrades often have the most difficult readjustment whereas men who cut a sorry figure during military service, or who were flawed in conduct or character, become quick successes upon their return.

Ernst and his comrades discover to their sorrow that civilian life has an inevitably devaluating effect on the ties of friendship which were developed during the war. Reunions of the group are depressing because they weaken the good memories.

> "In vain do I try to picture all these fellows in dirty uniforms again, and this Konersmann's restaurant as a canteen in the rest area. It cannot be done. The things here are stronger—the things that differentiate us from one another are too powerful. The common interest is no longer decisive. It has broken up already and given place to the interest of the individual. Now and then something will shine through

> from that other time when we all wore the same rig, but already it is dwindled and dim. These others here are still our comrades and yet our comrades no longer—that is what is so sad. All else went west in the war, but comradeship we did believe in; now only to find that what death could not do, life is achieving; it is driving us assunder."[2]

Through the story of Ernst Birkholz and his comrades Remarque provided a realistic, and necessarily gloomy, assessment of the post-war situation for a defeated Germany and its former soldiers. The novel, which is replete with disillusionment, turmoil, suicides, and infidelities, does not offer a new interpretation of the subject of post-war adjustment. As in the case of *Im Westen nichts Neues*, Remarque's treatment of the subject matter of *Der Weg zurück* gives the work its distinction and validity. This moving novel again bears the hallmark of autobiographical authority.

Remarque's first period of work on the novel in his rented apartment at the Hoberg home in Osnabrück lasted from November, 1929 until the early part of December. At that time he felt the need to take a break from his strict writing regimen. It was also necessary to return to Berlin to help settle the final details of his impending divorce from Jeanne.

After their divorce was granted in January of 1930 he and Jeanne traveled together to Switzerland for an extended vacation period in Arosa and Davos. With unconventional behavior of this type it is hardly surprising that news of their divorce was slow in reaching the public.

By summer Remarque was eager to bring *Der Weg zurück* to a conclusion. For that reason he returned to his apartment in Osnabrück and spent eight weeks there completing the novel. Even then he was not competely satisfied with what he had written. Despite that, his own eagerness to be finished with the project and to put an end to pressure from his publishers caused him to submit what he had done.

In the United States the novel ran in serial form in *Collier's* magazine. This original version was even more pessimistic than the later revised version. Suicide terminated the first story and there was also a generally larger content of gloom and doom. Remarque decided to change the ending of his novel and informed his publishers in 21 countries of that fact. In order to make them more amenable to his proposed changes, and the resulting inconvenience to them, he indicated his willingness to cancel contracts and return the advances he had received. However, whatever their degree of annoyance may have been, they were willing to accede to Remarque's wishes rather than ruffle the feelings of their literary luminary. Remarque disappeared from Berlin to work on a different conclusion. He managed to elude the publisher's representatives looking for him until he had time to return with the re-written ending for the novel.

Der Weg zurück fell far short of reaching the success of *Im Westen nichts Neues*. No one really expected that it would. After all, *Im Westen nichts Neues* was a commercial success unparalled in German publishing history. Its sequel was, however, gratifyingly successful. Apart from its intrinsic merit, the book could depend for its sales on the curiosity and eagerness of a readership predisposed to buy another Remarque book. Indeed, after *Im Westen nichts Neues* any book written by Remarque was a guaranteed financial success. Only the degree of success was in doubt.

As usual, however, Remarque was not to be allowed unmixed pleasure in the completion and favorable sales of *Der Weg zurück*. The predictable attacks of those critics and bitter adversaries already incensed by the impact and message of *Im Westen nichts Neues* were immediately forthcoming. In reality, attacks on Remarque had never really ceased.

There were also occasional complications in regard to the marketing of the new novel because some of the language in it was a bit too free and easy for censorship rules in a few countries. The most dramatic example of governmental censorship was the action taken by the Irish Free State which banned the novel, along with works by five other novelists, on June 2, 1931. Apparently it took a while for the linguistic outrages to register on the Irish censors. The story had earlier appeared serially in the Free State. Remarque's novel was in good company, or bad depending on the viewpoint, because works by Louis Bromfield and Knut Hamsun, among others, were also banned.

After the success of the film "All Quiet on the Western Front" it was inevitable that Hollywood would acquire the screen rights to the new book as well. Universal was once again the favored studio. This time, however, there was no rush to film the story. It was really too soon after "All Quiet on the Western Front" to put on the market a film with so many similarities. Universal was obviously in no hurry. There was a period of six years between the book's publication and the appearance of the film in the early summer of 1937.

James Whale directed and produced the film. R. C. Sherriff and Charles Kenyon did the screen play. A generally good cast was headed by John King in the starring role of Ernst. Other important parts were played by Richard Cromwell as Ludwig, Andy Devine as Willy, Spring Byington as Ernst's mother, Noah Beery, Jr. as Wessling, and "Slim" Summerville continued his role of Tjaden from "All Quiet on the Western Front". Although John King and his supporting cast gave creditable performances, the movie was flawed by an unfortunate tendency to slapstick humor not found in Remarque's story. This tendency had actually begun with the semi-comedic portrayal of Tjaden by "Slim" Summerville in "All Quiet". The humor became more heavy-handed in "The Road Back" with the increased emphasis on comedy for Tjaden and the casting of Andy Devine in the role of Willy. With Andy Devine in the part, Remarque's rough-and-ready, bluff Willy inevitably deteriorated into a near buffoon. This approach might have been acceptable for a run-of-the-mill war comedy but was a near-fatal flaw in a work with such a serious theme. However, despite Universal Pictures' unfortunate casting, or more likely because of it, the movie version of "The Road Back" was a commercial success. It can be appreciated as a better than average war film of the period if it is not compared too closely with the novel.

14

Prelude to Exile

At the beginning of 1932 Remarque's literary and financial fortunes were in excellent shape. His personal life was still somewhat unsettled. Since their divorce in January of 1930 he and Jeanne had maintained a relationship which allowed them to be together while at the same time preserving their, chiefly Remarque's, independence. For most of the two years since the divorce they lived together, went out to dinner, to the theatre and to other social events, and even traveled together to Switzerland and Holland. Their trip to Holland obviously gave rise to rumors of a remarriage. *The New York Times* for February 7, 1932 reported that the Remarques were planning a second marriage and intended to live in the Amsterdam suburb of Bussum. The report proved to be completely erroneous. Whatever may have given rise to the report, the Remarques never took up residence in Bussum and were not re-married until six years later.

It is possible that the reported residence in the Netherlands may have had a connection with Remarque's efforts to safeguard his growing wealth. The German government either was taken in by the report and feared it was true or had definite confirmation of a Remarque move. Whichever was the case, in April of 1932 the German government seized Remarque's Berlin bank account of 20,000 Marks and accused him of being in violation of governmental banking regulations. He was charged specifically with establishing a residence in the Netherlands and of banking his book royalties outside Germany. The second charge was certainly true. Remarque had no intention of having all his financial resources at the mercy of a

German government of questionable integrity and stability. The Berlin bank account seized by the government contained a relatively modest sum. The 20,000 Marks amounted at the time to only 4,760 United States dollars. Although the amount was not significant the action was another important step in the growing alienation between Germany and its most popular author.

For over two years Remarque had been the object of scurrilous attacks from many quarters. The very fact of the popularity of his books particularly infuriated the professional officer class and the ultra-nationalists, mainly the National Socialists, who considered him a despicable near-traitor because he had failed to glorify German militarism. Although he had suffered much emotional distress as a result of the attacks, he had managed to cope because of the large outpouring of popular support. His spirits were particularly lifted by the many supportive letters he received from his fellow veterans.

Despite the unpleasantness to which Remarque was frequently subjected it was a long time before he seriously entertained the idea of leaving Germany for anything other than vacation trips. Although he maintained a home in Switzerland, at this time it was still just a vacation retreat for use when pressures at home made it necessary for him to escape for a while. He never thought of himself as other than German. And none of his chauvinistic detractors had a greater love for Germany or a greater awareness of the problems facing her. Although Remarque always claimed he was not a political person he could not avoid being vitally affected by the rapidly changing political situation in Germany.

After the Reichstag election on November 6, 1932 had left Chancellor Franz von Papen without parliamentary support he was forced to resign. The Nazis with their 196 deputies were the largest group of the 584 delegates in the Reichstag. Because they were the most powerful single element in a badly divided Reichstag they were able to bring sufficient pressure to bear to effect the resignation of von Papen. This move, and the subsequent short-lived tenure of General Schleicher, opened the way to a compromise between contending factions which ended in President Hindenburg's appointment of Adolf Hitler as chancellor on January 30, 1933. After the disasterous fire at the Reichstag building on the evening of February 27, 1933 the Nazis capitalized on a questionable confession by a young Dutchman who admitted to being a Communist. It was a very convenient confession from the Nazis' point of view because it had the desired effect of creating a backlash of voter outrage against the Communists. This voter backlash became apparent following the elections a week after the Reichstag fire. In the elections the Nazis gained 92 more delegates. Strengthened by the public resentment against the Communists, the Nazis, through a series of emergency decrees suspending civil liberties and the freedom of the press, succeeded in creating an atmosphere in which it was relatively easy to browbeat opposing politicians and ultimately to bring about an end to the Weimar Republic. The coup de grace was provided when the Reichstag passed Hitler's "Enabling Act". This act gave the government, in effect Hitler, those powers formerly constitutionally held by the Reichstag. Germany was then a dictatorship.

Almost immediately under the new totalitarian regime literary figures such as Remarque, whose works did not conform to the party line, became one of several endangered species in the "New Germany". The barbaric and repressive actions of the Nazis were responsible for a mass exodus from Germany of intellectuals and creative persons in all fields on a scale unparalleled in modern history. It is possible that since Remarque was not a Jew or a Communist he could have made peace with the Nazis if he had chosen to "recant" and agreed to write only "suitable" books in the future. In reality, however, that was an option he never considered. Whatever his shortcomings, Remarque was a man of great integrity and fierce independence. He had no inclination to make peace with, or be subjected to the whims of, the hoodlums who were brutalizing his beloved country. All that was left for him now was to arrange the details of his journey into exile.

15

Exile in Switzerland

Fortunately for Remarque his exile was not to be as traumatic as that of most German writers who were forced to leave their homeland. He had the advantage of having an established summer and vacation residence on Lake Maggiore at Ronco near Ascona. He and Jeanne had been there on vacation as late as July of 1932. In fact, reports in mid-July from the American publisher Little, Brown and Company indicated that Remarque and another German writer, Emil Ludwig, had applied for citizenship in Switzerland. Little, Brown and Company was the American publisher at the time for both Remarque and Ludwig.

Remarque and Jeanne returned to Germany again, however, and the final break did not come until they left Berlin for Switzerland in the early morning hours of January 29, 1933. According to an interview he gave Robert van Gelder on January 27, 1946 he was very fortunate in the timing of his departure. As van Gelder tells it: "Remarque's agent found him one morning at about four o'clock and urged him to go to Switzerland and start work on a new book that he had contracted to write. 'There was fantastic luck again', said Remarque. 'I considered, should I order another drink and then go home to bed, or should I order another drink, get into my car and drive to Switzerland. I decided it would be better if I woke in Switzerland the next day and started work at once than if I slept in Germany and drove to Switzerland the next day. That is why I was in Switzerland when the Nazis came to hunt for me.'

The Nazis would have better served themselves Remarque says, had they followed him into Switzerland and killed him."[1]

It was not enough for the Nazis that Remarque and the majority of other outstanding literary figures had taken leave of Germany. Even in their absence the Nazis continued to berate them. Because they no longer could physically apprehend those writers whom the Nazis regarded as enemies of the state it was thought necessary to carry out a symbolic act of destruction. If the writer could not be seized his works could at least be destroyed. A suitably impressive symbolic display of this type was conceived and orchestrated by the Nazi master propagandist Dr. Josef Goebbels who had a special enmity for Remarque. The time was the night of May 10, 1933 and the location selected for the propaganda show was the square in front of the Berlin Opera House. The actors were Nazi students and assorted Nazi speakers who denounced the authors whose books were being destroyed. After each speaker had vilified the author or authors assigned to him, the books of those authors were thrown into the bonfire. The condemnation of Remarque made by the seventh speaker is typical of the tone of the others: "Against literary betrayal of the soldiers in the world war, and in the name of national education in the spirit of self-defense, I consign to the flames the works of Erich Maria Remarque".[2] At the completion of the propaganda show some twenty thousand books had been burned. This mindless destruction allowed the Nazis to vent their hostility and impotent rage against the objects of their hatred in the only way open to them. However, the Nazis did not appreciate the fact that they had also just given to the rest of the world a frightening and appalling insight into the barbarous mentality of the leaders of the Third Reich.

The book burnings also had another effect not foreseen by the Nazis; that of increasing book sales for those writers whose writings were destroyed. *Time* magazine for October 9, 1933 reported Emil Ludwig's comments in this regard as well as his account of how he and Remarque spent the evening of May 10, 1933.

"At the reception in Manhattan by the American Jewish Congress Dr. Ludwig boasted that the Nazi burning of his books and those of many another Jew and Pacifist, including Erich Maria Remarque, is helping to boost their world sales, quickening the flow of royalty checks to Switzerland where friends Ludwig and Remarque bank their money in gold francs. 'The night of the public burning of the books,' said author Ludwig, 'I invited my friend, Erich Maria Remarque, to drink with me. We opened our oldest Rhine wine, turned on the radio, heard the flames crackling, heard the speeches of the Hitler spokesmen—and drank to the future'."[3]

A Kyle Crichton interview with Remarque which was published in *Colliers* in 1939 has a humorous antecdote concerning an incident which took place the day of the book burning. According to Remarque, Otto Klement, his close friend and personal literary representative, was in his office not far from the Opera House shortly before the "event" was to take place.

"- - -two Storm Troopers presented themselves at Mr. Clement's office and announced that they had been assigned to see that no harm came to him during the sacred ceremony. Presently, they had become bored and asked if they could borrow something to read from the library. He invited them to help themselves. One selected *All Quiet on the Western Front*; the other took Remarque's *The Road Back*.

'They sat reading them,' says Mr. Clement, 'blissfully unaware that the government was burning those books only a stone's throw away'."[4]

Apart from the traumatic effect of enforced absence from his native land, exile held no real fear for Remarque, and only occasional minor inconveniences. Very few of his fellow exiles were as blessed as Remarque with a happy union of financial resources and bright prospects combined with great personal adaptabilty and resiliency. And few of his fellow exiles were more implacable than Remarque in his hatred of the Nazis even though his public statements did not at once mark him as one of the most militant. He was usually careful, however, to make a distinction between Germany and the hated Nazis who were temporarily running her affairs.

Each of the exiles had his own way of continuing the struggle against the Nazis. Many of them had been politically active against the Nazis before the takeover and continued that activity. The Communists, who had been so close to achieving their own takeover of the Weimar Republic, were particularly vitriolic in their attacks. Writers such as Bertolt Brecht and Anna Seghers never let up in their verbal and written assaults on Naziism or forgot their total commitment to international Communism. Many of the exiled writers were relatively incapable of providing any meaningful voice of protest. In most instances they were culturally uprooted, transplanted, and deprived of their reading public as well as their publishers in their new country. Even if new publishers and translators could be found their work would still depend for its success on readers in an alien culture.

Numbered among the elite group of exiles were the fortunate few who were not only commercial successes at home but also enjoyed international reputations. In addition to writers such as Remarque, Franz Werfel, and Stefan Zweig the group included, as its most critically acclaimed member, the estimable Thomas Mann. After his exile travels brought him to the United States, Mann frequently functioned as a self-appointed champion and spokesman for the German-speaking exiles in the United States. He was a good friend of Agnes Meyer and her husband Eugene Meyer, the publisher of the *Washington Post*. That friendship gave him entree to the Roosevelt White House. As a result of contacts with influential persons in government he was able in several instances to cut through bureaucratic restrictions to aid refugees.

Despite those efforts, the patrician Mann was not particularly popular with his fellow exiles. He was certainly a controversial figure during, and even after, the war with Germans who resented his hortatory wartime broadcasts to them over the BBC. Mann was forced into exile in Switzerland a few months after Remarque in 1933. Mann's daughter Erika indicated in a telephone call from Germany to her parents vacationing in Switzerland that it would be unwise for them to return home.

Mann and Remarque were never on close terms and Mann certainly did not enhance his standing with Remarque during a

1933 visit to Ascona. Remarque was later quoted as saying about that visit:

> "In 1933 he didn't want to be seen on the street with me in Ascona because he would have to lose his public in Germany. Mann also was never banned. It only became too much for him when he, the non-Gymnasium graduate, had his honorary doctorate from Bonn revoked. Then he placed himself at our head in America without asking us."[5]

These comments clearly show that Remarque's old resentments had not softened appreciably even seven years after the close of the war. Much of that resentment might have come from the fact that Remarque had also done much, financially and otherwise, to assist less-fortunate exiles. However, the very private Remarque would have been deeply distressed to think that his private assistance might be made public.

It is also to his credit that he did not accept an earlier offer by the Nazis which would have enabled him to avoid exile. The offer, originating from Goebbels, would have left him and his book untouched if he had been willing to attribute all responsiblity for the film "All Quiet on the Western Front" to his "Jewish" publisher Ullstein.[6] Remarque scorned the offer even though, ironically, he had nothing at all to do with the film. The Nazis had yet to learn, as others in dealing with Remarque had occasionally already learned to their sorrow, that behind the playboy facade there lay fierce pride and integrity.

Exile did not cause his playboy reputation to suffer. From his home base at Ascona he continued to indulge his taste for good living. For him that often meant driving his Lancia on vacation escapes to some of his favorite haunts in Switzerland, Italy, and France. In places such as Davos, St. Moritz, Venice, Rome, Paris, and the French Riviera, Remarque was a welcome and well-known guest. In the company of his ex-wife Jeanne, or of some other equally striking female companion, he made the rounds of fashionable nightclubs and restaurants enjoying to the full his celebrity status.

There were other times, much fewer in number however,

when the ambivalence of Remarque toward his way of life caused him to shun the celebrity haunts. As in the case of many persons who suddenly achieve wealth and fame, Remarque was frequently filled with doubts as to his own worthiness for the success he had achieved. He was a very sensible, practical person who had no illusions about himself or most of the other persons with whom he associated who had also achieved material success. At those times when he had had enough of indulging the bon vivant side of his nature he sought solitude in obscure bistros or escape in the hard work of writing. Very likely Remarque's constant awareness that he could never again be as successful with a book as he had been with *Im Westen nichts Neues* caused the words to flow less smoothly for him; and also was responsible for much of his increased devotion to drinking.

Remarque's enforced absence from his family in Germany was apparently less a source of emotional loss for him than a matter of concern for their safety and well-being. After his mother's death he had spent most of the time away from his father and his sisters Erna and Elfriede. Since the end of 1922 when he left Osnabrück for Hannover his return visits had become increasingly rare. There were various reasons for this situation. Primarily there was the fact that for him the focal point of affection in the family had been his mother. With her death the heart of the family was gone. He had a degree of love and respect for his father but there had never been a real closeness between them. Because of the family's frequent moves during his youth, and the cramped quarters in which his family lived when he returned from the war, there was actually no place he truly could call home. Another factor was his father's re-marriage which, while not opposed by Remarque, served as yet another reminder that the family unit was irrevocably altered. Peter Remark was again fortunate in marrying a good woman with whom he lived happily until her death. In 1935, two years after Remarque's last visit to Osnabrück before going into exile in Switzerland, Peter Remark moved to Bad Rothenfelde to live with Erna and her husband Walter Rudolph.

Little of substance is known about Remarque's early relationship with his sisters Erna and Elfriede. By the time he left for exile in Switzerland, Elfriede was grown and gone from home. Erna was married and had her own home.

An interesting but completely unsubstantiated rumor has it that after the success of *Im Westen nichts Neues* Erna, without the approval or knowledge of her brother, sold his wartime diaries and papers. If there is any truth to the rumor, Erna's action would hardly have served to endear her to Erich. However, if the story were true it seems likely that the diaries would have surfaced by now. That is, unless Remarque succeeded in regaining possession.

16

Drei Kameraden

1937 saw the completion of the third novel, *Drei Kameraden* (*Three Comrades*). Although Remarque never designated it as such, the work may actually be considered the final work in a trilogy which includes *Im Westen nichts Neues* and *Der Weg zurück*. With *Drei Kameraden* he essentially concluded his concern with the author-protagonist's re-entry into post-war society.

One of the principal themes running through his first two novels is that of comradeship. The third novel not only continues the theme but expands it by adding the new dimension of romantic love. *Drei Kameraden* might just as accurately have been entitled *Vier Kameraden* (*Four Comrades*) because that is the situation Remarque gives us.

The novel is not only an excellent study of friendship and comradeship between men but is the best love story Remarque ever wrote. There were to be other gripping love stories portrayed in his novels but none which had quite the same intensity or ring of authenticity.

The fact that Remarque dedicated this novel to "J. R. Z." (Jeanne Remarque Zambona) makes a very significant statement regarding his feeling for Jeanne at this time. Even though their marriage had been legally ended, the love story in the novel celebrated the real-life love they had shared. If it is true that every person has one great love in his life then this was Remarque's. Even though he was later to have well-publicized affairs and another wife, no other relationship apparently ever touched him as deeply.

Drei Kameraden is set in Berlin during the period immediately preceding the Nazi takeover. Three young men who had been schoolmates and comrades during the war are trying to make a success of a garage and automotive repair shop after having gone their separate ways at the conclusion of the war. The owner of the garage is Otto Köster who had been their company commander, served later as a pilot, and after the war had briefly been a student. Before he bought the garage he had also been a racing car driver. Otto was later joined in the operation of the garage by the second comrade, Gottfried Lenz, who had been knocking about South America for a few years without achieving anything of importance. The third comrade is "Robby" Lohkamp who is the narrator of the story. "Robby" serves as the Remarque-protagonist and as such his story is of paramount importance.

Despite the best efforts of the comrades the garage was on the verge of financial ruin. Repair jobs were scarce and prospects were bleak. The prize possession of the garage was Otto's car, affectionately named Karl. Karl was much like the comrades themselves in that there was more to him than met the eye. The three comrades enjoyed taking Karl on the road in order to lure the owners of newer and better looking cars into races on the highway. The owners of those more impressive looking cars then always learned to their chagrin that Karl was a finely tuned racing car which always won such races.

One of the outings, and the resultant race, led to a meeting with Patrice Hollmann who was eventually to be the love interest of "Robby" as well as the "fourth" comrade. Otto and Gottfried were much taken with the attractive Pat. Robby was completely smitten with Pat and, with much trepidation, began a courtship of her.

The relationship soon developed into love in spite of brief misunderstandings usually caused by Robby's feelings of insecurity when in the company of Pat's more sophisticated friends. At first Robby tried to conceal from Otto and Gottfried the intensity of his feeling for Pat. However, the attempted deception was not only unsuccessful but unnecessary. Robby's love for Pat had the unqualified approval of Otto and Gottfried.

For a while their life together was wonderful. Even financial problems could not adversely effect the happiness they shared. Unfortunately an old medical problem could. Pat's long dormant tuberculosis flared up during an idylic vacation by the sea. Robby's frantic phone call to Otto for help in bringing Pat's doctor produced instant results. Otto, driving Karl at breakneck speeds in the best tradition of Remarque fictive friendship, delivered Dr. Jaffe in time to provide the necessary treatment. It was now apparent that Pat could not survive many more attacks of severe hemorrhaging. Although Dr. Jaffe insisted that she go to a sanatorium at once, Pat resisted the suggestion in order to spend with Robby as much as possible of the time remaining to her. In the end, however, Robby and Dr. Jaffe prevailed and Pat went to a sanatorium in an attempt to delay the inevitable for a little longer.

In Berlin Robby, Otto, and Gottfried also were fighting a losing battle. It was necessary to sell the garage and go their separate ways economically. Robby had to go back to the job he had had as a piano player in a bar in order to eke out a subsistence income.

There was worse to come, however. One night Gottfried was shot to death by a Nazi during a street brawl. Although Robby and Otto looked through the city in order to find the murderer and avenge their comrade, another of their friends, Alfons, was the first to find the Nazi and wipe the slate clean.

As the result of a telegram from Pat containing the message "Robby, come soon!",[1] Robby was driven by Otto to the sanatorium. When they arrived it was apparent that Pat did not have long to live. It was to be merely a matter of the lovers sharing the last few days of their time together.

However, even those last few days were not free of financial worries. Robby had only enough money to last ten days at most. Pat's room at the sanatorium was paid for only for a few days. Robby was desperate and planned to return to Berlin in an attempt to raise some money. Otto, however, said that he would raise the money for Pat and prevailed on Robby to remain. Shortly after Otto's return to Berlin he sent Robby two thousand Marks. Instantly Robby realized the source of Otto's funds: the sale of Karl. For Otto that was almost the ultimate proof of friendship. He had once told Robby that he would rather part with his hand than with Karl.

When Robby thought about the sale of Karl he realized how interrelated all of his important relationships had been and what their loss meant.

> "We belonged together. Karl and Köster, Karl and Lenz, Karl and Pat. Angry and helpless I stamped the snow from my feet. Lenz was dead. Karl was gone. And Pat? With blinded eyes I stared at the sky, this grey, endless sky of a crazy God, who had made life and death for his amusement."[2]

It was necessary for Robby to overcome his understandable bitterness in order to make Pat happy during their last days together. Pat had good days and bad. However, she was determined to make as few concessions to her illness as possible. She rejected Robby's attempts to spare her by limiting her activities. Pat, well aware of the consequences of her decision, expressed her feelings in this way:

> "In the time when you were not here I did everything that they told me. I was nothing but one anxious prescription, and it hasn't helped. It only got worse. Don't interrupt me! I know what you are going to say. I know too what is involved. But the time that I have still, this time with you, —let me do as I will."[3]

Pat and Robby did spend their brief remaining time together in a bitter-sweet, carpe diem existence. Pat, frail and vulnerable, continued her gallant struggle against the inevitable. As her strength failed she became increasingly concerned with the fear that her remaining strength would not allow her to get through that period of the night which had claimed so many other patients in the sanatorium. As Robby put it:

> "She was afraid of the last hour between night and morning. She believed that with the end of the night the mysterious stream of life became weaker and almost expired—she dreaded only that hour and didn't want to be alone. For the rest she was so brave that I often had to clench my teeth."[4]

It was not long before she did indeed fail to survive that last hour of night before the morning. As the novel ends, Remarque leaves Robby, and the reader, alone to contemplate the impact of Pat's loss.

In this deeply moving love story Remarque has given his readers a unique opportunity to understand the intensity of the love he shared with Jeanne Zambona. There is absolutely no doubt that Jeanne is the physical and spiritual model for Pat. Robby's description of Pat fits Jeanne perfectly.

> "Her hair was brown and silky and in the lamplight had an amber sheen. Her shoulders were very straight but inclined a little forward, her hands were slender, a bit long and bony rather than soft. Her face was narrow and pale, but the large eyes gave it an almost passionate strength. She looked very good I thought."[5]

A Remarque trademark in the story is the Irish Terrier which Robby gave to Pat so that she would never have to be alone. Remarque, the avid dog fancier and trainer, often gave dogs, usually Irish Terriers, to his friends. His own favorite was an Irish Terrier named "Billy" which he had for many years. He had "Billy" at the time of his marrage to Jeanne and there are pictures, taken in Switzerland, which show Remarque, Jeanne, and "Billy" together. "Billy" is being held on a leash by Jeanne.[6] It is not surprising that Pat also decided to call her dog "Billy".

There is further autobiographical agreement in the fact that Jeanne's tuberculosis was transferred to her fictional counterpart. In both cases the condition was attributed to inadequate nutritional conditions during and after the war. In both cases also an early encapsulation of the disease broke out and brought about a re-occurrence of the pathological process. However, in Jeanne's case the disease was again arrested and controlled whereas Remarque allowed Pat to succumb to the illness.

One might raise the question as to why Remarque made this decision. Was it simply to enhance the drama of the love story? Did the ending merely serve to underscore Remarque's belief in the impermanence of male-female relationships? Was it just the logical ending for a love which had already achieved the ultimate in intensity, devotion, and commitment? It is, after all, rather difficult, if not impossible, for an inveterate reader of Remarque to imagine Pat as an aging "Hausfrau". Although it seems probable that all the above elements played a role in the choice of ending, a last possibility should be considered. Did Remarque, through the death of Pat, put a symbolic end to the most significant love of his life? Was this a cathartic self-admission that, even though their relationship continued after a fashion, love had died? It seems probable that this is the case.

Even though Remarque was well into the writing of *Drei Kameraden* before he went into exile in January of 1933, it was not until almost 1936 that he considered the work ready for publication. For this book, however, his German publishers were no longer available to him. Fortunately there was an alternate possibility in the Netherlands. The Dutch publishing house of Emanuel Querido had set up in 1933 a division to accomodate German language authors who had been forced into exile by the Nazis. The Querido Verlag was to become one of the most prominent outlets for emigre authors such as Remarque, his friend Emil Ludwig, Franz Werfel, and Heinrich Mann. Querido published *Drei Kameraden* in German in 1938.

An English translation of the novel done by A. W. Wheen had been published in Boston by Little, Brown a year earlier. Shortly before the April printing of the translation a serial version of *Three Comrades* began in *Good Housekeeping* in January of 1937. The last installment of the story appeared in the May issue. As was always the case with Remarque stories, *Three Comrades* was very well-received by American readers. It was not to be long until Americans would also have an opportunity to see Hollywood's version of Remarque's love story.

17

The Film Version of *Drei Kameraden*

Film rights to *Drei Kameraden* were acquired by Metro-Goldwyn-Mayer rather than by Universal Studios which had done movies from the first two novels. It was evident from the beginning that MGM intended to do full justice to the filming of this valuable screen property. The producer was to be Joseph Mankiewicz and the director Frank Borzagas. F. Scott Fitzgerald was brought back to Hollywood to write the screenplay.

The MGM commitment was also evident in the high calibre of the cast. The book role of Robby (designated as Erich Lohkamp in the movie) was played by Robert Taylor. Patricia Hollmann was Margaret Sullavan. The two other comrades, Otto Köster and Gottfried Lenz, were played by Franchot Tone and Robert Young respectively. Guy Kibbee and Lionel Atwill appeared as Alfons and Breuer. Monty Wooley was Dr. Jaffe.

There were to be many difficulties before the screenplay was ready for filming. Whatever his merit as a novelist might have been, Fitzgerald appears to have been a bad choice to capture the flavor and vitality of Remarque's dialogue. Fitzgerald obviously found it difficult, and in many instances impossible, to avoid taking basic liberties with the novel.

Among the most far-fetched was the ending of his screenplay. This scene was not the novel's ending of Robby with the dead Pat in her sanatorium room. His ending has "Bobby" and Köster walking away from a snow-covered cemetery on a hill in the city. The sound of machine gun firing is heard from the distance and Köster comments that there is fighting in the city. Then we learn: "As they continue on, they are suddenly four instead of two—the shadowy figures of Pat and Lenz, grave and tender, walk beside them toward whatever lies ahead."[1] Fade out. The screenplay ends.

Mankiewicz and MGM were less than pleased with the way the work was going and Fitzgerald was given E. E. "Ted" Paramore as a collaborator for revision of the screenplay. Fitzgerald's artistic sensibilities were offended by the unwanted assistance and the collaboration was a troubled one. Although Fitzgerald and Paramore shared screen credit for the workable screenplay which finally emerged, Joseph Mankiewicz might well have shared the credit because he rewrote several sections of the screenplay. Although Fitzgerald was embittered because of the Mankiewicz revisions, he should more properly have been grateful. Much of his work could only have been improved. Fred Lawrence Guiles in his book, *Hanging on in Paradise*, quotes Mankiewicz in regard to this episode.

> "Today Mankiewicz is slightly bitter about his few months of work with Fitzgerald. 'I pissed on the American flag. I dared to rewrite Scott Fitzgerald's dialogue when Maggie Sullavan pulled me off into a corner of the soundstage and said, 'You've got to do something about this dialogue for Christ's sake! I can't speak it'."[2]

Ironically, Scott Fitzgerald did have some reason to be grateful to Mankiewicz for the assistance. After Louis B. Mayer saw the film he gave Fitzgerald an extension of his contract.

Mayer was involved in a questionable incident before the film was released to the public. For reasons not entirely clear, he decided to show the film to a representative of the Nazi government. Not surprisingly, the Nazi was not pleased with the accurate portrayal of Nazi violence and suggested to Mayer that the Communists be substituted as the villains of the piece. Mayer was willing to go along with the suggestion until Mankiewicz, to his great credit, adamantly refused to agree to the change. "Three Comrades" was released in June, 1938. Ready public acceptance made it a great commercial and critical success. Frank S. Nugent in his review of the film for *The New*

York Times said: "It is a superlatively fine picture, obviously one of 1938's best ten and not one to be missed."[3]

Although Robert Taylor, Franchot Tone, and Robert Young were praised for their acting, it was the sensitive and moving performance of Margaret Sullavan which won the most plaudits. That performance, one of the best in a distinguished career, gained for her an Academy Award nomination.

Despite the praise given to "Three Comrades", the film version of Remarque's generally taut story is often marred by mawkish sentimentality. In many instances the action depicted in the screenplay is only an approximation of the original story. Sadly, the comradeship of Remarque's novel is supplanted by a kind of unconvincing fraternity-boy friendship. However, it is apparent that these flaws in the Fitzgerald-Paramore-Mankiewicz adaptation did not deter hosts of moviegoers from seeing and enjoying it. Perhaps to a nation just making its way out of the depression era an abundance of escapist sentimentality was more of a box-office advantage than a disadvantage.

18

A New Relationship Made and an Old Marriage Repeated

During the six years from the beginning of Remarque's journey into exile from Berlin to his departure for the United States on the eve of World War II, he maintained his residence in Porto Ronco. During that time, however, he traveled extensively in France and Italy and considered France almost a second home. Paris in particular won his heart. Although Remarque loved his beautiful home in Porto Ronco he also needed the vitality and diversity of urban living. Paris not only had that vitality and diversity but a unique dignity and beauty which had great appeal for Remarque the Romantic.

In the mid and late thirties much of the charm of his time spent in Paris, and other parts of France, was due to the company of attractive female companions. The most attractive was the Berlin-born, German-American actress Marlene Dietrich.

One would think it likely that their first meeting might have occurred in one of the popular Berlin watering places favored by Remarque and Dietrich in the 1928–29 period. According to Marlene, however, that was not the way it happened. In her autobiography, *Nehmt nur mein Leben . . .* , which was published by the C. Bertelsmann Verlag in 1979, Marlene placed their first meeting at the Lido in Venice. According to her account Remarque took the initiative and introduced himself to her. She was greatly impressed by his celebrity status.

When they met on the beach the next day Marlene had with her a book by Rainer Maria Rilke. Remarque's facetious comment to the effect that she had a taste for good books evoked an apparently defensive offer by Marlene to quote a few poems in an attempt to show him that she did not fit the stereotype of the actress lacking literary or intellectual interests. In Marlene's account the recital of these poems so impressed Remarque that he was amazed. The reader apparently is to assume that the Remarque-Dietrich relationship had as its basis a shared appreciation of poetry.

Dietrich's autobiography does not throw any new light on their relationship. Indeed it downplays the relationship to the extent that it appears to be merely a friendship between the actress and a rather poorly-defined writer of limited dimensions. Anyone knowing little of Remarque would receive an impression of a man who had an unerring ability to identify wines from all over the world, who loved to drive his Lancia at high speeds, who had difficulty with writing, and who was given to periods of melancholia. These brief glimpses are all accurate but somewhat misleading because of their fragmentary nature. It is also informative that no mention is made in the Dietrich book of Remarque's first wife Jeanne or his second wife Paulette Goddard.

Marlene Dietrich's rather bland, apparently self-serving, and abbreviated account of her relationship with Remarque is not really surprising. Indeed, if one takes into account her basically private nature and her fiercely protective attitude toward her family and friends, no other treatment is possible. Real candor appears to be lacking.

It may well be, however, that Dietrich's superficial treatment of her involvement with Remarque is the best indication of how important the relationship was to her. She was well aware of his aversion to any biographical probing of his activities which went beyond the superficial. She has certainly kept faith with Remarque's desire for privacy. His shade might even be moved to offer a posthumous apology for some unchivalrous comments he made about Marlene which were reported by his friend Victoria Wolff in the Munich magazine *Madame* for July, 1971.

In her elaboration on Remarque's fear that the confidentiality of the extensive correspondence he had with friends might be abused, she revealed his later practice of signing letters with a pseudonymn instead of his name, or with his nickname "Boni." For example, he signed his letters to her "the tyrant of the western world."[1] According to her, this precautionary measure dated from his sister Erna's high-handed and unauthorized sale of his wartime journals. Wolff then specifically stated:

> "He also did not trust Marlene Dietrich to whom he had written letters during the years of their love. Even two years ago when we met for the last time in the garden of the Baur au Lac (hotel) in Zürich he said 'Marlene is keeping all my letters in a bankvault. She is waiting for my death and then she will publish them. That would be horrible not only for Paulette, but I would hate it that friends would poke around in my private life'."[2]

Remarque's term "private life" has a rather hollow ring when one considers that the relationship with Marlene was prominently displayed over a period of years in at least four countries on two continents. They were frequently seen together in restaurants and nightspots. One of Marlene's biographers, Charles Higham, mentions particularly the time Dietrich and Remarque spent together at Fouquet's in Paris.[3]

On the basis of other accounts, there were also reported excursions into a world slightly more exotic than that of cafe society. One of those accounts is found in a book of memoirs based on the tape recorded recollections of Marthe Lemestre. Lemestre was the madame of the famous Paris brothel known as the "Sphinx." This establishment, like a few others of its type, was more than just a house of prostitution. It was really a combination salon and brothel. As a salon it was frequented by such celebrities as Mistinguett, Edith Piaf, Maurice Chevalier, Josephine Baker, Colette, Jean Cocteau, Wallace Beery, Clark Gable, Gary Cooper, Errol Flynn, and John Barrymore. Some of those also availed themselves of the other pleasures available in the "Sphinx."

Marthe Lemestre tells of a visit to the "Sphinx" by the Dietrich party:

> "Marlene was accompanied by her husband, Sieber, and novelist Erich Maria Remarque, author of *All Quiet on the Western Front*. It was really a wonderful event for me. - - -She and Erich often visited me when they were in Paris. Marlene dined very simply, downstairs in the dining room with the girls."[4]

There is another first-hand account regarding Remarque's association with a second brothel-salon in Paris. *Der Spiegel* published an article on October 11, 1976 which concerned the memoirs of Fabienne Jamet.[5] She was the madame of the famous house at 122 Rue de Provence. By its clientelle, which frequently included international celebrities, the establishment was referred to as "One Two Two" or, more often, simply "One." The bordello's salon could boast of the presence of notables such as Fernandel, the Duke of Windsor, Porfirio Rubirosa, and Ernest Hemingway. Of this group only Rubirosa went upstairs with the girls. The others were content to socialize and drink in the salon. "Content" may not be quite accurate in the case of Hemingway. It seems just as likely that he may have been reluctant to be the object of invidious comparisons which could devaluate his "macho" image.

Fabienne Jamet said that whenever Remarque was in Paris he paid a visit to "One." She also commented on the prodigious amounts of Bordeaux wine, Champagne, Vodka, and whiskey he drank which never seemed to make him drunk. Remarque also restricted his activities to the first floor and never went upstairs. It is likely that his reason for that choice was much the same as Hemingway's.

In any case, it seems that his ability as a lover was not enhanced by the over-fondness for the drink which increases desire but inhibits performance. Charles Higham mentions this problem specifically when he states, "He was a poor lover, often unable to achieve erections because of his drinking . . ."[6] Higham did not give a source for this assertion. It would be difficult to document such a claim because those persons most able to validate it are naturally the least willing to be quoted. It is, however, almost certainly true. The reader of some of the later Remarque novels can easily pick up references which indicate that Remarque had more than a casual concern with the problem of impotence.

Remarque's readers will also not be surprised to learn how much of his socializing and drinking time he spent in brothels. Many of his novels contain very sympathetic portrayals of prostitutes. It is readily apparent that Remarque had a fondness for the German and French prostitutes he had known. He succeeded in glossing over the more sordid aspects of their profession and usually depicted them as practical, decent business women. Although he did not go so far as to present his readers with the stereotype of the prostitute with the "heart of gold," he did sympathetically portray them as "survivors." Coming from Remarque, that was a high compliment.

In 1938 he turned his attention from the demimonde long enough to write a new chapter in his relationship with Jeanne. Since their departure from Berlin in January of 1933 they had spent some of the time together at Porto Ronco, although for the most part they were elsewhere pursuing their own interests. Jeanne's artist's eye had been greatly impressed by the beauty of "Casa Monte Tabor." She enjoyed the time she spent there and also took advantage of the painting opportunities it provided. Essentially, however, from 1933 it was understood by both that they were free agents. Despite the fact that the marriage had been dissolved since 1930 emotional bonds remained which were difficult to sever.

Even though much of the old love he had had for Jeanne was gone, he made a decision in 1938 which not only showed the existence of some remaining affection but was an excellent demonstration of Remarque's loyalty. At that time Jeanne was in great danger of being compelled by Swiss government regulations to return to Germany. According to governmental interpretation of her case, she was not Jewish and was otherwise not technically "politically endangered." She could therefore be denied further resident status in Switzerland and be made to return to Germany. This possibility of course was abhorrent to her and to Remarque. For Remarque the solution to the problem was clear. The decision was made by them to remarry so that Jeanne could once more enjoy the legal protection of his name. Therefore, on January 22, 1938 they were remarried in St. Moritz, Switzerland. Dr. Julius Robbi performed a civil ceremony which was witnessed by two members of the administrative staff of the Zivilstandamt (Civil Registrar's Office) for St. Moritz, Jakob Accola and Martin Cadisch.

For Jeanne, their second marriage served its purpose well. There were no more problems regarding residence in Switzerland. Money as well was never again to be a problem because financial support from Remarque continued for the rest of her life. Indeed, in later years Remarque often fretted about the generosity of that financial support.

19

Loss of German Citizenship

It was very fortunate for the Remarques that their legal position in Switzerland was secure because by March of 1938 the attention of the Nazi bureaucracy had turned to them.

On March 21, 1938 a letter of notification was sent by the Geheime Staatspolizei (Gestapo) "to the Reich Leader of the SS and Head of the German Police in the Ministry of the Interior" concerning "deprivation of German citizenship of the German-blooded writer *Erich* Paul Remark, born on June 22, 1898 in Osnabrück, last domestic residence: Berlin-Wilmersdorf, Wittelsbacher Street number 5, present residence: presumably Porto Ronco near Locarno (Switzerland)."[1] The letter bore the signature of a Dr. Lange.

In translation the complete text of the rather lengthy indictment reads:

> "The German-blooded writer *Erich* Paul Remark has German nationality status. He left the territory of the Reich even before the assumption of power and resides in Porto Ronco near Locarno in Switzerland. On the basis of a reference in a Paris newspaper he is said to be living at the present time in St. Moritz.
>
> Remark first became known as a result of an erotic novel 'Die Traumbude,' which appeared in the Schönheit publishing house in 1920 and was intended to propagandize nudism. Later Remark became an editor of the magazine "Sport im Bild" and assumed the pen-name 'Erich Maria Remarque'.
>
> Under this name he wrote the books 'Im Westen nichts Neues' and 'Der Weg zurück'. Both products are characterized by a particularly base and un-German conception of the meaning of war. German soldiership and heroism are dragged through the mud in this bungling work in a manner which can not be duplicated. Mention should particularly be made of the outpourings of indignation by the widest

circles of the German people, ruthlessly suppressed by the rules of the Weimar system, against the performance of the film, 'Im Westen nichts Neues,' named after the novel of the same name.

Erich Re-mark (sic), with support from the Jewish Ullstein Press, has for years, in the most sordid and base manner, insulted the memory of the dead soldiers of the World War and already, as a result of that, excluded himself from the German community.

With the money acquired in this manner he bought himself a villa in Switzerland. In Porto Ronco near Locarno he maintained, until recently, an active social life which was exclusively limited to emigrants, Jews, and communists.

To be sure, Remark recently has not been in evidence as a writer. Nevertheless, it can be assumed with certainty on the basis of the attitude evidenced by his books that he continues to be active in a manner inimical to German interests. His associations also unequivocally show that he clings just as much as he did earlier to the Jewish-Marxist seditious ideas.

Moreover, Remark has violated foreign-exchange regulations and also in this area acted contrary to the interests of the German people. Because of this currency violation he was given a fine of 30,000 RM.

I am therefore proposing to deprive Remark of German citizenship.

In the event that domestic inquiries should prove to be successful, I shall recommend the retroactive confiscation and seizure of his assets.

According to an account in the Paris newspaper of January 27, 1938, Remark is supposed to have re-married his former wife Ilse (nee) Zambona, born August 28, 1901 in Hildesheim. After the conclusion of the inquiry I shall, if appropriate, recommend the extension of the deprivation of civil rights to the wife and any children."

On June 3, 1938 the second step was taken by the Nazi bureaucracy in its attempt to strip Remarque of his citizenship. On that date a letter was written to the Foreign Office in Berlin by an official, whose signature is illegible, in the German Embassy in Bern. The letter provides a rather bland acquiescence in the procedure.

"The Reichsführer SS and the Head of the German Police, in a communication of April 25 of this year—S—PP(II B) Number 2833/38—, has requested the Embassy to take a position in the matter of the proposed deprivation of German citizenship of Erich Paul Remark. The consulate in Lugano reports concerning Remark that he owns his own house in Porto-Ronco near Locarno. In June of this year he again married Ilse (nee) Zambona from whom he was divorced.

His last book 'Drei Kameraden', which appeared in February of this year in the Querido-Verlag of Amsterdam, might be known there. Remark associates with the emigrant circles of Locarno. However, he has not otherwise been particularly prominent before the Swiss public.

I have no valid objections to make against the intended deprivation of civil rights."

The last approval in this sham governmental process came from the Reich Ministry of the Interior. That office circulated to appropriate agencies copies of a form dated June 8, 1938 which, when filled in with the pertinent names, dates, and file references, was able to dispose of the Remarque case as impersonally and expeditiously as it had thousands of others.

"In reference to the deprivation of citizenship proposal made by the Reichsführer SS and Head of the German Police on *April 25, 1938, S PP (IIB) Number 2833/38* forwarded for information.

I concur in the deprivation of citizenship of the *German-blooded Erich Paul Remark* and the proposed extension of it to include his *wife Ilse* (*nee*) *Zambona*."

(signed) Schumburg

The penultimate step in the procedure was taken on July 7, 1938 with the publishing of a list of persons whose citizenship had been taken away.

"German National Gazette
and Prussian Official Gazette
Number 155 of the Seventh of July, 1938
Proclamation

On the basis of section 2 of the law concerning the revocation of naturalizations and the deprivation of German citizenship which was passed on July 14, 1933 (BGB1.IS.480) I, in an agreement with the Reichsminister of the Foreign Ministry, declare that the following persons are deprived of German citizenship."

The alphabetized list includes 36 names, birthdates, and birth places. It begins with Adam, Wilhelm and ends with Weiss, Leo. Number 21 is: "Remark, Erich Paul, born June 22, 1898 in Osnabrück."

On July 12, 1938 a memorandum was sent from the Foreign Office to German diplomatic and consular representations directing them "when the opportunity presents itself" to confiscate the passports of those persons on the proscribed list. This memorandum was also signed by Schumburg. The proscribed list concluded with the words "the loss of German citizenship is extended to the following family members." Thirty-three names followed. The name of Jeanne Remarque was not among them. However, the Nazis with their distinctive blend of bureaucratic persistence and vindictiveness soon rectified that oversight. On September 14, 1938 a memorandum from a functionary named Lischka in the office of the Reichsführer SS and Head of the German Police in the Reichsministry of the Interior was sent to Department I of the same Ministry of the Interior to tie up some of the procedural loose ends.

> "To supplement my previous memorandum I am communicating the fact that Remark, according to a determination made by the German Consulat in Lugano in autumn of 1937, has again married his divorced wife Ilse Jutta (née) Zambona, born August 28, 1901 in Hildesheim.
>
> According to present information the marriage is childless.
>
> Furthermore I request the confiscation of the automobile IA69865 (the existence of) which was determined after (his) flight, and the declaration that it has reverted to the Reich.
>
> Further determinations of Remark's wealth have not been established at the present time."

The Remarque case was settled to the satisfaction of Nazi officialdom with a concluding memorandum from the Ministry of the Interior. This concise note, over the signature of an official named Duckart, states: "By the announcement of July 4, 1938—Remark was deprived of citizenship without the confiscation of his wealth and without the extension of the deprivation of citizenship to his wife. I request agreement henceforth in the retroactive confiscation of his wealth. The loss of citizenship will accordingly be extended to the wife."

The Nazi concern with the confiscation of Remarque's wealth was a meaningless exercise. They had locked the barn door a little too late in that particular matter. Perhaps, however, it satisfied their bureaucratic need to observe all the forms.

It was a different matter with the loss of citizenship. Apart from the fact that it was a moral injustice, the practical disadvantages of the Nazi action were serious. In the literal sense the Remarques had suddenly joined the multitude of stateless exiles. However, in this situation also the advantages of wealth and influence served to spare the Remarques, and others like them, from the harsher fate experienced by unknown and impoverished exiles. Moreover, the Remarques still had the advantage of residency permission in Switzerland. Later when the decision had been made to leave Europe for the United States, money and influence would make Panamanian passports available.

20

The Beginning of the Second Exile

From 1937 until he sailed for the United States in 1939, Remarque spent most of his time in France. A sizeable portion of that period was spent in the company of Marlene Dietrich. Apart from his romantic interest in this beautiful and famous woman with whom he shared so many common interests, Remarque needed her solicitous concern for his welfare.

Remarque's conduct, particularly his excessive drinking, often gave Dietrich good reason for concern. Charles Higham relates a story from the memoirs of the German exile song writer Max Kolpe (later Colpet) which underscores the point. Colpet, according to the account,

> "visited the couple at the Hotel du Cap at Eden Roc in the south of France, where he found her destraught over Remarque's frequent absences. Colpet wrote - - - that on one occasion Marlene called him in the middle of the night and begged him to help find the missing novelist. She mentioned that Remarque had a tendency to drive his sports car recklessly along the cliff roads, and might have crashed."[1]

Colpet went off into the night, looking in every bar for the errant Remarque. Finally, in desperation he checked a homosexual nightclub and found the object of his search. According to the account, Remarque was well-advanced in his drinking of Calvados and surrounded by convivial local homosexuals. In view of the fact that Remarque was a devout heterosexual, the opportunity to drink was the bar's only attraction for him. Colpet succeeded in persuading him to leave and drive back with him to the Hotel du Cap. Marlene was very grateful and relieved. "'At last I can sleep now.' she said.

Remarque continued to sneak out in this fashion, hoping Marlene wouldn't notice, but she always did."[2]

When Marlene had to return to Hollywood in the spring of 1939 Remarque decided to take his first trip to the United States. They did not travel together, however. It was better to be sensitive to appearances. Remarque booked passage on the pride of the Cunard White Star Lines, the "Queen Mary." The "Queen", which had been in service only since 1936, represented the ultimate in luxurious ocean travel. That was precisely the type of accomodation expected by Remarque and his acquaintances.

Remarque, traveling on a Swiss identification card because of the loss of his German citizenship, arrived in New York on March 23, 1939. His companion on the trip was his friend, and literary agent, Otto Klement. Klement served as his English interpreter when Remarque went beyond his linguistic depth. That happened quite often at this time although his command of English had improved considerably since the time of an interview in 1931. Editor Ray Long of *Cosmopolitan* magazine was reported in *Time* as saying that "Remarque later told him he had never been to the U.S. because he knew only these English phrases: 'How do you do? I love you. Forgive me. Forget me. Ham and eggs, please.' "[3] Although it is certain that Remarque had many occasions to use some of those phrases, essentially the Remarque sense of humor was at work because he was a far better student of English than that even at this early date. Over the years he developed an excellent command of English although he never lost his accent.

Also arriving on the Queen Mary were two well-known British writers, Marie Belloc-Lowndes and Frederick Lonsdale. However, Remarque was the literary celebrity in whom the newspaper reporters were most interested. A *New York Times* reporter interviewed him upon his arrival in New York. Remarque said that he had come to "study America, learn the language, and write a book dealing with the persecution of the Jews."[4]

When he was asked for his opinion regarding the likelihood

of war, he indicated that he thought it unlikely there would be war before June. He did, however, think there would be war by that date. He gave as a reason the small conflicts already "raging throughout the world." Remarque said that it was generally believed in Europe that war would begin "and that there will be 100,000 persons killed the first day. In his opinion the war would develop from 'the little fire in Japan,' and 'the little fire in Spain.' and spread throughout Europe until it becomes a major conflagration involving the whole world."

In the interview he praised the United States as the "salvation of the world" and Franklin Roosevelt as a great leader. "I have a great impression of President Roosevelt in his efforts for peace and I want to see what kind of people there are in this country who so impress every one in Europe."

Remarque remained in New York City only a few days to do some sightseeing and to attend to some business matters in regard to his latest novel *Liebe deinen Nächsten*, (*Flotsam*) which he had just finished. This novel, dealing with the plight of refugees from Nazi oppression, was to appear as a serial in *Collier's*, as a translation from Little, Brown and Company, and as a movie from Metro-Goldwyn-Mayer. The New York business transactions were largely left in the hands of Otto Klement while Remarque acquainted himself with the city. He enjoyed the excitement, vitality, and infinite variety New York had to offer and would have remained longer if his principal interest had not been in California.

Therefore, after a few days, he traveled to Los Angeles to renew acquaintances with Marlene, Josef von Sternberg, and some of his other friends in the California German exile community. The fabled Hollywood was not to Remarque's taste, however. Remarque was an urbanite who did not really care for the slower-paced life in California. In addition, the venality he encountered among persons associated with the movie industry must often have produced his famous Mephistophelian glower. The general atmosphere of the Hollywood "Lotus land" was alien to Remarque, although he was later to return to it for the same reason he made the first visit.

Kyle Chrichton wrote an interesting article about Remarque entitled "My Heart's in the Homeland" for the July 1, 1939 issue of *Collier's*. It was the result of an interview with Remarque which presumably was intended to attract reader interest in the serialization of *Flotsam* which was to begin with the next issue of the magazine. On the first page of the article there is a picture of Marlene Dietrich and Remarque sitting at a table in a Hollywood restaurant or nightclub. Marlene, very attractive in a white, hooded dress, appears to be lost in a reverie as Remarque lights a cigarette. The caption of the picture reads: "Erich Maria Remarque renews an old friendship with Marlene Dietrich on his last visit to Hollywood."

Shortly before the picture appeared they sailed back to Europe. Remarque left New York the middle of June. "To avoid the gossips, they traveled by different ships . . ."[5]

As the summer of 1939 drew to an end, the Hotel du Cap at Antibes was once again headquarters for the coterie of German friends. Remarque was there, along with Josef von Sternberg, Marlene, her husband Rudolph Sieber, and their daughter Maria. Also prominent among the guests at the hotel were the French movie actor Jean Gabin (who was later to replace Remarque in Marlene's affection), the English millionairess Jo Carstairs, and the vacationing Joseph P. Kennedy and his family. Joe Kennedy had been a Hollywood movie mogul during the 1920's and 1930's and was a very close friend of Marlene. By the summer of 1939 he had completed the second year of the three years he served as the United States ambassador to England's Court of Saint James. In her memoirs Marlene painted a very rosy picture of those relatively carefree late summer days at Cap d'Antibes. She particularly recalled the time when her daughter Maria and young Jack Kennedy swam to a nearby island and her concern that they might drown in making the attempt. As with many maternal fears, those were groundless because the children were very good swimmers. Although Jack was particularly remembered by her she expressed her affection for all of the Kennedy children.

Unfortunately the Antibes idyl was soon to end. Joseph

Kennedy had been strongly urging Remarque and his other friends to leave Europe as soon as possible because he was certain that the outbreak of war was imminent. Such advice coming from the ambassador to England was very persuasive. It, in combination with Remarque's survivor instincts, would likely have been enough to motivate him to transfer his exile to the United States. Any lingering doubt as to his decision was removed when Marlene decided to return to Hollywood. Joe Pasternak had called from Universal Studios to ask her to star with Jimmy Stewart in the western, "Destry Rides Again." Although her first reaction was to decline, von Sternberg, Remarque, and other friends urged her to accept Pasternak's offer.

Marlene's acceptance of the role made it necessary for her to return at once. Therefore, with the heart of the group leaving, the vacation was over and the friends drove back to Paris. Marlene soon afterwards sailed for the United States on the "Queen Mary."

Remarque's departure was delayed because of the numerous personal and business arrangements he had to make. There was also the important matter of trying to get identification papers in order for himself and Jeanne. At this point in their relationship Jeanne was hoping for a reconciliation which would bring them back together for good. However, he was still romantically interested in Marlene and was not willing, or inclined, to do more than maintain his nominal marriage. Despite this, however, he was greatly concerned that Jeanne also should be able to get papers which would enable her to go to the United States. Because of his connections he was able to obtain Panamanian passports for her and him. Although the passport was to cause trouble for her later in New York it served the purpose of getting her out of Europe.

With passport arrangements made for Jeanne, Remarque was ready to make his second trip to America. Jeanne was to leave later. She apparently thought he would be returning to get her. In the middle of August Remarque drove his Lancia to Paris after making a stop to pick up Marlene's daughter Maria.

In her memoirs Marlene mentioned that her husband drove from the south of France with all the people he could get in his Packard. Because of the chaotic traffic conditions caused by the movement of military units and civilians, Remarque and Sieber each had rather hectic trips to Paris.

Remarque drove from Paris to Le Havre where he was to board the "Queen Mary." He left his Lancia in a garage in Le Havre. When he returned to Europe three years after the war he found that his car was still there and in good shape. It had not been confiscated by the Germans because they were reluctant to do so on account of its Swiss licence. They had not looked into its ownership. When Remarque reclaimed the Lancia he paid for nine years of storage, had some minor mechanical adjustments made, and drove home to Porto Ronco.

Remarque, Sieber, and Maria Sieber were fortunate enough to be able to make the last peacetime sailing of the "Queen Mary." While she was sailing toward New York harbor the German army invaded Poland on September 1. The "Queen Mary" was accompanied part of the way by a British cruiser and arrived in New York just one day after Great Britain had declared war on Germany. There were 2,328 passengers on board when she docked September 4, 1939.

Time reported in its September 11, 1939 issue that Remarque "had little to say about World War II. Although he lost his German citizenship last year, has no country, and travels on a Swiss identification card, he had nothing but sympathy for the German people. 'Poor Germany,' he moaned. 'I cannot fight her.' "[6]

21

California Interlude

Soon after the arrival of the "Queen Mary" Remarque headed for California and a reunion with Marlene. Charles Higham quotes Jo Carstairs' secretary Viola Rubber as saying that Remarque checked into Marlene's bungalow at the Beverly Hills Hotel. According to that account he did his writing at night to the background of music provided by classical 78 rpm records "while Marlene smoked and walked about, her nerves screwed tight."[1] Their neighbors, the Herbert Marshalls, were reportedly not amused by the music accompanying Remarque's creative efforts.

Initially, governmental immigration regulations for the exiles curtailed Remarque's activities. He was restricted to his hotel accomodations from six P.M. until six A.M. each day. That was a real hardship for Remarque who loved nocturnal socializing and carousing. He was very fond of hotel life but not under those conditions. Marlene later was able to improve his morale by finding a house to rent so that he could have more spacious quarters to meet his friends during the restricted hours. The house he rented was in West Los Angeles at 1050 Hilts Avenue in the fashionable section of Westwood. He maintained his residence there until he moved to New York City in 1942.

Life in southern California was not an unmixed blessing for Remarque. The companionship he shared with Marlene and his friendships among the Hollywood German community were emotionally and socially sustaining. The general atmosphere of southern California was less appealing than the urban environment he preferred.

He particularly did not care for what he perceived as the

artificiality of the film colony. It was a strange criticism coming from Remarque. His attitude certainly did not hamper his own need for conviviality. David Niven, an actor noted both for his talent and his playboy reputation, mentioned some of Remarque's activities in his book, *Bring on the Empty Horses*.

"When Erich Maria Remarque was not wrapped around Marlene Dietrich or other local beauties, he acted as a sort of liason officer between the German-speaking foreigners, the Garden of Allah set, and Musso and Frank's Restaurant on Hollywood Boulevard where the brilliant William Saroyan and Budd Schulberg made their headquarters."[2]

Walking was another of Remarque's great pleasures. He was the stereotypical German in this respect. However, he felt somewhat frustrated in this activity while in California. He gave vent to those frustrations in a 1946 New York interview with Robert Van Gelder when he told how "he'd go out for walks and break them off and hurry back to his hotel and go to the bar and have a drink."[3] According to Remarque:

> "There always was some one in the bar, but the streets out there are deserted. No one walks. You know, that's ugly. In the country I take it for granted that I won't meet any one, but there are animals, the life of the country. But to walk in a city where there are rows upon rows of buildings and sidewalks extending for miles and people nowhere to be seen, only buildings and automobiles—ah, ghastly. Hollywood is ghastly anyway. I had nothing to do with pictures, never went near a studio, but the ghastliness of it crept into me and I had to come away."[4]

Remarque's recollection of never having gone near a movie studio is in error. It is typical of his often lofty generalizations which round off the truth of a situation. As a point of fact, Remarque often visited Marlene on the movie set while she was starring in the film "Destry Rides Again." Cameraman Hal Mohr, who was working on the movie, tells of an interesting exchange he had with Remarque at that time. In Mohr's words:

> "I was doing a picture with Marlene Dietrich at a time when Erich was pursuing Marlene pretty earnestly. He used to sit on the set with her, and once I tried to be friendly. 'Your name is Remarque. We could be

related. My mother was a Remarque.' And he got on his high horse, sputtering, 'This is not possible.' He was a pretty snobby man, but at any rate, there's no connection."[5]

Charles Higham also mentions Remarque's visits to the set of "Destry Rides Again" and the fact that he had "new dialogue for Marlene which was emphatically not suitable for a western."[6]

During the filming of "Destry Rides Again" a shadow temporarily passed over the Remarque-Dietrich relationship when Jeanne arrived in the United States from Europe.

22

Jeanne's Bureaucratic Welcome to America

When it became apparent to Jeanne that her sometime husband intended to extend indefinitely his planned six-week visit she decided to join him in the United States. Unfortunately she was also to learn that American bureaucracy is often largely indistinguishable from the European.

On October 15, 1939 she embarked at Bordeaux, France on the "SS Manhattan" which arrived in New York harbor on October 22. She was traveling on the strength of a Panamanian Consular passport issued by the Consul of Panama at Athens, Greece on September 30, 1937. It would soon be seen, however, that these credentials were of doubtful validity when subjected to the careful scrutiny of Immigration and Naturalization officers made more alert by the unsettled conditions of the time.

Examination of her travel documents resulted in her classification as a "Doubtful Visitor, No Immigration Visa." She was detained at Ellis Island in New York harbor until a hearing was held for her on October 25. At 1:35 P.M. of that day a "Board of Special Inquiry," consisting of Inspectors Galvin (chairman) and Bishara with a secretary and interpreter in attendance, met to consider her case. Jeanne was sworn in and gave her testimony in German. By way of preliminary information she stated her name, age (38), citizenship (Panamanian), birthplace, and birthdate. She provided basic facts about her trip to the United States and indicated she was a housewife traveling to meet her husband at the Beverly Hills Hotel, Beverly Hills,

California. She had one hundred thirty dollars and a return steamship ticket issued by the United States Lines good for third class passage from New York, unstated destination, on the SS "President Roosevelt" or "Harding." No sailing date was given. She was coming to the United States as a temporary visitor for pleasure and intended to remain six months. She also stated that she had a sister, Edith Schleuss, in Davos, Switzerland at the Alexander House.

At the heart of the matter was her Panamanian Consular passport No. 5 which was issued in her name by Nicolas Z. Typaldos, Consul of Panama at Athens, Greece, on September 30, 1937, and was valid until September 30, 1942. She had obtained passport visa No. 73 issued October 2, 1939 by Frank Cussans, the United States Consul, at the American Consulate at Bordeaux, France. The visa was granted to her as a non-immigrant, temporary visitor.

The following is a verbatim transcript of the hearing held October 25, 1939.[1]

"Q. You have the right to have a relative or friend present at this hearing. Do you wish to avail yourself of this right?
A. No

Q. Where is your legal place of residence?
A. In Porto-Ronco, near Lugano, Switzerland.

Q. How long have you lived in Switzerland?
A. Since 1933.

Q. Was it in 1933 that you left Germany?
A. Yes.

Q. Did your husband leave Germany with you?
A. Yes.

Q. Was your husband born in Germany?
A. Yes.

Q. Is your husband the well known author, writer of "All Quiet on the Western Front"?
A. Yes.

Q. Of what country is your husband a citizen?

A. Panama.

Q. Of what country was he a citizen prior to obtaining or acquiring Panamanian nationality?
A. Germany.

Q. Were you formerly a citizen of Germany?
A. Yes.

Q. Was your husband disfranchised by the Government of Germany
A. Yes.

Q. When?
A. 1937.

Q. Did you lose your German nationality at the same time?
A. Yes.

Q. Why were you and your husband deprived of your German nationality?
A. Because of his novel "All Quiet on the Western Front".

Q. Where were you and your husband at the time of your disfranchisement?
A. In Switzerland.

Q. How did you acquire Panamanian nationality?
A. My husband arranged this.

Q. Did you ever live in Panama?
A. No.

Q. Did you (sic.) husband ever live in Panama?
A. No.

Q. Did you ever live in Greece?
A. No.

Q. Did your husband ever live in Greece?
A. No.

Q. Did you or your husband ever visit in Greece?
A. No.

Q. Where did you obtain your present passport?
A. My husband gave it to me in Switzerland.

Q. Do you know how it got into his possession?
A. No.

Q. Did you (sic.) husband ever inform you how he acquired Panamanian nationality?
A. No. All I had to do was fill out certain papers—my name and my age.

Q. Apart from your Panamanian passport have you other documents indicating that you are a citizen and national of Panama?
A. No.

Q. Did the Vice Consul of Panama in New York talk to you yesterday and inspect your Panamanian passport?
A. Yes.

Note: Vice Consul Guillermo Fabrega, stationed at the Panamanian Consulate General, New York, conferred with his Consul General by telephone yesterday and advised that the Consul General would telegraph to the Immigration Department, Panama City, to ascertain if Jutta Ilse Remarque was on the register of naturalized Panamanians, and, furthermore, to ascertain if the passport which was issued to her in Athens, Greece, is valid. The Vice Consul stated he would inform this station immediately when word was received by the Consul General from the Home Government.

Q. When did you (sic.) husband come to the United States?
A. The last occasion on September 5, 1939.

Q. Was your husband previously in the United States?
A. Yes. He came here during the spring of 1939 the first time.

Note:
Ellis Island File No. 99454/979 contains evidence that Erich M. Remarque was admitted at the port of New York, March 23, 1939, ex SS "Queen Mary" as a temporary visitor for a period of six months.

Q. When did your husband leave the United States after his arrival in March, 1939?
A. I believe it was the middle of June, 1939.

Q. Why didn't you accompany your husband to the United States in September, 1939?
A. At that time my husband thought that he would stay only six weeks here and return after that time.

Q. Have you information that he was forced to change his original plans and will remain here indefinitely?
A. No. I did not.

Q. Did your husband come to the United States as a visitor the last time?
A. Yes.

Q. To what country will you go when your proposed visit in the United States is over?
A. Either to France, and if I can't go there, to a South American country.

Q. Have you a French visa issued subsequent to France's entry into the war
A. No.

Q. Have you a visa to go to any South American country?
A. No.

Q. If you are in fact a naturalized citizen of Panama will you go to that country to take up residence?
A. Yes.

Q. Can you return to Germany?
A. No.

Q. Have you any relatives in New York?
A. I have a half-sister, Hertha Zambona. I have the address in my baggage. She lives in the State of New Jersey.

Q. If a bond should be required as a condition to your temporary admission to insure that you will maintain the status of a visitor and depart from the United States at the end of a fixed time, who would furnish one in your behalf?
A. My husband or I can put it up myself. I have three thousand dollars transferred to my account in the Guaranty Trust Company, New York City."

At the conclusion of Jeanne's hearing, Inspector Bishara made a successful motion "to defer action for advice from the Panamanian Consulate General in New York as to the validity of alien's passport."

The next day at 2:30 P.M. Jeanne met with a "Board of Special Inquiry" consisting of Inspectors Galvin (chairman) and Warner, a secretary and an interpreter. The first item of business was the reading into the record of a letter from G. Lopez Fabrega, the Consul General of Panama in New York City. In his letter Mr. Fabrega stated that he had received a cablegram from the Secretary of Government and Justice in his country. This cablegram stated that the Remarques had never taken Panamanian nationality and were not citizens of Panama. He therefore requested that their passports be returned to the Panamanian Consulate.

With the introduction of this devastating piece of evidence the remainder of the hearing went as follows:

"Q. This communication is shown and explained to you, and after you have become acquainted with the contents thereof, you may make any comments you choose.
A. I told you I didn't know how my husband got it.

Q. When your husband came to the United States the last time, did he travel on the same kind of passport that you present for admission?
A. Yes.

(In German)

Q. Have you a passport issued by any other country?
A. No.

Q. Have you any other form of travel document visaed by an American Consular Officer?
A. No.

Q. Do we understand your husband is now at the Beverly Hills Hotel, Beverly Hills, California?
A. Yes.

Q. Before decision is rendered in your case, is there anything you would like to say?
A. I can only say that I presented my passport to the American Consulate, and he visaed my passport. I also applied for booking with the United States Lines and they furnished me with transportation.

Q. Are you satisfied from the contents of the letter from the Consulate General of Panama, that you are not a Panamanian citizen and therefore have no right to use a Panamanian passport?
A. I am surprised about it.

BY INSP. WARNER:

I move to exclude under Section 13 (a) (1) of the immigration act of 1924, as an immigrant, not in possession of an unexpired consular immigration visa; and also as an immigrant, not in possession of a valid passport as required by Executive Order 8029 dated December 27, 1938.

BY SECRETARY:

Seconded.

BY INSP. GALVIN:

Unanimous.

BY INSP. GALVIN TO ALIEN:

Q. This Board has voted to exclude you from admission into the United States under Section 13 (1) (1) of the immigration act of 1924, as an immigrant, not in possession of an appropriate unexpired consular immigration visa; and also as an immigrant, not in possession of a valid passport as required by Executive Order 8029 dated December 27, 1938. From the decision of the Board, you have the right of appeal to the Secretary of Labor in Washington. Do you wish to appeal?
A. Yes.

Q. What is your exact foreign address?
A. c/o my maid Rosa Krivetz, Porto-Ronco near Locarno, Switzerland.

Q. What was the cost of your passage to the United States?
A. $244.

Q. If you are ordered deported you will be returned to the country from whence you came by the steamship company that brought you here in the same class of travel and in like accomodations, and thereafter, you will have no right to apply for admission into the united (sic.) States until after the expiration of one year from the date of your departure, unless you first secure permission to do so in writing, from the Secretary of Labor. Do you understand?
A. Yes.

Q. The Secretary of Labor in her discretion, may order the steamship company to refund the full cost of your passage. Is that clear?
A. Yes.

* * * * * * * * * * * * *

3 P.M.

I hereby certify that the above, consisting of three pages, is a true and a correct transcript of the stenographic notes recorded by me.

(signed)
Sarah Sisser
Secretary "

When the "Board of Special Inquiry" voted to exclude Jeanne Remarque from admission into the United States it quickly became apparent that the Immigration and Naturalization Service was not dealing with the routine case of a friendless exile. Jeanne's more effective appeal was the one she directed to Remarque, not to Immigration and Naturalization. Quickly she had as her advocate Isaac H. Levy of the prestigious New York law firm of Battle, Levy, Fowler and Neaman. Mr. Levy informed Mr. James L. Houghteling, the Commissioner of Immigration, that either he or his law partner Mr. Battle would like to be heard when the Remarque case came before the Board of Review in Washington. Mr. Levy appeared before the Board at 2:00 P.M. on Wednesday, November 1.

Mr. Levy had also been very active in dealing with the Mexican Consulate in the Remarque affair. After learning that the Consul General was authorized to issue tourist cards to the Remarques, he stopped by to pick them up. He was given the card for Jeanne but was told that the consul in Los Angeles should issue Remarque's card. Through his good offices the Mexican Ambassador was moved to recommend to his government that the Remarques be admitted to Mexico as political refugees. The next step, now that Jeanne's admission to Mexico was assured, was to ask that she be released in Levy's custody and a transit visa issued.

On November 4, 1939 the Board of Review sustained Jeanne's appeal "as an in transit (alien) under $1,000. departure bond containing the condition that the alien will sail on the next available sailing from the Port of New York to Mexico."

The November 4 position was modified on November 7 "to allow the alien 30 days in which to leave the United States in any manner in which she sees fit, provided the surety on her $1,000. departure bond submits a proper consent to this change."

Deputy Commissioner Edward J. Shaughnessy of Immigration and Naturalization was informed on December 8, 1939 by letter from the Mexican Embassy in Washington, D.C. that Jeanne Remarque was "in possession of permission to go to

Mexico at the expiration of the extension to January 4, 1940 which was granted by you."

The matter was now officially settled. Jeanne could visit Remarque in California and then spend such time in Mexico as would be required before preparations could be made to apply for U.S. citizenship. It was a particularly interesting case because of the important persons whose interest it attracted. Before the bureaucratic skirmishing ended, the author Louis Bromfield had sent a telegram urging special consideration for Mrs. Remarque. The American Ambassador to Belgium, Joseph E. Davies, had cabled to express his hope that some relief could be given her which would be consistent with the regulations. Interest in the case was also expressed by Senator Robert F. Wagner, New York congressmen Bruce Barton and Sol Bloom who asked to be informed when the final decision was rendered. The concern evidenced by these prominent personages must certainly have helped to bring clarity to bureaucratic decision making.

23

Liebe deinen Nächsten: The Book and the Movie

"To live without roots takes a stout heart."[1] With this succinct statement before the beginning of his text Remarque provides a motto for his fourth novel which was the first novel to deal with the plight of refugees from Hitler's Germany. The title *Liebe deinen Nächsten,* which translates as "Love Thy Neighbor", provides another example of Remarque's irony. There are indeed many examples of love for one's fellow man in the book but, taken as a whole, the work might better be entitled "Man's Inhumanity to Man." The title of the English translation by Denver Lindley was *Flotsam*. This title effectively conveys the value most of the world placed on the European exiles of the Hitler era even if the title does not do complete justice to Remarque's point.

In this novel Remarque portrays the soldiers of a different kind of war. His characters are innocent victims of political and/or racial persecution. Through no fault of their own they have been forced into a purgatory of flight. As in his war novels, the overriding concern is survival. The exiles' dream is always for the legitimacy which passports, visas, and identification cards give to their existence. Their struggles are against hunger, physical abuse, unemployment, and an indifferent, or often harrassing, bureaucracy. Education and background have no bearing on the ability of the individual to cope with the new circumstances of exile. As is always the case in Remarque's novels, the principal characters are the resourceful, resilient individuals who possess the wit and motivation to survive.

These are the figures with which Remarque most closely identifies.

In *Liebe deinen Nächsten* the most important of these survivor figures are the double protagonists Josef Steiner and Ludwig Kern. Steiner, the older of the two, had to leave Germany because of his political activities against the Nazis. His wife Marie is still living in Germany. Ludwig Kern, a former medical student from Leipzig, is twenty-one at the beginning of the book's action in 1937. Kern and his father had been obliged to leave Germany because the elder Kern was Jewish.

Steiner and Kern met in Vienna in a refugee rooming house which was raided by the police who were looking for illegal aliens. While they were in jail the survival-wise Steiner took Kern under his wing. Their relationship in some ways is reminiscent of that of Paul Bäumer and Katczinsky in *Im Westen nichts Neues*. In each instance the didactic aspect of the friendship is extremely important. This instructive aspect is also important for Remarque's reader who learns with Kern what is required to survive as a refugee. Remarque moves the scene of the action from Austria to Czechoslovakia to Switzerland to France and finally to Germany where Steiner has returned to be with his dying wife Marie. In all of these locales Remarque shows through his characters what the prevailing conditions were which affected the life of refugees. The reader becomes acquainted with the official attitudes and regulations, the attitudes of the local population, practical means of earning a living, the best local restaurants and hotels for maximizing the effect of meager financial means, ways of obtaining fraudulent identification, local border supervision, and finally, regulations and penalties for illegal residence. In short, *Liebe deinen Nächsten* is a repository of exile lore; some of which Remarque learned firsthand but most of which he learned from the stories of exiles. The situation is reminiscent of the way in which he collected material for *Im Westen nichts Neues*.

Even as a stateless refugee Ludwig Kern was fortunate in having much to give meaning and comfort to his life. Not only was he adaptable and resourceful but he enjoyed the support and friendship of Steiner. Most important, however, was the love he shared with Ruth Holland. Ruth was a fellow refugee who had been forced to give up her university studies and leave Germany because she was Jewish. For both of them their love came to be the chief sustaining force in their lives. Their love in its happy times is quite similar to the best moments of the Robby-Pat love in *Drei Kameraden*. The most striking difference is the happy ending which Remarque grants to Ludwig and Ruth. Their good fortune comes as a result of the generosity of their benefactor Steiner and a few other of their exile friends. The money left to them by Steiner has made it possible for them to receive passage for two on a Portuguese freighter sailing from Bordeaux to Mexico (shades of Jeanne) with some money left over for a new start. Visas and entry permission for Mexico have been arranged through the Refugees' Aid Committee.

There is no happy ending, however, for Josef Steiner and his wife Marie. During the period of his exile from Germany Steiner has not tried to communicate with her to avoid endangering her. One day he receives a letter from her which is delivered by another exile. The letter tells of her hospitalization and is, in effect, a letter of farewell although no cause of illness is stated. Any Remarque reader, however, will instantly suspect that the disease is cancer. Steiner immediately calls the hospital and learns that Marie has only a few days to live. There is now only one course possible for him; he must return to Germany to see Marie. When Steiner announces his decision to Ludwig, Ruth, and his other friends it is clear to all of them that his return to Germany will almost certainly result in his death at the hands of the Nazis. His friend Marill tries to dissuade him; but to no avail.

To explain his reasons Steiner says:

> "Marill, she is still all there for me, she is alive, she breathes, her eyes are still there and her thoughts, I am still there behind those eyes—and in a few days she will be dead- - - But now, now she is still alive for a few days longer, the last days—and I am not to be with her? Try to understand that I must go. There is no other way. Damn it, the world

is ending; if I don't see her I'll simply break. I'll die with her.- - -I know what you mean. I understand it too. I'm not crazy. I know what the stakes are, but if they were a thousand times higher I'd still take that train and nothing could stop me."[2]

Steiner does take the train and is able to make his way back into Germany to his hometown to see Marie. Marie urges Steiner to leave after their reunion so as not to be caught by the Nazis. Although he will have none of it, the matter soon becomes academic because, when he leaves the room, he is taken into custody by three armed men. His old nemesis Steinbrenner is one of them. The nurse has reported his visit. When interrogated by a Nazi official, Steiner is asked to give the names of his fellow anti-Nazi political activists who have not yet been apprehended. Steiner deceptively agrees to do so with the understanding that he will be allowed two more days to spend with Marie in the hospital before he has to reveal the names. Although the terms are agreed to, the full time is not needed. His next visit was their last time together.

"Marie's breathing became shallow, then it came in gasps with pauses. Finally it was almost inaudible, and ceased, like a gentle breeze falling asleep. Steiner held her hands until they grew cold. He died with her. When he got up to go out he was an insentient stranger, an empty shell that had the motions of a man."[3]

As he leaves the room he is taken into custody by Steinbrenner who is elated at the prospect of lavishing his particular brand of sadism on Steiner. However, Steiner has different plans. They descend the broad stairway in the hospital. "The open bay window grew larger, came nearer; very near—he thrust Steinbrenner toward it, leaped against him, over him, and pitched with him into the space."[4]

* * * * * *

Given the subject matter of this latest novel and the success Hollywood had enjoyed with Remarque novels, the movie version of *Liebe deinen Nächsten* was not long in coming. It appeared in 1941 at the same time as the second printing of *Flotsam*. The movie was entitled "So Ends Our Night." It was released by United Artists and produced by David L. Loew and Albert Lewin. The movie was directed by John Cromwell from a screenplay adapted from the Remarque novel by Talbot Jennings.

The cast of actors chosen was excellent. The veteran actor Fredric March played Steiner and Frances Dee was his wife Marie. The promising young actor Glenn Ford was given the role of Ludwig Kern. Margaret Sullavan, who had been highly praised for her excellent performance as Pat Hollman in "Three Comrades," was cast as the most important female love interest, Ruth Holland. Ann Stein was the Slavic gypsy woman who befriended Steiner and Kern when they worked at the Prater in Vienna. The Nazi Steinbrenner's name was shortened to Brenner for the movie. This important cameo role was well-played, with appropriate malevolence, by Erich von Stroheim.

The movie was warmly received by theatre audiences but critical reviews were mixed. Critics such as Bosley Crowther of the *New York Times* were luke-warm toward the production. It was generally conceded that the cast was good but that more could have been done with the story.

24

The Last Years in Hollywood

On May 9, 1941 Erich and Jeanne Remarque appeared at the American Consulate in Tijuana, Mexico to make formal application for an Immigration Visa under the quota system. Their application forms indicated that they would be entering the United States at San Ysidro, California with a destination of 1050 Hilts Avenue in West Los Angeles, California. It is open to question as to whether they really intended to live permanently in the United States as their applications indicated. They certainly did want American citizenship, however, and this was the first official step toward that end. Formal declaration of intention to become a citizen of the United States was filed by Remarque October 8, 1941 in Los Angeles. Jeanne filed her declaration in New York City November 5, 1941.

The Hilts Avenue address was never intended to be the long-term residence of Jeanne Remarque. She remained only a short time before leaving for New York to take up residence in the Hotel Pierre at Fifth Avenue and 61st Street. They now went their separate ways because that was what Remarque wanted. He was quite willing to support Jeanne in comfortable style in a separate establishment but he required an independent life style and the freedom to enjoy an "open" marriage. With the steps taken toward her citizenship, and financial support provided, Remarque apparently now felt that he had done his duty for his nominal marriage partner.

In 1941 Remarque's romantic interest in Marlene Dietrich was in full flower. The relationship suffered a setback, however, when the French actor Jean Gabin appeared in Hollywood. Gabin, whom Marlene had met before the war in Paris, had been one of the group of friends vacationing in the south of France in 1939. Now he was in Hollywood because of Darryl F. Zanuck's offer of a contract at Twentieth Century-Fox. However, Gabin was even less pleased than Remarque had been with the Hollywood types and the general atmosphere of the film capitol.

The Hollywood nightspots now saw a new romantic couple as Gabin and Dietrich made the rounds. Remarque cooled his heels. Charles Higham succinctly expressed the differences in the two men. "Whereas Remarque had attracted Marlene because of his uncompromising, austere intellect, Gabin clearly drew her by reason of his earthy, perhaps rather stupid, but constantly alive peasant quality, his sheer manly virility."[1] Gabin's earthiness was apparently not enough to sustain a long-term relationship. Within two years he had departed Hollywood.

The Remarque-Dietrich relationship remained alive but tenuous until about 1942 when a wryly amusing incident, reported in a *Colliers* article of May 14, 1954, served as one of the final straws. A "Hollywood Friend" reported that Marlene had given Remarque several tropical fish for the aquarium in his Westwood home. Three of the fish were her particular favorites because their tail markings looked like the French tricolor. For that reason she called them the "French Fleet." Remarque, who loved tropical fish, was very pleased to have them. At first he was quite conscientious in caring for Marlene's gift but little by little the novelty wore off and he neglected their care. The terminal effect of that neglect became apparent one evening when Marlene and some other guests came to his home for dinner. Marlene checked the aquarium to see how the "French Fleet" was getting along and saw to her horrified surprise that the "French Fleet," along with some other fish, was now floating dead on the surface. As the "Hollywood Friend" put it: "The dinner went very badly; she kept referring to the fish, and everybody at the table could feel the tension. We all left immediately after dinner. I don't think she and Remarque saw much of each other after that."[2]

Reporter Joseph Laitin in Hollywood told of an interview he had with Marlene Dietrich in which he:

> "asked who her greatest and closest friend had been. That all depends she said, on what I meant by 'greatest' and 'closest;' did I mean the person she saw most now, or a long time ago; did I mean the person she loved the most, the person she'd most like to be with, the one who loved her most—? 'I just can't answer the question,' she said, and changed the subject. But just before I left her, the conversation turned back to her friends and I carefully raised the question again. She sat silently for a moment, staring straight ahead, then said in a very small voice: 'Mr. Remarque—but I don't see him very often now'."[3]

When Remarque was interviewed for the same Dietrich article his comments were brief and far less revealing. "She is a very great and generous artist and a very great personality. That is all I can say."[4] His remarks are precisely the response one would expect from a man of his pride and passion for privacy in matters which affected him deeply. Remarque was never less than a gentleman in his public statements no matter how acerbic his private comments may have been.

There is no comment on the record from Remarque as to his reaction to the humorous scenario made up by Marlene to describe what would happen at her funeral. It's unlikely he would have been greatly amused. The story was apparently a party standard with Marlene which was augmented with new details during the course of several narrations. Irving Hoffman and Joseph Laitin are quoted at some length in the *Collier's* article as they discuss the story.

> "Writer-Publicist Irving Hoffman: I wrote a column on the funeral story in the *Hollywood Reporter* a few years ago. Miss Dietrich tells the story at parties, reciting it in script form. According to the script, only men who have known her well will be permitted to attend the Dietrich rites—and her husband, equipped with a list, will be posted at the door to keep out gate crashers - - - the many men who have falsely insisted they have been her friend.
>
> Laitin: Her friends told me that the funeral story gets longer and longer as time goes on—and more hilarious, as she caricatures the men who will be admitted. Douglas Fairbanks, Jr., she indicated, will show

up in a full-dress Navy uniform, bearing a wreath from the Queen of England; French actor Jean Gabin (who is said to have ranked next to Remarque in her esteem) will be leaning against the church door, a cigarette dangling from his lips, disdaining to join the other mourners; Remarque, with characteristic vagueness, will be at the wrong church, mourning at the wrong funeral. Other men get similar treatment in the story—British actor Michael Wilding, Gary Cooper, James Stewart, John Wayne, and many more."[5]

One of Marlene's well-known admirers who did not figure in her funeral story was Ernest Hemingway. It certainly wasn't because he wasn't important to her or she to him. The "Kraut" and "Papa" were very close friends over a period of several years.

In a strange way, circumstances made Hemingway and Remarque rivals. Each had a reputation as a hard-drinking, fast-living, "macho" representative of what Gertrude Stein termed the "lost generation." Each was closely associated with the Paris of the 1930's and '40's and each was associated with a well-known novel dealing with the first World War; Hemingway's *A Farewell to Arms* and Remarque's *Im Westen nichts Neues*. A mystique had also developed around each man; a mystique partly of his own making and partly the result of the public perception of the man. The inevitable comparisons of *A Farewell to Arms* and *Im Westen nichts Neues* were frequently made, apparently by persons who had only a nodding acquaintance with the works. The only real similarity the works have in common is that each is set in the World War I period. There is no doubt that Remarque's novel remains the definitive work on the real war.

Apparently Hemingway was jealous not only of Remarque's literary success but also of his relationship with Marlene. This attitude came out clearly in Hemingway's conversation with his biographer A. E. Hotchner as reported in *Papa Hemingway*. Hemingway was elaborating on his relationship with Marlene:

"The thing about the Kraut and me - - - is that we have been in love since 1934, when we first met on the "Ile de France," but we've never been to bed. Amazing but true. Victims of un-synchronized passion.

> Those times when I was out of love, the Kraut was deep in some romantic tribulation, and on those occasions when Dietrich was on the surface and swimming about with those marvelously seeking eyes of hers, I was submerged. There was another crossing on the "Ile," years after that first one, when something could have happened, the only time, but I had too recently made love to that worthless M—, and the Kraut was still somewhat in love with that equally worthless R—."[6]

Hotchner has confirmed that the initial "R" indicated Remarque.[7] It is a pity that there is no comparable Remarque assessment of Hemingway.

Although Remarque's romantic involvement with Marlene was the most important of his relationships in Hollywood, he enjoyed a very active social life in general. Here, as in Europe, it was a social life on his own terms. Much of his socializing was done with friends in his own home or in theirs. In these controlled situations Remarque and his celebrity friends could find the privacy they ordinarily desired. Even his well-publicized forays into the world of Hollywood nightclubs remained essentially controlled because he and his fellow patrons were not really exposed to the general public. There were exceptions, however. Remarque often dropped in around midnight at a nightclub for a nightcap. On those occasions he was usually convivial and accessible to anyone who wished to share a drink or a story. When Remarque was in the mood, few people were more amiable.

As was to be expected, most of Remarque's friends in California were German or Austrian and were associated with the movie industry or were members of the exile community. Among his friends were the writers Walter Reisch, Franz Werfel, Carl Zuckmayer, and Lion Feuchtwanger; the publisher and literary agent Felix Guggenheim; producers Alexander Korda and Josef von Sternberg; actress Elisabeth Bergner and her husband Paul Czinner. He was also a frequent guest of the Jesse Lasky's at their Santa Monica beach front house.

During his residence in California, and indeed during all of the World War II period, there is no evidence that Remarque was a part of any organized exile activity against the Nazis. He did not contribute to any of the exile publications or participate in the lecturing or radio interviews so common among his fellow exiles. The reason for this lack of involvement on his part certainly did not come from a diminished hostility to the Nazis. For him the Nazis represented the darkest and most bestial side of man's nature. However, it was impossible for him to attack his beloved Germany. And also at the time it was obviously impossible to make a realistic distinction between the Nazis and Germany. There were other reasons for his failure to become politically involved. The most obvious was his declared position even before he achieved celebrity status. At that time he stated that he was not a political person. His position in this respect remained quite consistent. He also thought that the anti-Nazi statements he could make through his novels would be more effective, and reach a larger audience, than some of the more dramatic means chosen by others. *Liebe deinen Nächsten*, and its movie version, had done a good job in this regard. The next novel, which he had already begun, was to be another story of the exile plight. However, it would be another five years before *Der Triumphbogen* or *Arch of Triumph* would be released for publication. Not only was Remarque a painstaking writer whose writing had not gone particularly well in California, but one who preferred an interval of three to five years between his novels. It was always commercially desirable to have his readers eagerly anticipating the next release.

By January of 1942 Remarque was ready for a change of scene and routine. When he made the decision to move to New York he closed his Westwood home and set about making the arrangements for the housing of his extensive art collection.

25

The Art Collection

Remarque had started collecting paintings and other works of art as soon as his literary success could be translated into an income commensurate with his artistic tastes. His interest in art was a long-standing one; dating back at least to his Gymnasium years in Osnabrück. Shortly after World War I he was writing art criticism for Osnabrück newspapers and articles for his favorite publication, *Die Schönheit* in Dresden.

There appears to be no doubt that his interest in art was genuine. However, with Remarque there was also often present the element of snobbishness. He was a man committed to the enjoyment of the "best" things his celebrity and material resources could command. He broke no new ground by believing that those things were: the most beautiful women, the best of food and drink, the fastest cars, the best of accomodations, and now, the acquisition of masterpieces of art. Although it was important for him to have the best, it would be unfair to him to imply that undiscriminating acquisitiveness was the chief factor in his collecting. He bought only what appealed to him and was not motivated by a desire to use his purchases to make a later profit; although he was a canny businessman who enjoyed seeing his art works appreciate in value. As Remarque's collection grew, so did his detailed knowledge of art. He had a scholarly passion to learn everything possible about the artists and areas of his collecting interests.

Most of Remarque's art collection was kept in his villa in Switzerland before 1939. Shortly before the beginning of the war it was taken to the United States. It was in his Westwood house when he decided to make the move to New York City.

The collection was loaned to the Los Angeles County Museum of Art for an indefinite period. It was stored by the museum from January 13, 1942 until there was a special exhibit of his collection. That exhibit ran from November 22, 1942 through January of 1943. The collection was valued at $100,000., which was wildly conservative even at that time.

A listing of the works shown in the Los Angeles exhibit reveals an almost exclusive preference for nineteenth-century French painters. The artists represented were: Paul Cezanne, Edgar Degas, Honore Daumier, Eugene Delacroix, Pablo Picasso, August Renoir, Henri Toulouse-Lautrec, and Maurice Utrillo. Cezanne was best represented with three oil paintings and nineteen watercolors. Degas was next in importance with two oil paintings, four pastels, one gouache, and two drawings. Daumier had three oil paintings and two drawings. There was also one oil painting by Delacroix and a drawing by Picasso. Also included were two oils by Renoir, one oil by Utrillo, and two pastels by Toulouse-Lautrec.

In addition to this outstanding collection of paintings and water colors, other important areas of Remarque's collecting interests were represented in the Los Angeles exhibit. There were four Chinese bronze pieces dating from the Chou and Han dynasties. In addition there were nine pieces of ancient Chinese pottery: one vase from the Han dynasty and eight figural pieces from the Tang dynasty portraying musicians, dancers, and a buffalo cart with buffalo.

The collection also included two Egyptian paintings. Both were mummy portraits of women which were found in Fayum and dated from the first century.

A splendid group of seven oriental carpets completed the exhibit. Four of the carpets dated from the seventeenth century and three from the sixteenth century. The work of Persian and Armenian craftsmen predominated in this collection.

The Remarque collection, minus the Chinese bronzes and pottery, was next on public display in New York at the Knoedler Galleries at 14 East Fifty-seventh Street. This loan exhibition of the pictures was arranged by Sam Salz, Remarque's friend and art dealer in New York. The Knoedler exhibition ran from October 18 to November 13, 1943 and was a very popular attraction.

The New York showing was the last time his collection was on public display in the United States. After the war most of his art works were transferred to his home near Ascona. Although several items were on display from time to time in various Swiss museums, his collection essentially was one he had chosen to live with. Everything in it reflected his own tastes and had been selected chiefly for his pleasure and not just for his profit.

26

The Tragedy of Elfriede Remark Scholz

After closing his Westwood home Remarque moved to New York and took a corner suite in the Ambassador Hotel on Park Avenue. He lived and worked here until he moved some years later to an apartment at 320 East 57th Street.

1942 and 1943, the first years of his New York residence, passed rather uneventfully for Remarque. He was working on another exile novel which would be named *Arc de Triomphe,* (*Arch of Triumph*). That novel, however, would not appear until 1946. Life was good for Remarque. He could write at his usual leisurely pace without feeling the necessity of rushing a book into print. He could also enjoy a fairly modest social and public life which included visits with a few friends and occasional interviews with journalists. There were also frequent visits to fashionable restaurants and night spots such as "The Stork Club" and "21" where he became a regular.

On September 21, 1943 he settled an income tax dispute with the federal government regarding his 1939 income tax. The government disputed some of the deductions he had claimed for travel expenses and calculated that he owed $8,921.50 more in taxes. Remarque and the government agreed on the compromise amount of $3,892.50 to settle the matter.

In the autumn of 1943, at about the same time Remarque was settling his federal tax difficulties, his sister Elfriede in Germany was becoming involved in events which were to end in her tragic death. Elfriede, who was five years younger than Remarque, had become a "Damenschneidermeisterin" (a master ladies' tailor) and married a man named Heinz Scholz in Dresden in 1941. In 1943 she was the proprietress of a prosperous fashion salon in Dresden. Prior to that she had moved frequently. The municipal registry record in Osnabrück, for example, indicates moves to Duisburg, Rheydt, and the Hague in the years 1917 to 1923. She always returned to Osnabrück after each move. However, on March 26, 1926 she moved to Leipzig and, after that came back only for visits.

Elfriede and her brother had never been particularly close because of the difference in their ages and the divergence of their paths. They had also not seen each other for a number of years. Nevertheless, Elfriede shared Remarque's outspokenness; and that was a very dangerous quality in the terror-laden atmosphere of Hitler's Germany.

The specific outspokenness which brought her into conflict with Nazi authorities occurred in the spring of 1943. At that time, according to the charges made against her, over a period of months she made defeatist and subversive comments which were regarded as harmful to morale. Those charges resulted in a mockery of a trial which culminated in a death sentence against her. The basic details of the Nazi case against Elfriede are found in the official judgement:

In the Name of the German People

In the criminal case against
the master ladies' tailor Elfriede Scholz née Remark from Dresden, born on March 25, 1903 in Osnabrück, at the time in police custody because of seditious remarks,
the People's Court, First Senate, on the basis of the principal proceeding of October 29, 1943 in which there participated as judges:
President of the People's Court Dr. Freisler, presiding,
Provincial Court Director Dr. Schulze-Weckert,
SA-Senior Section-Leader Lasch,
SA-Senior Leader Hell,
General Labor Leader von Mangold, as representative of the Chief Public Prosecutor:
Supreme Court Councillor Prietzschk
finds that:
Mrs. Elfriede Scholz née Remark has over a period of months made immoderate, mischief-making, defeatist statements to the wife of a

soldier which intensified to statements that she would like to blow the Führer's brains out (that) our soldiers are beasts to be slaughtered (and) the Führer will have them on his conscience
she would hope for the combat soldiers that their wives would die in the bombing terror and (she hoped) for the women who believed in victory that their husbands would die in a foreign country.

As a dishonorable, fanatic, seditious propagandist of our war enemies she is forever without honor. She is punished with death.

Reasons

Mrs. Elfriede Scholz struck her landlady, the previously mentioned Mrs. Toni Wentzel, in many conversations as a woman who does not believe in our victory, who also scornfully, at any sort of setback, asks whether she (Mrs. Wentzel) still believes in victory. The previously mentioned Mrs. Wentzel has credibly testified that with calm certitude.

In addition, Mrs. Scholz for months has had a defeatist demoralizing influence on Mrs. Ingeborg Rietzel. She knew Mrs. Rietzel as her customer—she is a ladies' tailor—and had become friendly with her. Thus they sometimes met in the home of Mrs. Rietzel and sometimes also in the home of Mrs. Scholz. As Mrs. Rietzel has testified, she also revealed to her her scornful and ironic nature, particularly in remarks concerning the outcome of the war, she didn't believe in victory, and (asked) whether Mrs. Rietzel still believed in victory. Mrs. Rietzel still remembers precisely individual particularly striking demoralizing and defeatist utterances. Mrs. Scholz once said to her: "What kind of luck has he brought us? All of the people who go to the front are only cattle for the slaughter, all of whom he has on his conscience. If I were offered the opportunity, then I myself would blow out his brains. I would gladly bear the consequences. The German people then would at least be freed from this man. I would gladly sacrifice myself."
Or: "Does this idiot perhaps want to have all of our cities destroyed before he makes peace?"
Or: "I have traveled through the world and seen many peoples. If the enemies come in it won't be so bad. They are much better than we are always told, and Germany through its own fault is so hated in the entire world."
Or: "I wish for the women who are still 'for the war' (that is in this context that they believe in victory) that their husbands will be killed abroad. And for the men who are still out there fighting fanatically that their wives and children at home will be killed by the bombs."

Mrs. Elfriede Scholz admits, because of a general pessimism, to have expressed doubts concerning the outcome of the war. However she only did that in order to strengthen herself. She of course knew that Mrs. Rietzel is a faithful National Socialist; just as she knew that the husband of Mrs. Rietzel is an active officer and is, body and soul, a soldier and faithful National Socialist. She thought that she could be encouraged by the two of them. Moreover, she did not speak as Mrs. Rietzel has testified.

In reality however she made defeatist and demoralizing statements and also didn't at all have the intention to be converted to National Socialism by Mrs. Rietzel but on the contrary attempted to destroy the belief of Mrs. Rietzel. Mrs. Rietzel has presented before the court all of the previously mentioned testimony, and the scornful-ironic nature of Mrs. Scholz, with such convincing positiveness and with the impression of a thoroughly credible personality, with the (full) awareness of her responsibility as a witness without any malice, that no doubt can exist (that) it was as she testified. Moreover, the basic attitude of Mrs. Scholz's remarks, as reported by Mrs. Rietzel, is entirely consistent with the basic attitude of Mrs. Scholz attested to by Mrs. Wentzel. Both witnesses were not acquainted with each other when they were interrogated for the first time in this case and so testified.

If Mrs. Scholz wishes to attribute her pessimism in part to the influence of her brother, the author of the notorious pot-boiler *All Quiet on the Western Front*, she can still not excuse herself, particularly in view of the fact that, on the basis of her own testimony, she has not seen her brother for 13 years. She is, rather, a shameless traitress of her own (and) our own German blood, of our front, (and) of our life as a people, a defeatist, trouble-making propagandist of our war enemies (5KSSVO, 91b StGB.). For a woman so unprincipled and therefore devoid for ever of all honor there can be, if we ourselves do not wish to surrender, only one punishment: the death penalty.

Because Mrs. Elfriede Scholz is condemned, she must also bear the costs (of the proceedings).

(signed) Dr. Freisler Dr. Schulze-Weckert[1]

There is no evidence of an appeal, or the possibility of an appeal, for the sentence of death meted out to Elfriede Scholz. Although it is not known where she was incarcerated for most of the almost two months between sentencing and the execution of the sentence, she was moved to Plötzensee prison in Berlin before judicial murder was carried out.

Motivated by a feeling of pathological nostalgia for one of the barbaric practices of the Germanic past, the Nazis favored the headsman's axe as the method of execution for certain types of offenses. This was the method employed in the case of Elfriede Scholz. She was beheaded at 12:57 A.M., December 16, 1943 in Plötzensee prison.

On the day of her execution she was allowed to write a final, brief note of farewell to her sister Erna.

> Dear Erna!
>
> Now, for the first time, I am in Plötzensee and at midday today at one o'clock I will be no more. Everything that I leave belongs to you (as well as) the life insurance. Heinz has certainly not deserved that I still have affection for him. However, I forgive him everything, and all others (as well). A last fond greeting to you and Ludwig and the parents.
>
> Your Elfriede

Elfriede's note is very interesting not only because of what she said but also because of what was left unsaid. For example, one can only speculate about the reasons for her comments about her husband Heinz Scholz in view of the fact that almost nothing is known about their relationship and his fate. For what was she forgiving him? Was it simply for marital sins, for not being supportive of her, or something more sinister? More interesting, however, is Elfriede's failure to mention her brother. It may be that since they had been apart for so many years their relationship was only nominal, or less. It may also be that she was afraid that her last message might not be delivered to Erna if her brother were prominently mentioned. She may also have felt that Erich indirectly bore a large share of the blame for her tragic position because the Nazis' hatred of him had been directed at her. If Remarque had not been her brother the disposition of her case might have been different. Roland Freisler, the presiding judge at her trial, essentially confirmed this suspicion with his remarks to her at that time. Freisler indicated that because her brother was beyond the control of the court she would have to help atone for his guilt.

Such outrageous departures from judicial decorum and basic human decency were hallmarks of the "Volksgerichtshof" under Roland Freisler. This "People's Court" was the embodiment of the judicial reign of terror directed against any real or imagined enemies of the Nazi regime who were unlucky enough to be brought before it. Guilt was assumed. Freisler was the perfect person to carry out "Das neue Strafrecht" (the new criminal law) whose principles he had set forth in a book by that title which he co-authored. Freisler could not be expected to show any sympathy to anyone who had less than total commitment to Nazi ideals. He himself had been a dedicated member of the party since 1925 and, as politician and lawyer, advanced from local political positions to the Prussian Ministry of Justice in 1933. The next year he joined the National Ministry of Justice. He assumed his position as President of the People's Court in 1942 and was therefore in the position to serve as Elfriede Scholz's nemesis. It is regretable that this most notorious of the Nazi judges could not be called to account in a real court of justice for the outrageous crimes he committed against his fellow Germans. However, he did not escape a retribution which was rather more direct. On February 3, 1945 Roland Freisler was killed in the collapse of a building during an American bombing attack on Berlin.

After the execution of Elfriede Remark Scholz the Nazis made a nominal attempt to carry out the provision in the official judgment that she should bear the cost of the action taken against her. This included the cost of her execution. There is no evidence to indicate that a charge was ever made against the extremely modest estate of Elfriede or that Erna was ever billed. Either of those courses of action would have been logical. Instead, with grisly malice, the Gestapo sent Remarque a bill for 90 Marks for his sister's execution. The bill was found among his effects after his death.

A postscript was added to this tragic case after the war when Remarque, in an attempt to obtain a measure of retroactive justice, asked his attorney, Dr. Robert M. W. Kempner, to pursue the matter through legal measures. Dr. Kempner initiated a complaint of "judicial murder" which was directed to the General Prosecuting Office in Berlin. However, the attempt was frustrated because the women who had made the denunciations of Elfriede could not be located.

Fortunately, this frustration proved not to be the final word in the case. On the twenty-fifth anniversary of her execution the city council of Osnabrück, voted to honor Elfriede Scholz by naming a street "Elfriede-Scholz-Strasse." Cold comfort perhaps, but better than none.

Remarque, who was then living at his home in Porto Ronco, wrote to the Osnabrück City Council to express his appreciation for the honor they had given his sister. The *Osnabrücker Nachrichten* for January 24, 1969 reported that the letter read, in part: "I am deeply moved by the generous and noble gesture of the city of Osnabrück and would like to express to you from the heart my gratitude for that."[2]

A later article in the same newspaper written by Frau Ilsetraut Lindemann had more to say on the subject. That article appeared November 11, 1970, slightly more than two months after Remarque's death. Lindemann reported that she had written to Remarque earlier (presumably a year earlier, around the time of the City Council decision) and asked for information about Elfriede. Remarque responded with a friendly letter in which he indicated that if something were written about his sister he would like to be the one to write it. Lindemann went on to say that Remarque had never said anything about his sister in conversations with friends (the friends with whom she had talked, at any rate) and one would have to assume that he did not care to discuss family matters. Her assumption was right on target. No researcher or interviewer ever succeeded in extracting directly from him important information of a personal nature. Anything which touched him deeply he locked away inside himself. Remarque's standard reaction to probing inquiries was that his novels provided all of the important autobiographical information one needed.

27

Arch of Triumph: The Novel and the Movie

In 1946 Remarque's fifth official novel appeared. *Arc de Triomphe*, or *Arch of Triumph*, was the second novel dealing with the exile theme. As in the case of *Liebe deinen Nächsten* the story takes place in the period immediately preceding the outbreak of war in Europe. The setting this time, however, is Paris; a city which Remarque loved and knew well.

In contrast to *Liebe deinen Nächsten* this novel has only one male protagonist; a German exile doctor in Paris who calls himself Ravic. Ravic, whose real name is Ludwig Fresenburg, has been living in Paris for more than two years and supports himself by doing ghost surgery at the hospital of Dr. Durant. Durant is an aging society doctor who is making a name for himself by exploiting, through "ghost" surgery, skills which made Ravic-Fresenburg chief surgeon at an important hospital in Germany. The jealousy and resentment shown to Ravic by nurse Eugenie and Doctor Durant are offset by the friendship and appreciation of Ravic by his French medical colleague Doctor Veber.

Ravic is one of Remarque's most memorable and self-sufficient protagonists; a prototypical survivor who has mastered the skills necessary to cope with life as a stateless exile while at the same time remaining faithful to his innate sense of decency and human dignity. In short, Ravic is almost a mirror image reflecting many facets of the character of his literary creator.

Although Ravic is depicted as a person of great emotional strength and courage, Remarque does not hesitate to show the areas of his vulnerability. Ravic shares with his fellow exiles the uncertainties of a life without official sanction and documentation in which one can suddenly be taken into custody by the authorities and deported. However, unlike most of the exiles, his medical ability has gained for him a position, however tenuous, which is more than adequate for his material needs. Deportation as well holds fewer fears for him than for most because he has already experienced the procedure and knows how to cope with the unfeeling French bureaucracy. The threat of deportation represents only an endurable inconvenience for a person as resourceful as Ravic.

The reasonably well-ordered exile life Ravic has made for himself is considerably complicated by the appearance of Joan Madou. Joan, a mediocre actress and singer, was wandering one night through the streets of Paris in a dazed and potentially suicidal condition as a reaction to the sudden death of the man with whom she had been living when Ravic took her in his charge. His solicitude, purely humanitarian at first, gradually develops into a bitter-sweet and problematic love. Joan attaches herself emotionally to Ravic and he, fearful that she might commit suicide in her despair, feels obligated to look after her. The self-sufficient Ravic certainly does not intend to fall in love with Joan. However, he is drawn to her despite himself. The love that he comes to shares with Joan is beset with difficulties arising from her neurotic possessiveness and unpredictability. Ravic, a logical man, is often at a loss to understand Joan's attitudes and her often arbitrary actions. Joan wishes only to be loved but not necessarily understood. In several long conversations Joan and, particularly, Ravic attempt to clarify their relationship. These conversations, although often tiresome, do serve the purpose of developing the characters for the reader and of demonstrating the skill Remarque has in writing believable, and often powerful, dialogue.

Ravic's frustration in dealing with the alternately fascinating and exasperating Joan grows as he attempts to cope with an erratic relationship in which the stability of predictable behavior is absent. After suffering through Joan's infidelities, and the resultant emotional anguish involved in trying to resolve their different ways of looking at their relationship, Ravic attempts to break away. That proves difficult to do because Joan calls on him for help later when she is living with an actor. The first time she calls it is a false alarm and merely an attempt to effect a reconciliation. The second call, however, is a true cry for help after she receives what proves to be a fatal gunshot wound from her lover. Because she does not say specificially why she wants Ravic to come to the apartment he at first refuses. It is only when the actor comes to get him, and confesses his deed, that Ravic goes to her aid. By this time it is too late for effective medical treatment. Ravic has Joan taken to Veber's hospital but does not operate because nothing can be done due to the nature of her wound. In a scene reminiscent of the last moments of Pat in *Drei Kameraden,* Ravic and Joan say their goodbyes with mutual pledges of love. As a progressive paralysis begins to effect her respiration Ravic accedes to her request and gives her an injection to end her suffering.

Joan's suffering ends just as France's suffering begins. German troops have invaded Poland and France will soon be at war. Ravic knows that it is now time to appear before the authorities under his true name of Ludwig Fresenburg because the danger of deportation to Germany or even to Switzerland is over. As the novel ends with Ravic being driven by the French police to his place of internment, Remarque describes a darkness which not only symbolizes the tragedy of Ravic's loss but also the darkness of war and suffering which was descending upon Europe. "The car drove along the Avenue Wagram and turned into the Place de l'tEtoile. There was no light anywhere. The square was nothing but darkness. It was so dark that one could not even see the Arc de Triomphe."[1]

Although the relationship of Ravic and Joan is the most important and interesting one in the novel, there are several other noteworthy characters and subplots. Among the most memorable characters is Ravic's friend, the Russian Boris Morosow who works as the doorman of the Scheherazade night club. Morosow has been a refugee in Paris for fifteen years and serves as Remarque's prototypical exile figure and in some ways is reminiscent of the old veteran "Kat" in *Im Westen nichts Neues*. Boris is Ravic's friend, chess opponent, drinking companion, and confidant. He is survival-wise and shares with Ravic the ability to reduce life to its essentials. He also shares with Ravic a compulsive desire to exact vengeance for past wrongs. In Boris' case it is the hope that he will have the opportunity to settle accounts with his father's murderers. Unfortunately, that hope remains unfulfilled. However, Ravic is allowed his revenge in full measure. The story of how he achieves that revenge constitutes the most important of the novel's subplots.

In 1933 Ravic ran afoul of the Nazis by helping two friends escape the Gestapo. One friend was a Jewish writer and the other was a comrade from the war who had saved Ravic's life in 1917 by carrying him back from No Man's Land where he was lying, bleeding to death from his wounds. When the Gestapo brought Ravic in for questioning his interrogator was a sadist named Haake who supervised a three-day period of torture in an unsuccessful attempt to extract information from him. Haake also tortured Ravic's girl friend Sybil in an equally unsuccessful interrogation. Neither Ravic nor Sybil had the information Haake sought. Both Sybil and Ravic fought back against their torturers. As a result Sybil was sent to a concentration camp for women where she hanged herself. Ravic was also sent to a concentration camp but escaped from the camp's hospital.

The full horror of those events is brought back to Ravic with painful clarity when he suddenly catches a glimpse of Haake on the street in Paris. Unfortunately the Haake figure vanishes into the crowd. However, any doubt as to whether Ravic was merely hallucinating ends when he sees Haake dining in Fouquet's restaurant. Because he is also a patron at the time, Ravic has an opportunity to collect his composure and to study his target. There is no mistake; it is the same person. Upon leaving the restaurant Ravic is stopped by Haake. Haake has noticed the scar on Ravic's forehead and, ironically, mistakes for a dueling scar the scar which provides evidence of Ravic's torture at his hands. Haake is pleased because he thinks he has had a lucky meeting with a fellow German. Ravic encourages his mistaken assumption and cultivates the chance acquaintance in order to find an opportunity to kill him. By taking advantage of Haake's desire to visit some of the famed Paris brothels, Ravic is able to set up an appointment with him two weeks hence when he will return to Paris. Ravic uses the time to plan what he hopes will be a perfect murder.

After a temporary mix-up caused by Haake's inability to remember their meeting place, Ravic gets his opportunity to exact a full measure of Remarque-style vengeance. A drive in a rented car toward a promised evening of pleasure in a nonexistent house of assignation allows Ravic to take Haake well away from the city before his suspicions become aroused. When that happens, a sudden braking stop sends Haake crashing against the dashboard and the windshield. Ravic takes advantage of a stunned Haake and uses a concealed monkey wrench to render him senseless. The execution is completed with Ravic's manual strangulation of Haake, his subsequent burial of the body, and the meticulous obliteration of all evidence of the Nazi's identity.

The killing of Haake is not only a perfect murder it is also one of the best examples of Remarque's fictive justice. It represents a cathartic settling of accounts which is an emotional necessity for Ravic and a vicarious catharsis for the reader. Even though justice is not always meted out appropriately in the real world the Remarque reader can usually find it administered in the novels in a form which is both imaginative and satisfying.

Unfortunately there are no guaranteed happy endings for many of his appealing and sympathetic characters. This is true of Goldberg the Jewish refugee who, defeated by the hardships of exile and the infidelity of his wife, hangs himself in his room. It is also true of the young prostitute Lucienne Martinet whom Ravic tries to help against all odds. It is also poignantly true of Ravic's thirty-four year-old American friend Kate Hegstroem.

Kate is the second most important female character in the novel, second only to Joan. Unlike Joan, however, there is no ambivalence in the relationship with Ravic. They are simply good friends. Ravic had removed her appendix and a friendship blossomed even on short acquaintance. Her operation had been his first in Paris and he considered her lucky for him. Life had not been particularly good for her, however, because she had recently gotten a divorce from a charming Austrian who lost his charm for her after he became a Nazi stormtroop leader. She had returned to Paris to seek Ravic's medical advice to explain her hemorrhaging. An exploratory operation reveals a shocking fact; Kate has cancer and it is so widespread as to be inoperable. Ravic can not bring himself to reveal to Kate that she has terminal cancer and allows her to believe that all will be well. However, Kate does learn the truth when she spends a period of recuperation at her home in Florence and consults with Dr. Fiola, a physician recommended to her by Ravic. Kate reacts to the knowledge of her condition with the character and grace one has come to expect from such sympathetic Remarque characters. Upon her return to Paris from Florence she does not reproach him for withholding the knowledge from her but merely said as they were about to take leave of each other after their first meeting: " 'Why didn't you tell me what was wrong with me?' she asked lightly as if she were asking about the weather. He stared at her and did not answer. 'I could have stood it,' she said and the ghost of an ironical smile with no reproach in it flitted across her face. 'Adieu, Ravic!' "[2] There were other meetings of Kate and Ravic as their friendship continued in Paris. The most notable was their attendance at the great social event of the summer in Paris, the Monfort Ball. Ravic escorted the wealthy and socially prominent Kate. In his description of the conspicuous affluence of the costume ball, counterbalanced by the Communist demonstrators outside on the street, Remarque provides a striking scene which brings to mind not only the ostentatious life style of the French nobility before the Revolution but also the decadence of a France on the eve of its fall to the armies of Nazi Germany. There is, however, no indictment of Kate Hegstroem even as Remarque describes in less than flattering terms the costumed party-goers who share her financial circumstances.

Kate is obviously a character close to Remarque's heart. It

may also be said that her cancer is, in a strange way, a sign of the author's favor. In his novels only sympathetic characters are allowed the disease from which his mother died. And Kate is indeed a sympathetic character. The wonder is that Remarque chose to limit their relationship to friendship instead of love because Kate has many of the characteristics of Remarque's most memorable fictional female love interests who share comradeship as well as love. If Remarque had chosen to make the character who shared Ravic's love a blend of Joan and Kate he would have simplified Ravic's life and created a far more sympathetic character.

Joan, however, is the character with the greater emotional impact who remains a haunting, enigmatic figure despite the best efforts of Ravic, and the reader, to understand her. What, if any, was her prototype among the women in Remarque's experience? The most obvious, and perhaps most likely, answer is Marlene Dietrich; obvious because it was she who had had the most recent emotional impact on Remarque. With Joan's blond hair, wide-set eyes, high cheek bones, and general body structure she certainly is physically very much like Marlene. Charles Higham in *Marlene* clearly equates Marlene with Joan:

> "Theirs (Marlene and Remarque) was a loving friendship, which he oddly echoed in his novel published at the end of the war, *Arch of Triumph,* in which he is dimly seen in the illegal doctor Ravic, and she, more in her twenties persona of a struggling actress, can be discovered in the character of a girl, Joan Madou, with whom Ravic falls in love. One can only regret the fact that she, with her toughness, tenderness, and melancholy, did not play the part in the film version, instead of the cheerful, self-assured Ingrid Bergman."[3]

One can agree with Higham to the extent that a much younger Marlene would have been an excellent casting for the part of Joan. However, the determination of Joan's counterpart in real life is not as simple. Remarque's first wife Jeanne, who apparently served as the model for Pat in *Drei Kameraden*, must also be considered. Physically and emotionally Jeanne had much in common with Joan. From the first of his significant fictive love relationships, that of Pat and Robby, to the last, Robert and Natasha in *Schatten im Paradies,* Remarque appears to have kept before him the lasting memory of his love for Jeanne. Therefore it seems plausible to regard his creation Joan as an amalgam of his memories of Jeanne and Marlene.

Arch of Triumph continues the exile theme started in *Liebe deinen Nächsten* but offers a more readable story. One interesting and unusual verification of the novel's impact, and reader identification with Ravic, may be found in the immediate celebrity status in America of Calvados, apple brandy from Normandy, which was one of Ravic's favorite drinks. Relatively unknown to the American public until this time, Calvados stocks were quickly exhausted by the demands of the sudden fad. Norman suppliers likely developed a sudden, profound appreciation of the power of literature. Indeed, distillers in general have had reason to be grateful for the wide occurence of their products in Remarque's novels.

The lasting impression of *Arch of Triumph,* however, is not that of fads but rather the bitter-sweet love of Joan and Ravic and the integrity and strength of one of Remarque's most impressive protagonists. At the end of the novel he is a man as alone as he was at the beginning, awaiting with strength and quiet heroism whatever an arbitrary fate has in store for him.

The success of this fifth novel made inevitable a screen version of the story. For Remarque this was five movies for five novels; a commercially enviable situation. There were to be problems, however.

The film was made by a newly-fledged corporation, Enterprise Pictures, organized by David Loew and Charles Einfeld. It was released by United Artists in 1948. The movie was produced by David Lewis and directed by Lewis Milestone who had received an Oscar for his direction of Remarque's first filmed novel "All Quiet on the Western Front." In addition to his work as director of "Arch of Triumph" Milestone also collaborated with Harry Brown in writing the screen play.

Because a turbulent love relationship is at the heart of the novel the casting of strong principals was vitally important. Charles Boyer was chosen for the Ravic role and Ingrid Bergman was persuaded to play Joan, although she had reservations at first. With the casting of this team Enterprise Pictures had brought together again the actors who had had great success in the 1944 MGM film "Gaslight." Ingrid Bergman won an Oscar for her superb performance in that film as a distraught wife being driven insane by her murderer husband. Charles Boyer also seemed a good choice to capture the strength and dignity of Ravic.

Casting for the other parts was not as satisfying. Although Louis Calheren was sufficiently urbane and witty as Ravic's confidant Boris Morosow he did not capture the full dimensions of the character. The choice of Charles Laughton to play the sadistic and menacing Haake was unfortunate because the Laughton mannerisms detracted from the role's potential credibility. Many of the interesting and important supporting characters in the novel did not survive the transition to the screenplay. Some deletions in the interest of streamlining are understandable; the decision to remove the Kate Hegstrom character is not.

Unfortunately the success of the novel, and two fine leading actors in the film, did not translate into movie success. The production was a commercial failure and only a very qualified artistic success. Ingrid Bergman received 175,000 dollars in cash for the film, with the further promise of twenty-five percent of the net profit. The latter provision of the agreement became strictly academic when there was no profit. There was, instead, a loss of approximately 2,000,000 dollars.

The concensus critical view was that the film had concentrated too greatly on the love story to the detriment of the exile theme. Bosley Crowther's review which appeared in *The New York Times* of April 21, 1948 was right on target. It was Crowther's belief that the film did not effectively express "the bleak atmosphere of pre-war Paris against a vast sense of continental doom. - - - Rather this over-drawn picture, upon which much time and coin were spent, is just a hermetically sealed love story played by beauteous Ingrid Bergman and Charles Boyer."[4] However, in regard to that love story Crowther continues:

> "- - - too much of a good thing—even of Bergman and Boyer is too much. - - - That, in the end, is the trouble with 'Arch of Triumph' on the screen: an over-indulgence of personalized romance to the disadvantage of the broader theme. - - - They're just actors in a slow, expensive film—a film, we might add, in which a blighted romance is all that stands as the tragic symbol of a tottering world."[5]

There is perhaps more truth than one might wish to acknowledge in Crowther's incisive judgement that " 'Arch of Triumph' is simply the story of a strong, sad man who falls in love with a tramp."[6] It may also be that it was the wrong time so soon after the war to present this intensely dramatic film. Whatever the reasons, the efforts of Bergman and Boyer were not enough to ensure success.

The financial problems of the film also caused difficulties for Remarque in receiving compensation for the film rights to the novel. In April, 1949 a breach of contract suit was filed in Los Angeles by his attornies against Enterprise Studios. The complaint stated that the studio had entered into an agreement to pay 50,000 dollars for film rights. The money was to be paid in 10,000 dollar installments. Remarque's suit alleged that the first installment due the past January was not made. This was the only time that Remarque had to resort to court action over film rights.

In a 1952 interview with *Der Spiegel* Remarque offered the following comments about the film.

> "I naturally can not take a stand and say: that is a bad film. - - - They used the most popular actors of that time, the director of *Im Westen Nichts Neues* and a top writer for the scenario. Then all of that promptly missed the mark. I was happy when I had my money and I never went to the studio. Only months later did I see the film by chance. If it had been up to me, Garbo would have played Joan. She visited me and said: 'That is a role for me'. However one should not interfere."[7]

28

Der Funke Leben (Spark of Life)

In New York in August, 1947 Remarque officially became a citizen of the United States. This brought to fruition a process which had begun on October 8, 1941 in Los Angeles with his formal declaration of intention to become a citizen. He was proud of his American citizenship and felt he had made a good adjustment to life in the United States. Remarque was quoted as saying, perhaps too euphorically, in 1945: "I am no more German for I do not think in German nor feel German, nor talk German. Even when I dream it is about America, and when I swear, it is American."[1] One can accept the spirit of the statement if not its total accuracy.

Despite the pleasure he took in his life in the United States, the attraction of Europe, particularly his home in Switzerland, was very strong. After war's end Remarque was able to return for extended visits to his beautiful home on Lake Maggiore. For several years he continued the visits to Ascona while maintaining his principal residence in New York. Remarque was quoted as saying:

> "I now think of New York as my home. It is an unbelievable city. There is virtually everything here. I am very happy to have become an American. I have met exceedingly cultivated people in America. Americans have an innate sense of freedom, whether they realize it or not. They act toward each other that way. It is so easy to mix with others. This freedom is something it is very hard for a European, who has not observed it, to conceive of."[2]

The freedom of which Remarque spoke was particularly appealing to a man who had so recently escaped the oppressive atmosphere of Nazi Germany. Despite the military defeat of

Germany he was well aware that the spirit of Naziism was still strong in many Germans. For this reason he decided that his next novel should portray as graphically as possible the worst of the Nazi horrors—the concentration camp. There was some professional risk involved in this decision because the subject would represent a complete departure from his practice of writing about experiences and/or places about which he had at least some first-hand knowledge. In this case he would have to make use of stories he had heard, and survivors' accounts he had read, to supplement with specific technical details his excellent narrative skills and background knowledge.

Remarque also well knew the risk he was taking in writing a novel dealing with a topic about which there was a surfeit of recent accounts. There was as well the danger that many of his readers would wish to put the horrors of the war behind them. In an interview with Robert Van Gelder, Remarque indicated his concern:

> "The novel that I am working on is dated, it is dated now. The scene is a concentration camp—can you imagine anything more dated? But if it is a good book it will be widely read and through it some people who did not understand before may be made to understand what the Nazis were like and what they did and what their kind will try to do again. It is so dated, do you suppose anyone will read it?"[3]

His approach to the telling of his concentration camp story was determined by his perception of the difficulty most people have in comprehending and relating to large-scale tragedies.

> "The difficulty is, you see - - - that our imaginations can not count. When I saw five million died—the figure is a blank. Five million deaths does not equal one death. Five thousand dead in a concentration camp—there is that same difficulty. The figure is blank. But if I say five died, then perhaps. And if I say one died—a man I have made you know and understand—he lived so, this is what he thought, this is what he hoped, this was his faith, these were his difficulties, these his triumphs and then he—in this manner, on this day, at an hour when it rained and the room was stuffy—was killed, after torture, then perhaps I have told you something that you should know about the Nazis."[4]

Remarque also makes clear the personal family reason he had for writing a book about Nazi atrocities in his simple dedication of *Der Funke Leben* (*Spark of LIfe*): "To the memory of my sister Elfriede." Remarque never publicly mentioned the tragic death of his sister—or, for that matter, anything else which deeply affected him. It is in the novels that one will find the true Remarque feelings. By writing this account of Nazi inhumanity he had paid his final respects to his sister while at the same time striking out at the Nazis with the only weapon available to him.

Consistent with his comments as to how one should cause people to relate to large-scale tragedy, Remarque proceeded from the specific to the general. He built his novel around a nuclear character designated through most of the story simply by his concentration camp number "509". It is only toward the mid-point of the novel that the reader is informed that "509" is a former journalist named Friedrich Koller who had been sent to the camp because he had refused, under torture, to divulge the whereabouts of persons the Nazis were seeking. By designating Koller by number rather than by name Remarque succeeds in conferring on him "Everyman" status. His fate, therefore, serves as a symbol for the greater tragedy of the hosts of victims who lost their lives because of Nazi crimes.

Der Funke Leben begins its story in the spring of 1945, shortly before the end of the war. Its setting is the Mellern Concentration Camp. The name and place are fictitious although from Remarque's descriptions of the camp and the town below he is almost certainly using his hometown of Osnabrück as the model. Mellern is a labor camp—not an extermination camp as such. It is almost a distinction without a difference, however, for the exhausted and sick inmates who die at the hands of brutal and sadistic SS overseers.

Set slightly apart from the main labor camp, and separated by a wire fence, is a group of barracks. This area is known as the "small camp" and is populated by those prisoners too weak to work. It is in effect a "dying area" reminiscent of the hospital "dying room" found in *Im Westen nichts Neues*. Within the "small camp", in Barrack 22, is a comparatively hardy group of survivors who call themselves the "veterans". 509 is part of this group. The most important of the twelve members of the typically Remarque "in group" of survivors are Lebenthal, Karel, Ahasver, Bucher, Westhof, and Berger. It is interesting to note that Remarque's "Everyman" character is the only one in the novel designated by number.

509 and his fellow prisoners are fighting the same basic battle fought by all of Remarque's main characters: the battle of survival. The locale is different and the circumstances are somewhat different but the continuity of concern remains.

The stories of the individual veterans in the small camp are used to point out past Nazi atrocities. Karel, the youngest, is a Czech boy only eleven years old. His parents had been gassed and, along with others, their ashes sold to German farmers for use as fertilizer.

The oldest of the veterans is a seventy-two year-old Jew who received the name Ahasver because of his ability to survive a dozen concentration camps. He serves as a protector of a young inmate who has been driven insane by the SS's use of him as an attack object to train their dogs. In the process he lost his ears and his reason. He is referred to as the "sheep dog" because he now believes he indeed is a German sheep dog. Ahasver has trained him to his commands so that he can hide him when the SS men come to the barrack.

More important to the story is the doctor Ephraim Berger, the room senior. Berger was assigned by the SS to work in the crematorium. There he filled out death certificates and, more important for the Nazis, extracted gold teeth from the corpses awaiting cremation. Berger had been sent to the camp by a former patient who was a high-ranking SS man. The Nazi had syphilis and wanted to eliminate the doctor who knew about his illness. Even though Berger has no official opportunity to serve in a medical capacity he is able to do much to alleviate the suffering among his fellow prisoners. Berger who, like Ravic, represents the best of the medical profession, is allowed by Remarque to survive to experience the liberation of the camp by the American Army. The treatment of injuries to camp inmates resulting from a last spasmodic effort by the SS to destroy the camp allows Berger an opportunity to restore his confidence in long-dormant medical skills.

In almost all of the novels there is one character who is the quintessential survivor; in *Der Funke Leben* that character is Leo Lebenthal. Lebenthal is also a scrounger whose proficiency can only be matched by Katczinsky in *Im Westen nichts Neues*. Lebenthal's ability as a trader meant the difference between marginal survival and starvation for the veterans in the small camp. Whether the transaction involved trading a gold tooth from a dead body to corrupt Nazis for food or supplying Nazi memorabilia to souvenir-hungry American G.I.'s, Lebenthal was always quietly and efficiently successful. Remarque's portrayal of Lebenthal is unambivalently favorable and shows the admiration he felt for the practical businessman. This is particularly true of Lebenthal who always shared the fruits of his success with his comrades in order to help maintain the physical dimension of the "spark of life".

The reader is presented with a complete rogue's gallery of Nazi types who shrink from no act of sadistic barbarism. The SS men who operate the camp are the perfect representatives of a regime which is evil incarnate. Sadists such as the SS camp leader Anton Weber and the SS squad leader Guenther Steinbrenner have unlimited opportunities to give free rein to their natural instincts for cruelty. The SS men vie with each other in attempting to discover new ways of inflicting torture and terror on the helpless inmates. Worse than these, because he purports to be a representative of medicine, is the surgeon Major Wiese. Wiese conducts medical experiments on prisoners until that enterprise is thwarted by the camp commandant—not for humanitarian reasons but because of the commandant's dislike of the surgeon.

The camp commandant, Obersturmbannführer Bruno Neubauer, is clearly the most interesting of the Nazi characters. Perhaps this is because Remarque makes him more fully dimensional by providing an abundance of evidence concerning his motivations and family situation. Neubauer spent most of his time in the camp but went frequently to his impressive home on the outskirts of Mellern where his wife Selma and his daughter Freya lived. The enemy air raids on Mellern had jolted Neubauer from his smug complacency and had also caused panic for Selma, whose former faith in the system has been shattered. After all, she and most other Germans had believed that Germany would never be subjected to enemy bombing. They had faith in Hermann Goering and the Luftwaffe and thought he was safe in making his boasting statement that people could call him Maier if German soil should ever be bombed. Neubauer could not bring himself to accept the fact that their world had changed and the Nazi master's exploitive privileges had come to an end. There would be no more French silk dressing gowns for Selma, no more French champagne, and no more Russian slave laborers to tend the spacious grounds. There would also be no further opportunities to terrorize businessmen such as the Jew Max Blank by committing them to a concentration camp and then buying their property for ridiculously low prices. In Blank's case it was an office building in Mellern which, in effect, Neubauer received as a gift after Blank had been sufficiently "educated" in the camp. Neubauer had also acquired a tobacco shop in the same manner. But then the bombing raids on Mellern came and destroyed those ill-gotten acquisitions. With typical Remarque-style justice, Max Blank is allowed to savor the spectacle of Neubauer surveying the damage and lamenting his losses.

As Neubauer's situation becomes increasingly dangerous Selma urges that they sell their real estate holdings and prepare to flee. She has secretly acquired through the years a number of pieces of jewelry and gemstones which now can be taken easily when they flee. Because, she reasons, "The same thing can happen to us that happened to others when you came to power - - -."[5] Neubauer is appalled by her statement and says: "The way you talk! One day you are hysterical with fear of a few bombs—and the next you talk like a Jew who'd cut one's throat for cash."[6]

Selma looks at him with the contempt his comments deserve. "She looked at his boots, his uniform, his revolver, his mustache. 'Jews don't cut throats. Jews look after their families. Better than many Germanic supermen. Jews know what to do in dangerous times.' "[7]

Selma's protestations are to no avail, however, because Neubauer, after considering all his options, has decided to stay and hold out. "Otherwise it would look as though I had a bad conscience."[8] Although at the time it appeared that Selma had acquiesced, when Neubauer later returned to their home he discovered that Selma and Freya had gone leaving a note asking him to follow and giving a Bavarian village as the address.

After the bombing raids on Mellern, and after an old newspaper seen by the prisoners reported that the American Army had crossed the Rhine bridge at Remagen, the mood of the camp changed. Even though the brutality continued it was apparent that the S.S. knew that their days of control were numbered. Among the prisoners there gradually could be expressed the previously unmentionable hope that rescue might be possible.

The first organized resistance movement among the prisoners began in the larger camp and eventually had its effect among the veterans in the small camp. At first the nucleus of the resistance was the Communists. They were the most tough-minded and, as Remarque put it: "Though they cooperated with the others, they never entirely trusted them and pursued their own special aims. They always protected and promoted their own people first."[9] Lewinsky and Willy Werner were the Communist leaders. As it became apparent that the Nazi grip on the camp, and even on the Mellern area, was loosening, the inmates received unexpected help from the outside. Labor groups of prisoners working to clear away the rubble of the Mellern bombings occasionally found pieces of revolvers left there for them to find by workers in the local weapons factory.

One of these revolvers was given to 509 by Lewinsky so that

it could be hidden in the small camp where the chance of its discovery would be less. For 509, who was being menaced by the brutal block senior Handke, the possession of a weapon meant the return of a feeling of security and self-respect. There was also an awareness that he no longer had to think of himself as a number but could again become a human being. Friedrich Koller had re-emerged to reclaim his identity.

As events raced to a conclusion for the Mellern camp the Nazis tried to sanitize the operation—to the extent that was possible. A transport of 2,000 prisoners from the camp was organized to reduce the size of the operation. Neubauer was disappointed that the embarassing problem of the maltreated prisoners couldn't simply have been disposed of by a fortuitous Allied bombing raid on the camp. However, since the Allies had not cooperated with the fulfillment of his wish, Neubauer attempted to make a few ridiculous, cosmetic changes at the camp in the hope that these would make his record look better when the American troops liberated the prisoners. Those changes included a change of clothing for the prisoners, increased use of disinfectants, and—the final substantive touch—the planting of shrubs and flowers, particularly primroses, for color.

When the day of departure came for the S.S. guards most of them left without ceremony. However, it was different for Camp Leader Anton Weber's group who felt that a "celebration" was in order for his group. In keeping with their nature, this was to involve the burning of the wooden barracks and the shooting of inmates who attempted to escape. However, the result of this escapade was not quite what Weber had intended. Friedrich Koller was inside the burning barrack and used his hidden revolver to wound Weber. In the resultant confusion and exchange of gunfire as the camp resistance fighters, led by Lewinsky and Werner, took over the camp, Koller crawled outside to Weber. As their eyes met, Koller, also mortally wounded, suddenly felt that it was at this moment the most important thing in the world that his eyes hold the look longer than those of Weber. "It was like a duel and a divine judgement. If he could hold out now, then that which had been so important for him that he had risked his life for it, would also hold out."[10] This final duel had to be won against Weber because what he represented "- - - had to be annihilated, it was evil incarnate; the anti-Christ; the mortal sin against the spirit."[11] Koller did indeed win his duel and expired only moments after Weber died. Through this symbolic confrontation Remarque allows the "spark of life" in his "Everyman" character to survive the Nazi "evil incarnate" represented by Weber. With the appearance of the first American tank an official end was also written to the evils of the Mellern camp.

The spark of life was not extinguished with the death of Koller. It was present in survivors such as Berger, Lebenthal, Ahasver and hundreds of other unnamed inmates. It was also present in the young prisoners Josef Bucher and Ruth Holland.

Bucher, one of the Veterans, was only twenty-five but had been in Mellern for seven years. His only "offense" had been that his father was the editor of a Social Democratic newspaper. Josef had worked as a carpenter for a while in the women's camp and had become acquainted with Ruth. They had occasionally been able to meet secretly to talk at that time. When his work detail was changed they were sometimes still able to talk at night with each other through the barbed wire which separated the women's camp from the small camp. Ruth and her family had been taken to another camp—this one an extermination camp. Her family had all been sent to the gas chambers. She had been allowed to live only because the Nazis needed young women for their soldiers as well as for the Ukranians who had allied themselves with the Germans. It had been so traumatic for Ruth that she vomited after almost each experience. Finally the Nazis sent her to Mellern. Her nightmare experiences had taken their emotional and physical toll. She now had gray hair and was missing several of her teeth. Although she was a few years younger than Josef she felt many years older. Despite the physical evidence of her tortured past, Josef loved her and tried almost constantly to reassure her of that fact. He had even provided the most tangible assurance of his love by sharing with her his part of the few morsels of precious food the Veterans were able to scrounge. Nevertheless she found it difficult to accept his assurances of love and his belief that they would be able to transcend the nightmarish past. In Josef's view the rules for people in the camp were different from those for ordinary people in ordinary situations. "They debased us, but it's not we who are debased."[12] Josef quoted 509 when he said, "All the things they did to us don't mean anything as long as we don't feel like it."[13] Ruth remained unconvinced. "She didn't believe any of those things which he anticipated with so much certainty—and yet in her, too, there was a last hope to which she clung."[14]

When they left the camp in order to turn that hope into reality they headed across the primrose-covered meadow and toward the white house which had seemed to them a symbol of order and normalcy when they observed it through their imprisonment. When they arrived they discovered to their amazement that a bomb had fallen behind the house and destroyed everything except the facade which was visible from the camp.

> " 'It never was a house. All this time.'
> 'It is good that we didn't know it was destroyed.'
> They looked at it. They had believed that as long as it existed, they too would exist. They had believed in an illusion. In a ruin with a facade. There was irony in it, and at the same time a strange comfort. It had helped them, and in the end that was all that mattered."[15]

Perhaps their love would also prove to be an illusion. Perhaps Ruth was right to believe that the enormity of their personal tragedy could not be overcome by rationalization and good intentions. That was not important now, however. Remarque imitated life in that he also gave his characters no guarantees of happiness beyond the moment. The love Ruth and Josef shared is not really comparable with any other love relationship in Remarque's novels. It is, however, vitally important for this novel because of the hope, however tenuous, that this particular spark of life will not flicker and go out.

Remarque allows these survivor-lovers to have the last word in the novel as they enjoy the luxury of being alone at last.

> " 'It is good to be alone for once, Ruth.'
> 'Yes. As though we were the last men.'
> 'Not the last. The first.' "[16]

There is reason for a modicum of hope for the future of individuals such as Ruth, Josef, Berger, Lebenthal, and the others. Remarque apparently is less sanguine in regard to the Germans—indeed, mankind—in general. In one of the novel's most appallingly brutal scenes Remarque describes the cold-blooded, wanton murder of a member of a work detail of prisoners in Mellern. The fifteen-year-old leader of a troop of Nazi youths had railed at the prisoners as "Jewish swine" and "traitors" and then stepped forward, pulled a pistol, and shot one of the prisoners full in the face. The boy callously watched the prisoner die and expressed regret only because he had no more bullets to fire. When the boys marched off they could be heard singing:

> "When Jewish blood spurts from the knife
> Everything goes twice as well."[17]

Remarque appears to be saying, "What improvement can one expect from the future when a new generation of Germans has this sort of mentality?"

The attitude of the unnamed young Nazi murderer was determined by the generation represented in *Der Funke Leben* by Weber and Neubauer. Weber and Neubauer also typify different Nazi reactions to defeat. The Weber types can be expected to end violently in a last act of defiance whereas the Neubauers after defeat try to delude themselves and others that they were simply doing their duty. Remarque had absolutely no tolerance for the Neubauers of Germany. Neither did the American soldiers who heard the excuse from former camp commander Neubauer. Neubauer tried to disassociate himself from the surrounding signs of human outrage by saying to the corporal: "There were orders. Duty—."[18] The corporal indignantly rejected that excuse and said to another soldier: "In the next few years those will be the two commonest excuses in Germany—I acted under orders and—I knew nothing about it."[19]

Der Funke Leben is clearly Remarque's strongest attack on Nazi totalitarianism. It is understandable that the communists, particularly the East German communists, would wish to applaud his attacks on a competing form of totalitarianism which had recently been their mortal enemy. There is an irony in their praise which would be appreciated by Remarque in one of his blacker moods. Remarque was anti-Nazi but certainly not pro-communist. He had no illusions about the true nature of communist methods and goals. His attitude in this regard is most clearly expressed in *Der Funke Leben* and in his later play "Full Circle." In the novel, 509's conversations with Lewinsky and Werner are used to state his position in unequivocal terms.

The Mellern communists saw their short-range goal as that of total domination, nationally as well as internationally. When Werner told 509 that there had to be an organized party to take over from the Nazis the following exchange ensued.

> " 'Your party, you mean. The Communists.'
> 'What other?'
> 'Any others,' said 509. 'So long as it's not totalitarianism.'
> Werner gave a short laugh. 'You fool! Only a totalitarian. Can't you read the signs on the wall? All intermediate parties have crumbled. Communism has remained strong. The war will come to an end. Russia has occupied a great part of Germany. It's by far the strongest power in Europe. The time of coalitions is over. This one was the last. The Allies have helped Communism and weakened themselves, the fools!' "[20]

509 then asked Werner the key question that would be uppermost in the mind of one who had suffered so much at the hands of one form of tyranny.

> " '. . . supposing you won and had the power, what would happen to those who are against you? Or those who are not for you?'
> Werner was silent for a moment. 'There are many different ways,' he said then.

'I know some. Killing, torturing, concentration camps.'
'Among others. Depending on what's necessary.'
'What an advance over the Nazis! Worth while living for!'
'It is an advance,' declared Werner, unperturbed. 'It's an advance in aim. And also in method. We don't do anything for the sake of cruelty. Only out of necessity.' "[21]

509, with great irony, explained that he had also heard that point of view when Weber stuck lighted matches under his fingernails in order to extract information. The point was not wasted on Werner because it was his address, among others, which Weber was trying to obtain. A further irony was that, although 509 had failed to divulge the information, Werner was later betrayed by a fellow communist. Werner again, as he had done twenty years before, asked the former journalist Koller (509) to join the communists and share the future which now would belong to them. 509 once again posed to Werner a variation of his former question.

" 'I'd also like to know how long it would be, if your party came to power, before you locked me up?'
'Not long. You are still dangerous. But you wouldn't be tortured.'
509 shrugged his shoulders.
'We'd lock you up and let you work. Or shoot you'
'That's comforting. That's how I always imagined your golden age to be.' "[22]

Werner previously had good reason to respect Koller as an antagonist. Before 1933 Koller had been an editor whose newspaper had attacked both the Nazis and Communists. Both parties had wanted to eliminate Koller but the Nazis had the first opportunity. Koller was dangerous because he was for something which, as he told Ashasver and Lebenthal ". . . now seems rather pompous and ridiculous. For humanness, tolerance and the right of the individual."[23] Those qualities mentioned in Koller's last sentence indicate what Remarque considered worthy human goals for governments and individuals. When such ideals are not respected, the concentration camp, or some other manifestation of man's inhumanity to man, will be the inevitable result.

Although Remarque honored his murdered sister Elfriede by dedicating *Der Funke Leben* to her memory, the reader will look in vain for any character or event having a direct relationship to her "offense", trial, or execution. There is, however, one statement which appears to indicate that Elfriede's fate was very much on his mind. On one occasion when Neubauer's wife Selma was urging him to get away from Mellern and he, frightened that their conversation would be overheard, said: "Take care for God's sake! Where's the maid? If anyone hears you, we're lost. The People's Court knows no mercy. One denunciation is enough."[24] There was certainly no mercy for Elfriede. Remarque had also not missed the point that by murdering his sister the Nazis symbolically were also murdering him.

The success of *Der Funke Leben* was not followed by a movie version of the book. This was the first of Remarque's novels, which was not filmed. The reason for this omission seems obvious. The unrelentingly tragic impact of the book would have been almost impossible to translate to the movie screen. Even if a reasonably accurate version had survived the transition from novel to movie scenario it is difficult to imagine any significant boxoffice success for such a film.

29

Zeit zu leben und Zeit zu sterben: The Novel and the Movie

In the summer of 1953 Remarque moved from the Ambassador Hotel on Park Avenue into an apartment in the Ritz Towers on Park Avenue at 57th Street. By that time he had essentially completed work on his seventh novel, *Zeit zu leben und Zeit zu sterben*, the translation of which is "A time to live and a time to die." However, when the English translation appeared it was given the title *A Time to Love and a Time to Die*. The substitution of "love" for "live" was apparently thought to make the product more commercially desirable. The German original, as well as the English translation by Remarque's friend Denver Lindley, appeared in 1954. The English translation, although not the German original, had the dedication "To P. G.". The "P. G." referred to was screen actress Paulette Goddard with whom he had had a close relationship for almost two years. Miss Goddard was living in an apartment in the Ritz Towers in 1953 when Remarque moved there to take an identical apartment, on an adjoining floor.

Apart from indicating his affection for Paulette Goddard, it would not appear to be particularly apropos to dedicate a novel such as *Zeit zu leben und Zeit zu sterben* to her—or indeed to anyone with whom he was in love. To be sure, the novel contains the standard, poignant love affair favored by Remarque but otherwise is essentially just another study of the Nazi nightmare. He appears to have been attempting a partial return to the formula he used for *Im Westen nichts Neues*. This time, however, the combat situations which frame the story have been reduced radically in order to allow him to emphasize the impact of the war on the German homefront. The homefront for this novel is the city of Werden; a fictitious name to represent his Osnabrück home. Even though Remarque couldn't or, for emotional reasons, wouldn't "go home again", he liked to take the characters with whom he most closely identified back to that setting and vicariously experience their adventures and misadventures.

Ernst Graeber is the latest in the series of Remarque protagonists which began with Paul Bäumer in *Im Westen nichts Neues*. Like Bäumer, Ernst Graeber is a private soldier. He had been a corporal but he beat up a lieutenant and was broken in rank because of the assault. Even though he was not assigned to a disciplinary company after the incident, there was no chance of further promotion. Like Bäumer, Graeber was a good soldier and a combat veteran. He had previously served in France and in Africa and at the beginning of the story is fighting on the Russian front.

Graeber has the standard supporting cast from the Remarque stock company of soldier characters. Differing somewhat from the usual is the company commander Rahe, a highly decorated soldier and a decent human being, who is kindly disposed toward Ernst and helps him to expedite his furlough. In view of Remarque's use of words such as "schoolmaster" and "Lieutenant from the time of the first war" it is logical to speculate that Remarque's friend Hanns-Gerd Rabe may have been at least a partial inspiration for the sympathetic Lt. Rahe.

The Nazi menace among the combat troops is the former concentration camp block warden Steinbrenner. In everything but a chronological sense the S.S. man Steinbrenner may be considered a continuing character from *Der Funke Leben*. Because that novel took the reader to the end of the war in Germany, Steinbrenner could hardly have been sent from the concentration camp to the Russian front. In all other ways the characters are the same as Remarque continues the portrayal of a type—the ultimate product of the Nazi system. Steinbrenner has absolutely no redeeming or sympathetic features. Unfortunately he does not lack courage or zeal in carrying out whatever course of action his Party loyalty dictates. This is usually some form of killing involving Russian soldiers or Russian civilians suspected of guerrila activity. Steinbrenner is always the first to volunteer for firing squad duty. Most of his fellow soldiers dislike and fear him because they are aware he is a Gestapo informer.

As a good Nazi Steinbrenner also has a pathological hatred of Jews. He has a convenient target for his Jew-baiting in Private Hirschland who is either three-quarters Aryan as he sees it or one-quarter Jewish as Steinbrenner chooses to see it. When Ernst Graeber is about to leave the unit for his furlough, Hirschland asks him to tell his mother at home that everything is going fine with him. In answer to Ernst's question as to why he couldn't write her the same assurance, Hirschland says that because he is part Jewish his mother won't believe that the situation is as he says.

When Ernst later sees Hirschland's mother she tells him that she has received word that her son has been killed. Upon his return to the company after furlough Ernst is surprised to see Hirschland still alive. It turns out that Steinbrenner, during temporary duty as the company clerk, sent Hirschland's mother an official notification of her son's alleged death. Shortly after the discovery of Steinbrenner's sadistic joke, Hirschland, with typical Remarque irony, was actually killed, thus making a correction of the first report unnecessary.

In this novel Remarque doesn't have any characters who are strong advocates of Communism as was the case in *Der Funke Leben*. The closest he comes is the former Communist Immermann to whom he has given a "Devil's Advocate" role. Immermann earlier was sent to a disciplinary company because of his outspoken criticisms and former party affiliation. He was transferred to Rahe's company because his mechanical skills were of more use to the Nazis at the front. Immerman takes delight in needling Steinbrenner. He can be completely candid in his criticisms of the Nazis and the war because he has no real fear of retribution. Immermann, in much the same way as the hospitalized soldier with a head injury in *Im Westen nichts Neues* who could get away with outrageous behavior, has a "hunting license." He and Immermann can do and say things that the other soldiers can only think. Ernst is rather uneasy around the plain-spoken Immermann and doesn't want to be involved with anything which would endanger his up-coming furlough. Ernst is enough of an old soldier to know that you keep your mouth shut when conditions are not safe.

Despite his youth Ernst Graeber is indeed an old soldier. He is one of a very small number of surviving comrades from the original group. The only friend from that group still surviving is Fresenburg who is commander of the Fourth Company. Fresenburg is also from Werden and Ernst has known him a long time and respects his opinions. Before leaving for furlough Ernst visits his friend in order to say goodbye as well as to talk with someone whom he can really trust. Fresenburg, who is older than Ernst, has no illusions about the Nazis and the prospects for victory. His observations about German inhumanity, arrogance, isolation, and guilt cause Ernst a good deal of uneasiness and discomfort—even though these are also his feelings which he has attempted to suppress. Fresenburg's bitter comments are not what he had hoped to hear from him.

> "He had met Fresenburg because he wanted to get away from Immermann, Sauer, and Steinbrenner; he had wanted to talk to him about the peaceful old city on the river; about the lindenbordered road and about old times. But now it was even worse than before. Everything seemed jinxed these days. From the others he had not expected any help. But he had from Fresenburg, whom he had not seen for a long time in the confusion of the retreat—and it was just from him that he heard now what he had so long been unwilling to admit, what he had intended to think about only after he was home, and what he was more afraid of than anything."[1]

Before they said goodbye, Fresenburg asked Ernst to give his regards to their old History and Religion teacher Pohlmann who still lived in Werden.

Ernst's return to Werden for his three-week furlough was a journey of discovery—and the discoveries were for the most part painful. He had seen the destruction of war in other countries where he had served but had managed to block out of his mind the possibility that the war had really come home to Germany in the form of bombing raids. The effect of bombing was brought home for some of Ernst's fellow soldiers also going home on furlough when they were told that furloughs to the Rhineland were canceled. The reason for the cancellation, although unstated, was the widespread destruction of rail and other facilities in the area. The fate of those soldiers who were being deprived of the opportunity to return home to their families intensified the apprehensions he had been attempting to suppress.

> "Once more the ghostly and intangible something was there that had haunted him so long and that could never be wholly grasped, that eluded him and came back and stared at him and had a hundred ill-defined faces and no face at all. He looked at the rails. They led toward home, security, warmth and peace, toward the only thing that was left."[2]

The "ill-defined faces" began to take on definition when his train stopped outside of Werden rather than at the main station in the heart of the city. As he continued toward home, by bus and on foot, uppermost in his mind was the safety of his parents. His relief at seeing the first undamaged streets soon vanished as his nostrils picked up the smell of fire-damaged buildings. When he hurried to his home on Hakenstrasse (also a former Remarque address in Osnabrück) he was dismayed to see that his address, along with others in the neighborhood, was now just a pile of rubble. Inquiries to the neighborhood air raid warden, the registry office, and the missing persons bureau were to no avail. It seemed as if the war had swallowed up Paul and Marie Graeber. Ernst was now forced to confront the reality of that war in a way he had never done before.

Ernst's search for information about his parents took him to the Ziegler and Loose families who were friends of his parents. Neither family knew anything. The Zieglers were terribly afraid of something and appeared to have some one hiding in the apartment. The Loose family had lost two children to the bombing and fire. Mrs. Loose had become mentally disoriented as a result. Loose was worried because they had already been reported for some of the things his wife had said and told Ernst: "You don't know what it has been like here during the last year with everything getting worse and worse. No one could trust anyone else any longer. They were afraid of one another."[3]

After visiting the Loose family Ernst next stopped at the home of Dr. Kruse, his former physician. There he talked with Dr. Kruse's daughter Elisabeth whom he had known when she was a young girl. Now she was an attractive twenty year old. Elisabeth told him that her father had been sent to a concentration camp four months before because an informer had denounced him to the Gestapo. The informer presumably was Mrs. Lieser, a Nazi zealot who had been assigned lodging in the Kruse household. Mrs. Lieser epitomizes for Remarque the terror of denunication which numbered his sister Elfriede among its countless victims.

It was, surprisingly, another Nazi, Alfons Binding, who proved to be the most helpful of all the persons encountered during his furlough. Binding, a commander in the S.A., was a dimly-remembered classmate who had always liked Ernst and was impressed by his combat experiences. Binding spontaneously offered to help Ernst in his search for his parents. He also asked Ernst to be his guest in his suburban villa with its well-stocked wine cellar and pantry containing representative plunder from all the occupied countries. Ernst was overwhelmed by such generosity from this unlikely source. The irony was not lost on him that the "first human being who wants to help me unreservedly and offers me food and lodging has to be an S.A. commander."[4] Although he kept Alfons at arm's length, Ernst was too much of an old soldier not to take advantage of Alfons' generosity in sharing his provisions of food and drink. Those supplies enabled Ernst and Elisabeth to live comfortably and pleasantly during Ernst's furlough. Ernst appreciated the goodwill shown him by Binding but was shocked by his attitudes and his friends. Alfons had caused one of his former teachers with whom he had trouble in school to be sent to a concentration camp for "reeducation." For Alfons the war was a splendid opportunity to achieve gratification of any sensual desire or malicious instinct. Despite his weakness, Alfons was at least generous and faithful to his friends. Unfortunately, with the exception of Ernst, his friends were persons such as Heini the sadistic former member of the Security Service of S.S. who was now commander of the concentration camp. Alfons listened with a combination of horror and admiration to the stories Heini told of his exploits—particularly the one about making flame throwers out of Russians by pouring vodka down their throats and lighting it. Ernst, who had also heard Heini's stories, was so appalled by the incarnate evil of the man that later when he found himself following Heini on an otherwise deserted street he decided to kill him. Fortunately for Heini's longevity a woman suddenly appeared at the end of the street. Shaken by realizing how close he had come to doing something foolish—at least at that place—Ernst suddenly understood that he had to talk with someone whom he could trust with the dark doubts he had brought home from the field. Whatever the cost of the clarity he sought he was willing to pay it. Ernst suddenly thought of Fresenburg and his request that he pay a visit to Pohlmann.

After the melancholy procession of informers, victims, opportunists, and sadists, Pohlmann represented an affirmation that human decency still existed even in Nazi Germany. When Ernst visited him to find the answers to his questions he felt that he was "again a student facing an examination about his life."[5] There was, however, a comfort and reassurance in being with his former teacher and his world of books. "Here was embodied the past that had once been—kindness, tolerance, and knowledge—and the rubble outside the windows was what the present had made out of it."[6]

The answers Ernst received in his meeting with Pohlmann were the answers that he himself had instinctively known. He was now faced with the prospect of returning at the end of his furlough to fight for a corrupt and wicked government which had long ago lost the war and was only continuing to fight because it had no other option. The possible choices for ways of refusing to serve that government were all impractical or morally unacceptable for Ernst because they put others in jeopardy. Pohlmann had helped to put the dilemma into focus but it remained for Ernst to make his own decision. Pohlmann, who blamed himself and his generation for seeing the Nazi evil and allowing it to happen, had made his decision earlier. That decision had already resulted in his dismissal from his teaching post and his surveillance by the Gestapo. The Gestapo had good reason to be concerned. Pohlmann was involved in unspecified underground activities and at the time of his conversation with Ernst was harboring a Jewish refugee known only as Josef. Although Josef, one of the most interesting of Remarque's survivors, eluded the Nazis, Pohlmann was arrested by the Gestapo and taken away to an almost certain death. Through the character of Pohlmann, Remarque again demonstrated his faith in the invincibility of the human spirit and in the ultimate triumph of humanity over tyranny.

Fortunately, Ernst's furlough in Werden was not exclusively a time of soul-searching and concern for his parents' safety. It was also a time to fall in love with Elisabeth Kruse. Their relationship has none of the problematic qualities and the rough emotional edges so often found in his love stories. Unfortunately, without the controversy, their love seems rather bland. There is, however, no doubt of the sincerity of their love or of the emotional security it provides for each of them. For Elisabeth, worried about her father in the concentration camp and harassed by the Nazi informant Frau Lieser living under her own roof, her love for Ernst was her sole emotional support. For Ernst, their love gave some meaning to an increasingly alien world. Their relationship is unique among Remarque's fictive lovers in that they are granted a happy marriage, albeit a very brief one. The sanctuary provided by their love against the unpleasant reality around them lasts only for the last few days of Ernst's furlough. Then he leaves his loving and, as we later learn, probably pregnant, Elisabeth in order to return to a war he despises.

Upon his return to the front, Ernst finds the military situation even more hopeless than before. Although it has not changed for the better, he has. Unfortunately the price he has to pay for a practical demonstration of his new idealism is very high. The test of that idealism comes when he has to make a choice whether or not to allow Steinbrenner to murder four Russians suspected of guerrilla activities. He makes the only choice a Remarque protagonist could make by terminating Steinbrenner and releasing the prisoners. After making this dramatic commitment to human decency, Ernst tries to convince the suspicious Russians that they are really free by throwing down his own rifle. One of the fleeing Russians repays Ernst by killing him with that rifle.

Although there is bitter irony in the fact that Ernst's humane instincts caused his own death, no other ending would have been as effective. Ernst had to die because his new questioning attitude and willingness to act on his convictions would have condemned him sooner or later. Only the manner of his death was in doubt. The novel's ending shows clearly the impossibility of separating Remarque the idealist and Remarque the pessimistic realist.

A Time to Love and a Time to Die is unique among the novels for its detailed treatment of the war's impact on the German civilian population. Remarque's concerns range from the physical destruction of German cities to the moral harm caused by the Nazi blight on the German soul. It is apparent in this novel that the judicial murder of his sister Elfriede at the hands of the Nazis left its searing emotional mark on him. There are several references to informers, to "defeatism" and beheading which make it clear that Remarque is speaking the name of that particular demon in order to exorcise it from his psyche—to the extent that a literary catharsis can achieve that. The clearest reference to Elfriede's tragedy is inserted almost casually, but with a shock effect, in the simple account of Ernst's purchase of a bunch of jonquils which he intended to give Elisabeth for their marriage ceremony. The flowers were wrapped in paper and Ernst's attention was drawn to the paper in which they were wrapped.

> "Under the yellow blossoms appeared the picture of a man open-mouthed in front of some sort of tribunal. It was a photograph of the presiding officer of a People's Court. He read the text. Four persons had been put to death because they no longer believed in a German victory. Their heads had been hacked off with an ax. In the Third Reich the guillotine had long since been discarded. It was too humane."[7]

This statement is as close to a personal expression of grief for his sister as one is likely to find in the works of the intensely private Remarque.

Ernst Graeber's story is unique among Remarque novels not only because it is the only example of a protagonist's marriage but also because it is the only novel which even touches upon the subject of possible parenthood for a protagonist. Because Remarque's principal characters often serve as surrogates for the expression of his own views, the discussion between Ernst and Elisabeth on the subject of children is significant. Elisabeth catches Ernst by surprise when she expresses the hope that she is pregnant. He responds to her hope with a notable lack of enthusiasm and raises a few objections which she neatly answers. She makes the additional point that it is not just *a* baby that she wants but *his* baby. The entire matter may be academic because her pregnancy is only a hope at this point. Their talk has been enough, however, to cause Ernst some introspection on the subject. "He thought over what she had said about a child. It was as though suddenly a wall had been broken through. An opening has appeared and behind it, wavering and indistinct, a garden, a bit of the future. Graeber had never thought beyond that wall."[8]

The thought that life might indeed go on for him beyond the "wall" was new and intriguing. Perhaps there could be more than living merely for the moment; a life which "might sometime become an assured possession to be handed on to an alien, unborn existence in a future that had no end and was full of tenderness he had never known."[9]

Unfortunately, even at the end of the novel there still remains the question whether Elisabeth is indeed expecting a child. Perhaps the uncertainty is meant to imply a slight hope that Ernst may have fathered a child who will grow up in a better world than he did. The real significance of this small part of the novel is that for the first time the fifty-six year old Remarque has provided some insight into his own mixed emotions concerning parenthood.

A Time to Love and a Time to Die makes many harsh and frequently bitter judgments of the German people for their involvement, or acquiesence, in this black period of Nazi rule. Remarque held up the mirror and many Germans were made to feel guilty about the reflection they saw. How painful this experience was may be seen by examining some of the circumstances surrounding the editing and publishing of the German edition of the novel.

Remarque's German publisher, Kiepenheuer and Witsch in Köln, released *Zeit zu Leben und Zeit zu sterben* in 1954. Within a short time questions arose about several changes and omissions in the German edition. The newsmagazine *Der Spiegel* in its issue of December 15, 1954 reported the details of the "censorship" controversy which apparently began when the Copenhagen newspaper *Information,* a publication for former Danish resistance groups, reported that comparisons of the Danish, English, and German editions showed the German to be different in some ways. The suspicion was that certain alterations had been made in the German edition with a view to sparing German sensibilities.

According to *Der Spiegel* there was an immediate and energetic offical denial from Kiepenheuer and Witsch. The publisher's statement said in part, "The publishing house would never submit an author such as Erich Maria Remarque to censorship and Erich Maria Remarque, for his part, would never submit to censorship."[10] The offical denial went on to say that Remarque had merely expressed the request that the publisher should check the "question of Milieu, of terminology and other things relating to the external aspects of the novel."[11] According to *Der Spiegel* the publisher's statement indicated that they had gone through the manuscript carefully and returned it to the author with suggested corrections. "It was, of course, expressly left to the author to accept or to disapprove these changes."[12] The statement concludes by saying: "Mr. Remarque, for his part, accepted a part of the changes and the minimal omissions and disapproved others. The manuscript, which was revised by Remarque and returned to the publisher as ready for printing, appeared as a book without any additional change in this final revision."[13]

A comparison of the German edition and the English translation shows several points of divergence. One of the most important of those involves the partial rehabilitation of the arch-villain Steinbrenner. In one episode in the English translation Graeber and Sauer were discussing the "Sicherheitsdienst" or S.D., the security service of the S.S., when this exchange resulted: " '. . . They don't come this near the front. Wasn't Steinbrenner with the S.D. earlier?'

'I think he was in a concentration camp. Block warden or something like that.' "[14] This passage is missing in the German edition.

A more suspicious omission is Steinbrenner's elaboration on the ways he and his future wife and children would exploit Nazi parenthood assistance and racial stipends. This is particularly true of statements such as: "Selective breeding of the race! We've not only got to root out the Jews, we've also got to replace them with pure-blooded Germans. A new race of leaders."[15] When Graeber asked if he had "rooted out many Jews," Steinbrenner answered: "If you could see my conduct records you wouldn't have to ask. Those were the times!"[16] He then goes on to say that he has applied for a transfer to an S.S. division where one can really get ahead because in that kind of service hundreds of Russians or Poles can be killed in one afternoon. Slightly more than two large paragraphs of this type of self-indicting evidence have been excised.

The concluding part of the foregoing scene depicting the meeting of Graeber and Steinbrenner has also been removed. The missing part deals with Graeber's rebuke of Steinbrenner for his cruel act of sending Hirschland's mother a telegram notifying her falsely of the death of her son. Not only have all references to the half-Jewish Hirschland been eliminated, even the name is changed. A few rather innocuous early references to what was originally his character are now made to a soldier named "Hirschmann."

Chapter XX has suffered the removal of a small, but bitter, reference to the S.S. The reference was in a section in which Ernst is reflecting on the matter of forgiveness for the crimes committed during the war.

> "What would never be forgiven? he thought. After this war there would be horribly much to forgive and not to forgive. A single lifetime would not be enough for that. He had seen more dead children than these—he had seen them everywhere, in France, in Holland, in Poland, in Africa, in Russia, and all had had mothers who wept for them, not the Germans alone—if they still could weep and had not already been liquidated by the S.S. . ."[17]

The last fourteen words following the ultimate dash in the above quotation did not survive editorial revision.

Another relatively minor omission is noted in the episode involving the sadistic S.S. man Heini. Heini has been a guest in Alfons' house and has elaborated in gleeful and sadistic detail on his treatment of Russians. " 'Vodka,' Heini muttered. 'We swilled it in rivers! And then poured it down the beasts' throat and lit it. Made flame throwers out of them. Children, how they hopped around! You'd die laughing!' "[18] Caught up in the pleasure of listening to Heini's account, Alfons said to Ernst:

> " 'First a layer of wood and then a layer of people, and each layer having to have its own wood and then lie down on it and be shot in the back of the head—that's something, eh?'
> 'Yes, that's something.'
> 'And the women! Can you imagine what went on with them!'
> 'Yes, well enough. Would you like to have been there?'

'With the women?'

'No, with the others. At the burning pyre and the Christmas trees covered with hanged men and the mass machine-gunnings?''[19]

The entire foregoing exchange between Alfons and Ernst is not found in German editions.

The most significant of the omissions is in Chapter XIII of the Lindley translation in the section of dialogue between Ernst and Professor Pohlmann. Ernst realizes that the war is lost and if he were to return to the front he would only be helping to fight for a lost and evil cause. Pohlmann asks if he must go back. Ernst then mentions, and rejects, alternatives such as desertion, refusal, and self-mutilation. More significantly, the conversation turns to the matter of guilt and complicity in Nazi misdeeds. Ernst says: "But where does personal responsibility begin? We cannot simply take refuge behind the fact that we were acting on orders."[20] The painful pertinence of this question of guilt, even nine years after the end of the war, was apparently unwelcome in the Kiepenheuer and Witsch edition because approximately one page of material found in the English edition is not included.

Even a cursory examination of the German and English texts reveals several differences. All of the changes noted have the effect of muting criticism of one kind or another. Some sections have obviously been "sanitized." However, the situation is a somewhat confusing one. If the changes made, whether by the publisher or by Remarque, were intended as a serious attempt at censorship it was a rather poor effort because there are just as many damning indictments left as those which have been omitted.

Although it took four years, *A Time to Love and a Time to Die* made its way to the screen in 1958. The movie was produced for Universal-International by Robert Arthur and directed by Douglas Sirk. Orin Jannings is credited with the screenplay.

It is not certain what degree of collaboration, if any, there was between Jannings and Remarque. It is a matter of record, however, that Remarque by July 21, 1957 had reportedly spent several weeks adapting his novel into a screenplay. Philip Scheuer's column in the *Los Angeles Times* for that date reported on that activity and on some of Remarque's feelings about the film project.

He was not particularly pleased with the fact that Universal-International Studios had not yet settled on a definite title for the film. The working title at this time was "There's a Time to Love." Remarque preferred "And a Time to Love" or give up on his title. " 'But, of course,' he adds, 'they won't do that because they want to capitalize on at least a part of the original title. It was a Book of the Month and has had quite some success.' "[21]

Remarque credited director Douglas Sirk with persuading him to work on the screenplay. Remarque had met Sirk in New York and "found him an extraordinarily understanding and capable man." He went on to say: "A writer has to know—and trust—a director. There's an old rule for writers, 'When they make your book don't go near the studio!' or you'll end up with a fine pair of ulcers."[22]

Filming of the movie began in West Berlin in August of 1957 with a solid and talented, if not star-studded, cast. John Gavin had been chosen for the role of Ernst Graeber and the Swiss actress Lilo Pulver was Elizabeth Kruse. Veteran actors Keenan Wynn and Don Defore took the parts of soldiers Reuter and Boettcher. Actor and former stuntman Jock Mahoney played Immermann. The part of Ernst's Nazi benefactor Alfons (now called "Oscar") Binding was played by Thayer David. Charles Regnier had the cameo role of the Jewish fugitive Josef. Dorothea Wieck was the Nazi informant Frau Lieser and Kurt Meisel played the S.S. sadist Heini.

The most interesting casting was Remarque in the role of the anti-Nazi Professor Pohlmann. It was an excellent choice. Remarque couldn't have found a better part if he had created the character with himself in mind—as he may well have done. With Douglas Sirk's encouragement he finally got a chance to act—twenty-eight years after he had flatly rejected consideration for the role of Paul Bäumer in "All Quiet on the Western Front."

Remarque was quite pleased with the experience and recommended a similar acting experience for anyone who writes for the stage or screen. He soon became aware of the fact that dialogue in a novel does not always "play" if it is to be spoken. Therefore one should be able to appreciate the difficulties involved in transposition from one medium to another.

"Every playwright ought to try acting just as every public prosecutor should spend some weeks in jail to find out what he is meting out to others."[23]

Remarque discovered that acting is not as effortless as good actors make it seem. For his five minutes on screen he had to work twelve hours a day for two days. He didn't enjoy waiting around for the shooting of scenes. And a case of stage fright at the beginning didn't help either. However, all in all, it was a satisfying experience. In a Berlin interview he indicated what director Douglas Sirk's reaction to his work had been.

"Sirk said I was good - - - I don't know if he was lying, but he told me that two more days on the set and I would have become a real actor."[24]

It must have been a heady experience for Remarque because in the same interview he indicated a willingness to expand on his acting career by taking a small part in a stage play. Perhaps he had in mind his own play which in revised form was to appear on the New York stage as "Full Circle." In any event, nothing came of his passing interest and his acting career began and ended with one brief appearance in the limelight.

The choice of John Gavin to play the male lead was in some ways reminiscent of the decision by the same studio twenty-eight years earlier to cast Lew Ayres as the lead in "All Quiet on the Western Front", Each actor, although not a complete unknown, was just beginning his career. Before appearing in "All Quiet" Lew Ayres had appeared in only one movie—"The Kiss" in 1929. John Gavin had done a little better. He had appeared in two 1957 movies—"Four Girls in Town" and "Quantez". Starring in a Remarque movie, however, did not mean the same thing professionally for the two men. The "All Quiet" book and movie had made such a great impact that Lew Ayres achieved an instant stardom which has been justified by the distinguished acting career he has had since then. John Gavin was not as fortunate because the vehicle in which he starred was not as well known and did not offer the same dramatic opportunity for rapid professional advancement. However, a solid job of acting in "A Time to Love and a Time to Die", as well as many subsequent acting successes on the stage, in movies, and on television, have given him impressive theatrical credentials. His later election to the presidency of the Screen Actors' Guild and his appointment as the U.S. Ambassador to Mexico are indications of well-deserved success in larger arenas.

Remarque was quite pleased with the selection of Gavin to play Ernst Graeber and was quoted as saying "I think we have a good man."[25] Gavin, however, was somewhat apprehensive. It was his first important picture and he was "green, raw, and frightened".[26] Despite that, he remembers being comfortable in the role and feeling a lot of empathy with Ernst Graeber because he himself had been in service.

Apart from the filming of the scenes they shared, Gavin remembers seeing relatively little of Remarque. An invitation to Remarque's New York apartment subsequent to the filming of the movie gave them an opportunity to become better acquainted under more relaxed circumstances.

The final screenplay for "A Time to Love and a Time to Die" contained a number of changes from the Denver Lindley translation. Among the most striking changes are the following: (1) Hirschland, who suffered so much abuse from Steiner, soon disappeared from the screen version. The script called for him to kill himself because of his guilt at being on the firing squad which executed Russian prisoners. (2) In the book Alfons Binding told Ernst that he had put their former teacher Burmeister in a concentration camp to repay him for a school grievance. In the movie Binding told Ernst that it was Pohlmann he had sent to the camp. (3) In the book Ernst made the decision not to tell Elisabeth that her father had died in the concentration camp and buried the box containing the ashes purportedly his in a cemetery. In the movie he told her about her father's death. (4) In the movie Ernst told Elisabeth that he had received a letter from his mother which satisfied his concern for his parents' safety. In the book he also received a letter but did not tell Elisabeth—presumably because he was reluctant to reveal his good news while she was still concerned for the welfare of her father. (5) In both the book and the movie Ernst was shot to death by the Russian prisoners he had released. The movie version did not contain the ironic ending which had Ernst being shot by his own rifle which he had thrown away in a gesture of renunciation of any further killing. Instead, Ernst, who still had his rifle, was killed with the weapon of the dead Steinbrenner.

Given the constraints imposed by the movie format, "A Time to Love and a Time to Die" is reasonably faithful to the book. It is a streamlined version which does not really suffer from the changes. Remarque's close involvement with the project gave him an influence on the final product which most authors never enjoy.

Unfortunately the movie was not received with particularly laudatory critical acclaim. Fortunately most reviewers were not as hard on the movie as Bosley Crowther was in his review of July 10, 1958 in *The New York Times*. Crowther set the tone of his criticism by writing:

> "Gen. William T. Sherman's famous comment on the fundamental nature of war is illustrated to the point of downright tedium in 'A Time to Love and a Time to Die.' No theme is solidly stated, no philosophical comment is implied—other than the obvious one of General Sherman, and that's what nice Germans went through in World War II."[27]

John Gavin is dismissed as "a good-looking, awkward young man whose speech, attitude and dull delivery betray the tyro from Hollywood."[28] Gavin's soldier-friends Keenan Wynn and Don Defore, in Crowther's opinion, "might as well be acting automobile salesmen in Sioux City, Iowa."[29] Lilo Pulver, he concedes, is "winsome" even though she acts "with the airs and manners of a well-fed ingenue."[30] He goes on to add that "except for a case of German-accent, you'd never dream she'd been near a bombed German city in World War II."[31]

Crowther was also less than thrilled by Remarque's only movie appearance and gave him short shrift. "Stumbling around in a small role of an aging school teacher is Mr. Remarque who might better have saved himself embarassment by staying as far away from this pastiche as he could."[32] After being so pleased with his participation in the movie, Remarque must have been disappointed and chagrined at Crowther's cavalier dismissal of his efforts.

Apparently implied in negative criticism of the film is disappointment that it is not "All Quiet on the Western Front". Perhaps this attitude is natural, even inevitable, in view of the fact that "A Time to Love and a Time to Die" is based on Remarque's only book dealing directly with the situation of a German soldier in World War II and as such is somehow expected to have an impact similar to that of its famous predecessor. That expectation, if indeed it existed, was unrealistic. No one associated with "A Time to Love and a Time to Die" would have claimed that the two movies were comparable in their essential elements.

Even though it lacks the stark dramatic intensity of "All Quiet on the Western Front", "A Time to Love and a Time to Die" is a well-done, well-acted film which, for the most part, is true to Remarque's story. Remarque's presence in the film lends it an additional interest and credibility. Rarely, if ever, has an author had a like opportunity to present as a film actor the same humanitarian message he expressed in his book.

30

Der schwarze Obelisk *(The Black Obelisk)*

Throughout the 1930's Remarque divided his time between his New York apartment and his home in Ascona. There were also trips to favorite haunts such as Rome and Paris.

He almost came to grief during one short trip in 1954 when returning to Ascona on March 19 driving a new automobile he had bought in Italy. For reasons unknown, probably excessive speed, Remarque crashed the car into a wall near Locarno. Although he was shaken up and bruised he escaped serious injury.

Three months after his accident Remarque received news of his father's death. Peter Remark had died in the small resort town of Bad Rothenfelde, not far from his former home of Osnabrück. He had moved there to be with his daughter Erna and her husband Walter. Remarque went to Bad Rothenfelde to be with his sister at their father's funeral. This was to be his last trip to the Osnabrück area. With his father's death, the last real emotional motivation for a return home was gone. Certainly the Osnabrück hometown of his youth no longer existed except in nostalgic memory. Subsequent invitations extended to him by friends such as Hanns-Gerd Rabe and by civic authorities met with polite evasions or vague promises of a future visit which was never to materialize.

1954 and 1955 saw no let-up in his writing. After publication of *A Time to Love and a Time to Die* in 1954, Remarque concentrated his efforts on the completion of a screenplay commission he had agreed to do for an Austrian movie to be entitled "Der

Letzte Akt" ("The Last Act"). The screenplay was based on Michael Musmanno's 1950 book *Ten Days to Die* which dealt with Hitler's last days in his Berlin bunker. Judge Musmanno was a Pittsburgh Common Pleas Judge who had a distinguished war record and had served as a judge at the International War Crimes Trials in Nürnberg. In order to gather the material for his book he interviewed large numbers of persons who had been in the bunker or had known Hitler previously.

Remarque's episodic style was very effective in presenting the atmosphere of confusion and panic among Hitler's inner circle as the end approached. It was also fitting that an exile such as Remarque should have an opportunity through his screenplay to depict the final fate of those persons who had caused so much evil in the world.

"The Last Act" was a Columbia picture directed by G. W. Pabst. The film, starring Oskar Werner and featuring Albin Skoda as Hitler, opened the annual film festival at Edinburg, Scotland in August of 1955.

Even before beginning the screenplay for "The Last Act" Remarque had been at work on his eighth novel, *Der schwarze Obelisk (The Black Obelisk)*. This heavily autobiographical novel provided a way for him to make a bitter-sweet, nostalgic literary return to Osnabrück even though he was very reluctant, even emotionally unable, to make the same visit in real life.

The Black Obelisk is more directly autobiographical than any other of his novels. The Remarque-protagonist, Ludwig Bodmer, is a veteran of World War I who has returned to his hometown of Werdenbrück, a scarcely disguised Osnabrück, and has made a fairly successful transition to civilian life. He is employed as a salesman, and general factotum, in the firm of "Heinrich Kroll and Sons, Funeral Monuments". Remarque's own employment in the Vogt Brothers' firm during 1922 was the inspiration for Bodmer's occupation.

The action of the novel takes place in 1923 during the chaotic period of German inflation. Economic difficulties share the stage with the political unrest marked by the emergence of

National Socialism. On the whole, however, life is basically good for Ludwig Bodmer and his friend Georg Kroll. Georg, a war comrade of Ludwig, shares the ownership of the monument firm with his humorless, chauvinistic brother Heinrich. Remarque uses the Heinrich character to illustrate the dangerous excesses of nationalism to which he attributed most of the blame for Germany's woes.

Ludwig, like Remarque in 1923, has literary ambitions and is only marking time at Kroll's until he can get the right job in Berlin. Georg has no ambition to leave Werdenbrück and contents himself with reading about the activities of the social elite in Berlin and elsewhere. Before Ludwig gets his coveted job offer from Berlin, Remarque takes his readers through the only slightly-disguised world of his own Osnabrück youth.

Despite the hazards of their precarious economic existance, Ludwig and Georg manage not only to cope but to live life with a zest and penache rarely found among Remarque's characters. With their delightful, bantering exchanges, they are a refreshing change from the gloom-and-doom atmosphere of most of the earlier works. To be sure, *The Black Obelisk* has its own grim moments but, in general, the tone is much more light-hearted than Remarque readers are accustomed to. The novel not only has more characters than any of his previous novels but also more clearly comedic ones which help to make this story the most humorous.

The scene of much of the comedic give and take is the Walhalla Hotel and Restaurant owned by Eduard Knobloch, a "fat giant" with a brown toupee. Knobloch, who fancies himself a poet, has an adversary relationship with Ludwig and Georg because he thinks they took unfair advantage of a special offer on books of coupons for meals at his restaurant. They bought up large numbers of books at relatively low prices and, to Knobloch's deep annoyance, continued to eat meals for which they previously paid only a fraction of the current price.

The Werdenbrück "Poet's Club" has its meetings at the Walhalla Hotel. It is apparent in his descriptions of the activities of the club that Remarque, a pretty fair poet himself, does not spare the literary neophytes his satirical attention. Hans Hungermann and Otto Bambuss, literary rivals for pre-eminence in the club, are the principal objects of that attention. The chief comedic interest is in Bambuss who is writing a twelve sonnet cycle when his poetic inspiration disappears. Ludwig suggests that the virginal Bambuss needs a visit to the "Iron Horse", a prostitute at the local bordello, in order to instill in him new poetic inspiration. However, to rival Hungermann's great delight, the sex therapy has just the opposite effect. Bambuss never added another line after the first eleven perfect sonnets. Perhaps it is significant that although Remarque makes sport of the literary maneuverings of Hungermann, Bambuss, and Knobloch, he does not do the same with the Remarque character Ludwig. It should also be said in fairness, however, that Ludwig does not appear to take his own literary efforts very seriously.

As Remarque takes Ludwig through the scenes of his own youth the reader makes the acquaintance of several memorable supporting characters who contribute to the novel's often bizarre humor.

One of the most interesting of these is Oskar Fuchs, a business competitor in the tombstone business. He is known in the trade as "weeping Oskar" because of his practice of smelling cut onions before visiting a home in which there has been a death. Usually he makes the sale because the family is touched by his obvious grief over their departed loved one.

Retired Sergeant Major Knopf is both a source of amusement for Ludwig and Georg as well as a petty annoyance for the tombstone business. Knopf is a great drinker who makes a practice of urinating on the firm's showpiece, a black obelisk, in the garden behind the Kroll business when he returns from his evening's drinking. Ludwig breaks him of the habit by speaking into a drain pipe and giving him a military dressing-down for his filthy habit. Knopf gets the impression that the hollow-sounding disembodied voice is that of the Kaiser and flees in a state of frightened sudden sobriety.

There are numerous other characters who make their contributions to the lighter side of the story. Some of the most interesting are: Herbert Scherz, a "collector of clubs", who joins as many fraternal organizations as possible in order to insure a splendid turn-out for his own funeral; Wilke, the amorous coffinmaker; Renee de la Tour, the attractive singer with the disconcerting ability to roar out commands in a bass voice; the philandering Lisa Watzek who has an affair with Georg; Kurt Bach the wise-cracking sculptor; and Frau Beckmann whose common-law husband makes money by betting with innocents who don't know of her ability to pull nails out of a wall with her buttocks.

Humor in *The Black Obelisk* is not for the prudish or overly fastidious. It is raucous, often outrageous and crude, but always possessed of a wonderful zest and vitality. The heavy concentration of humorous characters and situations is tantalizing evidence of what Remarque might have achieved in other novels if the possibility for extensive humor had not been smothered by the gravity of the subject matter.

Although the tone of *The Black Obelisk* is generally far less sombre than that of the other novels, one nevertheless finds the intrusion of some problematic concerns. Those occur in the sections of the story which relate to Ludwig's employment as an organist for Sunday mass at the little church of the local insane asylum outside of town. As Remarque did, Ludwig supplements his income from the monument firm by tutoring students and by playing the organ in return for a modest stipend and Sunday breakfast after mass.

During his Sunday visits, Ludwig gets better acquainted with his former priest Bodendiek and meets Doctor Guido Wernike, both of whom serve the inmates of the asylum. Remarque uses the conversations between Bodendiek and Ludwig to give expression to many of his own vitriolic indictments of God and religion, specifically the Roman Catholic faith of his youth. Bodendiek, the imperturbable defender of the faith, has a ready answer for each of Ludwig's questions or accusations. However, none of the answers which Bodendiek so glibly supplies really satisfies Ludwig or lessens his alienation; an alienation caused by the trauma of war and by his mother's tragic death from cancer. When in the course of the discussion Bodendiek indicated that a person humiliated in this life will be exalted in the next as a kind of compensatory justice, Ludwig gives the example of a woman whom Bodendiek immediately recognizes as being Ludwig's mother. Ludwig describes her as

> "a woman who had cancer for ten years, who survived six frightful operations, who was never without pain, and who finally doubted God when two of her children died. She gave up going to mass, to confession, and to communion, and according to the rules of the church she died in the state of mortal sin. According to those same rules she is now burning for all eternity in the hell which the God of love created."[1]

Bodendiek has no satisfactory answer when Ludwig asks if this represents justice. It certainly didn't represent justice to Remarque whose mother was the model in this situation, and who, as a consequence of the manner and circumstances of his mother's death, never again was able fully to accept the teachings of the church.

If Bodendiek is the vicar of the soul, his colleague Dr. Wernicke is the vicar of the mind for the inmates. The fascinating account of the mental illness of one of those inmates, and Ludwig's relationship with her, is an intriguing story within a story.

An interview which Remarque gave to *Newsweek* in 1957 provides some insight into the approach he took to the novel and also indicates the importance he attached to the story of the girl he called Genevieve Terhoven.

> "I had been thinking about writing *The Black Obelisk*, about treating that early part of my life, for years. But there were so many difficulties. I wanted to write about Genevieve, the girl in the asylum. I thought I might do a novel just about her, but it seemed to me it would have been too static, with not enough interest. Then I gradually came to feel that I wanted to write about all the other things at the same time—the tombstone business and so on—and that Genevieve could be part of the

whole. Scenes with her could be worked in among others, and the whole thing might be moving. I hope it is.

Once I had seen my way, it came easily. Ten years after the first war many things had come together for me and I suddenly wrote *All Quiet on the Western Front* in just four weeks. *The Black Obelisk* took a year. I don't know what ever happened to Genevieve."[2]

The novel's Genevieve is an attractive twenty-year-old girl who has been committed to the asylum for treatment of her schizophrenia and for six weeks has been undergoing treatment from Dr. Warnicke. Ludwig never knows which of Genevieve's two delusional personalities he will encounter: the bitter, unattractive, and lewd Jennie or the dreamy Isabelle with her child-like but profound questioning. He also does not know what identity will be assigned to him by Genevieve when she is Isabelle. He might be the boring Rolf, the seducer Raoul, or Rudolf, a likeable young man whom she loves. Ludwig in turn is captivated by the charming Isabelle who views the most commonplace things in a fresh and questioning way. The moments of chaste and idyllic love they share come to an end, however, when Dr. Wernicke's treatment succeeds in eliminating Genevieve's Isabelle and Jennie personalities. The cured Genevieve has no recollection of Ludwig or their love and leaves the asylum in the company of her mother. Ludwig never sees her again. One can only speculate whether the girl Remarque knew in the asylum also won his heart or whether he was merely intrigued by the conversations he had with her.

The novel essentially concludes when Ludwig leaves Werdenbrück for a new job in Berlin. Only two additional pages are required for a summing up which reveals that most of the characters became victims of the war. Ludwig speaks for Remarque when he says: "I never saw any of them again. Occasionally I planned to take a trip back, but something always interfered and I thought I had plenty of time. Suddenly there was no more time. Night broke over Germany, I left it, and when I came back it lay in ruins."[3]

The Black Obelisk is a nostalgic remembrance of Remarque's world that was but is no more. In it he pays tribute to good times, good friends, and the indomitableness of the human spirit. Remarque recognized the uniqueness of this work when he said: "It is the first of my novels which is not tragic, being, in fact, rather gay."[4]

He also indicated in the same interview that he was negotiating for the sale of movie rights to *The Black Obelisk*. Apparently no agreement could be reached because the story has not been filmed. More's the pity. It could have been—and might yet be—one of the best Remarque movies.

31

The First Play, The Second Divorce, and the Third Marriage

The success Remarque had as the writer of the screenplay for "The Last Act" may have caused him to turn his hand to the writing of a drama on a closely related subject. Once again the setting is Berlin near war's end as Russian troops complete the capture of the German capital. Remarque named his first, and only, play *Die letzte Station* (*The Last Station*) and completed work on it in 1956.

As with "The Last Act", one can still hear offstage the sounds of bombing and shelling which not only mark the death of a city but also the passing of the Hitler nightmare. This time, however, the concern is not with the Götterdämmerung" of the Nazi overlords in the bunker but with the fate of characters more typical of Remarque: concentration camp fugitives, an attractive widow, S.S. men, and Russian soldiers.

When the play had its world premiere on September 20, 1956 in the Renaissance Theatre during the West Berlin Cultural Festival its title had been changed to *Berlin, 1945*. The new title, unlike the old, gave some indication of what the audience might expect. The play was directed by Paul Verhoeven with Heide Marie Hatheyer and Kurt Meisel in the principal roles.

The first night audience expressed its enthusiasm for the cast and author by more than twenty curtain calls. Remarque was in attendance for the first performance and appeared on stage in response to requests from the audience. However, he made no response to the expressions of approval but instead merely stood there and, without changing expression, stared back at the audience. It was obvious that he was not yet prepared to be a full participant in a love-feast with Germans. There was still too great a residue of bitterness from the past.

Berlin, 1945 met with very favorable critical response and ran for approximately sixty performances at the Renasisance Theatre. Professor Raeck, the owner and manager of the theatre, later made the play available to German television for a series of Sunday drama presentations. Conditions, however, were not particularly favorable for the television presentation. The actors were not at their best because they had not performed in the play for over a year. A second disadvantage was the fact that the Renaissance Theatre could not be used for the production because Gore Vidal's play *Visit to a Small Planet* was being presented and scenery changes would have been too expensive. The performance consequently had to be filmed in a television studio. The ad hoc quality of the entire venture made for an uninspired presentation at the January 5, 1958 performance. Revitalization of the play would have to await its later adaptation and performance in the United States as *Full Circle*.

Remarque's future wife, actress Paulette Goddard, was in the audience for the premiere performance of *Berlin, 1945*. She was, in fact, the only member of that audience whose presence was acknowledged by him when he reluctantly responded to calls for his appearance on stage. Upon arriving on stage he made only one bow and that was in her direction.

The close relationship they had enjoyed since 1953 was moving ever closer to an official engagement announcement. Before that could happen, however, his marriage to Jeanne Zambona Remarque had to be dissolved. Their marriage, which had served its purpose of protecting and supporting her when she was most vulnerable to financial and bureaucratic vicissitudes, had for a long time been a marriage in name only. It was now only a matter of arriving at a financial agreement of the principals to allow an amicable divorce and a subsequent Remarque-Goddard marriage.

That was achieved by May of 1957. On the twentieth of that month Jeanne was granted a "friendly" divorce from Remarque in Juarez, Mexico. Judge Ignacio Martinez Aguiyo granted the divorce on the basis of incompatability. That non-prejudicial term served the purpose of obtaining the quick and uncontested divorce on which they had previously agreed.

In an interview which Jeanne gave to the *El Paso Herald Post* on May 21, 1957 before she flew back to New York there was no obvious evidence of bitterness or sadness. She was quoted as saying: "It's all very friendly. - - -He sent me a beautiful bouquet of lilies of the valley just before I left New York."[1] They were both living in New York at the time. Remarque was living in an apartment in the Ritz Towers on Park Avenue at 57th Street and Jeanne was in her fifteenth year of residence at the Hotel Pierre. Jeanne put the best face on their separate living arrangements by saying: "You know artists - - - We always had separate places."[2]

She claimed not to know whether Remarque intended to remarry. When asked whether she intended to remarry she replied with a smile: "I'll let you know." Then she quickly added: "No, of course not."[3] She was less than forthcoming about Remarque's plans because she was well aware of his intention to wed Paulette Goddard. In her own case, however, there was certainly no thought of another marriage. Her financial position was secure and she would be able to indulge her artistic inclinations wherever she wished. There had also been health problems. Jeanne mentioned this in the El Paso interview. "I have been terribly ill. I had an emergency major operation, but I had not time to recuperate. Now I am going to Europe and rest for two months. I am going to stay inside the house and just rest."[4] Her plans were to visit Amsterdam and Munich and then visit a friend in Italy for a longer stay. Jeanne's post-divorce vacation trip to Europe was to lead to later residence in Italy and on the French Riviera.

In the summer of 1957 after the divorce Remarque was staying at the Bel-Air Hotel on Stone Canyon Road in Los Angeles. It was during this period that reports began to appear concerning a future Goddard-Remarque marriage. On August 23 the *New York Times* reported that Paulette had told friends that she and Remarque would be married at St. Moritz, Switzerland the next Christmas.[5] *Newsweek* for September 2 announced that their "longtime friendship" was ending happily with her announcement of their plans for a Christmas marriage in Switzerland. She was quoted as saying: "Ah, St. Moritz is so romantic in the winter." When she was asked why the announcement was so long in coming she answered: "I believe in five-year engagements."[6] Complications must have arisen, however, because *The New York Times* for November 29 quoted the manager of the Palace Hotel in St. Moritz as saying that the wedding of Paulette Goddard and Remarque, which had been scheduled for February of 1958, had been canceled. No specific reason for the cancellation was indicated. The manager said that they were "just advised by Remarque that all arrangements are off."[7] Perhaps it was decided that the locale of his second marrage to Jeanne should be avoided this time around.

Although the location was changed, the February wedding date was retained. On February 25, 1958 Paulette Goddard, Remarque and their wedding attendants, Mr. and Mrs. Robert Morris and Mr. and Mrs. Halsey Cowan of New York, drove up from New York City to Branford, Connecticut for what had been intended as a quiet wedding ceremony. Mr. Cowan, of the law firm of Wilzein and Halpern, had made the wedding arrangements with Branford Judge Cornelius J. Driscoll. Judge Driscoll performed the late afternoon marriage in his office in a brief civil ceremony which lasted only ten minutes. Because word had gotten out about the marriage, crowds of journalists, photographers, and persons trying to get a glimpse of the celebrities, made a media event of it.

There was only time to answer a few questions before the Remarques drove back to New York with the Cowans. The newly-weds' immediate plans were rather modest. There were plans for a party later that evening in New York during which there was to be a private screening of his latest movie "A Time to Love and a Time to Die." Future plans included nothing more exciting than a continuation in New York of their respective professional activities. Paulette mentioned returning to Broadway with a new play and indicated she was considering television and movie offers. In its coverage of the wedding *The New Haven Evening Register* quoted Remarque as saying that he and his wife would go to Europe in June for "background" on a new novel he was writing.[8]

Erich Maria Remarque and Paulette Goddard brought a lot of marital experience to their union. It was his third marriage and second wife. She had formerly been married to Edgar James, comedian Charles Chaplin, and actor Burgess Meredith. All of those marriages had ended in divorce. This marriage, however, was to last until Remarque's death.

32

Der Himmel kennt keine Günstlinge (Heaven has no Favorites)

The novel on which he was working at the time of the marriage was *Der Himmel kennt keine Günstlinge*, (*Heaven has no Favorites*). Remarque dedicated both the German edition of the novel and the English translation by Richard and Clara Winston to "Paulette Goddard Remarque".

Given the nature of the work, a trip to Europe for "background" hardly seems to have been necessary. The story is vintage Remarque and the locales are all places with which he was very familiar. Nevertheless it was presumably a pleasant means of combining at least a modicum of business with a pleasant trip for the newly-weds.

In *Heaven has no Favorites* Remarque indulges in a little literary wish-fulfillment when he selects a race car driver as his protagonist. The character, a successful driver known to the reader only as Clerfayt, is first encountered driving his racing car "Giuseppe" along Swiss mountain roads to his destination at the Bella Vista Sanatorium where his friend and co-driver Hollmann is being treated for tuberculosis. While there Clerfayt meets the beautiful Lillian Dunkerque who is also a patient. Dunkerque, half Belgian and half Russian, is twenty-four and has been in the sanatorium three years. She is romantically involved with the emigre White Russian Boris Volkov who is an out-patient at the sanatorium. Lillian, however, is not a person given to long term commitments and is growing restless in the relationship. She is also eager to leave the sanatorium and take her chances with her illness so that she can have a chance to live life on her own terms. The growing closeness between Clerfayt and Lillian appears to offer that opportunity and Lillian goes with him when he leaves the sanatorium after his visit with Hollmann. She is determined to live life for the moment while awaiting her death under conditions of her own choosing. Escape from the mountains symbolizes life for her although it will inevitably be a shorter one than if she remains. Clerfayt can understand her choice because he had been a prisoner of war during World War II and had made his own escape in order to survive.

After a painful leave taking from Boris Volkov who desperately wants her to stay, Lillian leaves the Bella Vista with Clerfayt for their destination of Paris. Lillian wishes to see her parsimonious uncle Gaston who is in charge of her inheritance money and has been doling it out in small monthly amounts. It is her intention to get all of her money from him so that she can make the most of the time left to her. Clerfayt is returning to Paris to sign a racing contract and to be reunited with Lydia Morelli, his beautiful and sophisticated lover. Something unexpected happens along the way back, however.

Remarque adds to the autobiographical flavor by taking Clerfayt and Lillian through the Ticino Canton to Ascona, Porto Ronco, and Lake Maggiore. Clerfayt, who lived in Ascona for a year, becomes a Remarque surogate who takes Lillian, and the reader, on a tour of some of the author's favorite haunts. Although the Ascona idyl is very brief, it provides sufficient time to make lovers of Clerfayt and Lillian.

Once in Paris Clerfayt goes his way to attend to career matters and to resume his relationship with Lydia Morelli. Lillian, intoxicated by her sudden freedom, devotes herself to a sudden expensive love affair with Balenciaga fashions and, in the process, causes her franc-pinching uncle Gaston accute discomfort. Her growing wardrobe serves as an emotional buffer against the inevitable. Hung around her room they function as fetishes to protect her against the terrors of the night. "Lillian had always been afraid of the night. Night was associated with suffocation, with shadowy hands reaching for her throat, with the frightful and unbearable loneliness of death."[1]

When Clerfayt sees her again he is struck by the change in Lillian. The woman he sees now has "the magical sureness of a beautiful woman."[2] Gone is the awkward adolescent quality he remembered. Clerfayt's assessment of her new maturity is strikingly confirmed by Lillian's performance when she is unfairly subjected to the jealous verbal barbs of Lydia when Lillian and Clerfayt meet Lydia and her escort at a restaurant. Lillian acquits herself very well and gains new respect from both Clerfayt and Lydia. Clerfayt's respect soon changes into love. Lillian returns that love—although as always on her own terms.

It is at this point that the reader has the unusual, almost unique, experience of seeing a Remarque protagonist thirsting to exchange his prized independence for what he thinks is the prospect of wedded, domestic bliss; a condition anathema to almost all of the characters with whom Remarque most closely identifies and, indeed, basically inimical to his own nature.

Clerfayt and Lillian live together as Clerfayt resumes his racing career. Lillian, however, soon becomes alienated by the profession she regards as little more than a frivolous tempting of fate. She is painfully aware that life and death are too great to be played with. She also feels that she is being trapped in a routine which is robbing her of some of the precious time still remaining to her. Her need for change causes her to go alone on a trip to Venice. Here she experiences a small hemorrhage while attending a play and has to recuperate in her room for a week. After her recovery she returns to Paris and to Clerfayt. She is surprised and troubled to learn that he wishes to marry her and settle down in Toulouse as the owner of an automobile franchise. In her view, being in that situation would be the equivalent of being locked up.

Lillian manages to evade a definite resolution of the issue until Clerfayt's departure to participate in the "Mille Miglia" race through Italy. She remains in Paris and receives radio reports of the race until a call from Clerfayt in Brescia informs her that he has completed the race in sixth place. Upon his return they go to see a house Clerfayt owns on the Riviera. Lillian again has the feeling that she is about to become a captive to a place and routine which would contradict the choice she made when she left the sanatorium. Moreover, Clerfayt has begun to urge her to see a doctor. She can foresee that he may next suggest her return to the hospital.

A trip to the casino produces big winnings for Clerfayt who has a sixth sense for gambling and racing but not for the wishes and feelings of Lillian. His uncharacteristic domestic urges have even caused him to propose using his winnings to have his house redone for their future home. When Clerfayt and Lillian collect the money which he won from his long gambling streak they are told of another very successful gambler who broke the bank twice in one night. They learn to their surprise that this legendary gambler is Boris Volkov, Lillian's former lover whom she left at the sanatorium. However, the Boris Volkov of legend seems to bear little resemblance to the conservative, rather dependent Boris Volkov Lillian remembers who urged her to stay at Bella Vista. Unfortunately, the Boris of her memory also seems distressingly similar to the new Clerfayt with his plans for domestic happiness.

When Clerfayt learns of Volkov's past he becomes convinced that it is because of him that Lillian has been evading his marriage proposals. He believes that she wishes to return to Bella Vista and Boris Volkov. With sudden clarity Lillian understands that it is necessary for her to leave Clerfayt at the earliest moment. However, because she wants no quarrels to cloud their last days together she consents, as a subterfuge, to marry him in the autumn. Comforted by her decision she is able to enjoy the time she has with Clerfayt before he drives in the Monte Carlo race.

Tragedy strikes Clerfayt just as he is about to take the lead in the race. The leading car he is on the point of overtaking wrecks and spills oil across the road. Clerfayt is unable to avoid crashing into the car. His car is also struck from the rear.

Clerfayt suffers severe injury to his face and chest and is taken unconscious to the hospital where he dies a short time later.

Lillian has difficulty comprehending the sudden tragedy which seems so terribly wrong. "It was all not true, it was not right, it could not be so—it was not Clerfayt who should be stretched out on the hospital bed, but she, she alone, and not he; it was a horrible distortion; someone had put across a dreadful, sinister joke."[3]

While Lillian is attempting to settle matters relating to Clerfayt's death his sister, who hated him and whom he hated in return, appears on the scene and attempts to exploit his death by threatening law suits against all parties involved in any way. She even tries to extort from Lillian the property assignment Clerfayt made out for her. Lillian does not allow herself to be intimidated. She terminates the embarassing confrontation by throwing the water and wilted flowers from a flower bowl into the sister's face.

After Clerfayt's death Lillian is quite uncertain where she should go and what she should do. Even though she had previously made the decision to leave him, she is not prepared for the sudden series of tragic events. In her need for comfort she places a telephone call to Boris Volkov but learns to her dismay that he "has left". Familiar with the euphemistic terms in use at the sanatorium, she interprets that to mean that he may have died. That is not the case, however, because when Boris reads of Clerfayt's death he comes to join her and meets her at the station as she is on the point of taking the train to Zürich.

When they meet again all of the old difficulties and misunderstandings have been stripped away and there remains only the "last consolation: that the person you loved was not dead, was still living, still breathing, no matter what his feelings were or what had happened. Neither weakness nor pity had prompted Boris to come, but rather the lightning-flash of this ultimate knowledge - - -."[4]

Boris and Lillian decide to return to Bella Vista. Her symptoms of illness have becomes more pronounced and it seems likely that, as a doctor in Nice predicted, she will not survive the summer. Despite the severity of her condition, Lillian asks Boris to drive her back to the sanatorium instead of following the doctor's suggestion to be taken in an ambulance. As they are driving up to Bella Vista they meet Hollmann driving away. He is cured of his tuberculosis and is off to take Clerfayt's place driving for the old firm. Hollmann is taking Clerfayt's place "as Clerfayt had taken the place of another, and as another would some day take Hollmann's".[5]

The final paragraph in *Heaven Has No Favorites* is strongly reminiscent of the concluding paragraph in *All Quiet on the Western Front*. Paul Bäumer's death is reported by saying: "He fell in October 1918, on a day that was so quiet and still on the whole front, that the army report confined itself to the single sentence: All quiet on the Western Front."[6] The report of Lillian's death reads: "She died six weeks later, on a bright summer afternoon so still that the landscape seemed to be holding its breath."[7] Each character falls victim to a different kind of war and the end is reported with almost objective detachment.

There is slightly more elaboration on Lillian's fate. We learn that Boris had discovered Lillian's body after she had hemorrhaged and suffocated in her bed. Her dying had been extremely difficult. However, in death her distorted features relaxed and regained the beauty Boris remembered. The concluding sentence says that Boris "believed also that she had been happy, insofar as any human being can ever be called happy."[8] This final comment ends the novel on a depressingly down-beat note. Remarque readers will not be greatly surprised by this further evidence of the darker side of his philosophy. It does seem somewhat inconsistent, however, coming from an author who spent so much of his time, energy, and personal wealth in hedonistic search of pleasure. At first glance one assumes that *Heaven Has No Favorites* is Clerfayt's story. It soon becomes apparent, however, that it is essentially the story of Lillian whose attitudes most consistently reflect those of Remarque. It is equally apparent that Remarque also strongly identifies with both Clerfayt and Volkov who in reality are, if not identical, at least blood brothers. Through these characters it was possible for Remarque vicariously to break the bank at Monte Carlo and to be a winning professional racing car driver. The weakness of Clerfayt and Volkov lay in their straying from the ideal Remarque protagonist's philosophy of living for the moment. In what Remarque considers a bourgeois desire to hold love too tightly, both Clerfayt and Boris try to impose their own wishes on Lillian. The attempt fails completely in the case of Clerfayt. Only death prevents him from learning of Lillian's desire to leave him. Boris, after his initial mistake, is given a second chance to accept love without conditions. The irony about love affairs, in Remarque's view, is that the more tightly you try to hold your love the more likely you are to lose her.

Remarque's fascination with death has never been more clearly expressed than in this novel. Death in many forms is constantly lurking in the wings. It can claim a Clerfayt who has tempted it once too often in his profession. It can also claim Lillian and her fellow patients at Bella Vista who constantly live with its pathological reality. The awareness and inevitability of death permeates and dominates the story from beginning to end. There is no escape for Remarque's characters just as there is no escape for anyone from the common ultimate fate of man. The important thing for Remarque is that his principal characters remain true to his philosophy; that is, with full awareness of the transitory nature of life, they extract a full measure of its pleasures while at the same time remaining true to their own code of decency and honor.

References within the novel date the action as occuring post World War II. However, with very minor changes it could easily have been post World War I. The Remarque experiences which serve as the basis for the story all antedate 1939.

Persuasive evidence that the basic essentials of the story line existed at least as long ago as 1947 may be found in a movie of that year which was based on a short story by Remarque. The story, entitled "Beyond", was written in the early 1940's and sold to United Artists. When the studio finally got around to making a movie of it called "The Other Love", it did not star Marlene Dietrich, as Remarque had wished, but Barbara Stanwyck. Stanwyck played an American pianist named Karen Duncan who was a tuberculosis patient in a romantic sanatorium in the Swiss Alps. While there she developed a relationship with her physician Dr. Anthony Stanton, played by David Niven, which was temporarily suspended because of her disenchantment with him and subsequent decampment from the sanatorium. After her escape to the outside world in which evidence of pathology was less obvious but just as real, she began her own version of Lillian's "gathering rosebuds". During her attempt to extract the most pleasure from the time remaining to her, she became involved with Paul Clermont, a Monte Carlo playboy acted by Richard Conte. However, Dr. Stanton came to find her, declared his love, and persuaded her to return to the sanatorium for treatment. The lovers were married before her death.

It is readily apparent that "Beyond" was modified by Remarque to become *Heaven Has No Favorites*. Karen Duncan became Lillian Dunkerque, Anthony Stanton became Boris Volkov, and, in the most major character change, Paul Clermont became Clerfayt.

"The Other Love" was the sixth Remarque story to be made into a movie. It was directed by Andre De Toth and produced by David Lewis for Enterprise. Harry Brown and Ladislas Fodor did the screen play.

Even though David Niven and Barbara Stanwyck were good actors, they were perhaps not the proper matching of lovers for this rather melodramatic love story. Bosley Crowther, in his *New York Times* review of the movie, gives faint praise to David Niven, and the back of his hand to Barbara Stanwyck. In his criticism of her he says that "- - - it might have been more appealing if Barbara Stanwyck, in the principal role, were a little less stony and truculent, showed a little more gentleness and grace. As it is, Miss Stanwyck's manner suggests remarkable durability. It is hard to perceive any pathos in her arrogant attitude."[9]

It is doubtful whether Richard Conte's feelings toward Crowther were any kinder than Barbara Stanwyck's when he read: "- - - Richard Conte performs the playboy like a poker-faced poolroom shark."[10]

Whatever the merits, or demerits, of "The Other Love" may be, it was certainly no worse than the later "Bobby Deerfield" which was, very roughly, based on *Heaven Has No Favorites*. The novel came out in 1961 but the movie wasn't made until sixteen years later, seven years after Remarque's death.

"Bobby Deerfield" was a Columbia Pictures/Warner Brothers presentation produced and directed by Sydney Pollack. The executive producer was John Foreman and the screenplay was written by Alvin Sargent. The movie was filmed on location in Europe at places mentioned in the novel or at places very similar to those found in the novel. The filming was done at LeMans and Paris in France, Lake Como and Florence in Italy, and Leukerbad in the Swiss Alps. As a result, one of the chief strengths, perhaps the principal strength, of the movie is its travelogue quality. The Remarque reader will, however, regret the omission of scenes of the Ascona-Lake Maggiore-Porto Ronco region; Remarque's home area to which Clerfayt took Lillian in the novel.

Studio advertising always carried at the top of its promotional picture the question: "Who is Bobby Deerfield?" Anyone who had read the novel would ask the same question since Bobby Deerfield was not a character in *Heaven Has No Favorites*. One soon discovered that the Frenchman Clerfayt had been metamorphosed into an American Grand Prix driver named Bobby Deerfield. Clerfayt/Deerfield was played by Al Pacino who had starred in such films as "The Godfather" and "Dog Day Afternoon." Lillian, who retained her name in the transition from book to movie, was played by Marthe Keller. Keller was essentially a European actress although she had appeared in the American films "Marathon Man" and "Black Sunday."

The part of Lydia was played by the well-known French actress Anny Duprey who was making her debut in an American film.

The scenario made an apparent attempt to be generally faithful to Remarque's story although a number of changes were made. Deerfield is a far more brooding, introspective character than Clerfayt who, by comparison, seems less problematic and far more likeable. Much of this is due to Al Pacino's grim and wooden portrayal of the character. Marthe Keller does better in capturing some of the essence of Lillian but almost entirely lacks her vulnerability.

In general, the movie is disappointing to any one with a knowledge of the book. The skeletal structure of much of Remarque's story is present but the characters are imposters.

33

Die Nacht von Lissabon, *(The Night in Lisbon)*

The year after the publication of *Heaven Has No Favorites* Remarque had an opportunity to make money from a movie studio without selling the film nights to a novel. When Cornelius Ryan completed his screenplay for the 1962 movie "The Longest Day", the producer, Darryl F. Zanuck, reportedly sent copies of the movie's script to various authors he considered representative of the countries which participated in the D-Day fighting in Normandy. Zanuck selected James Jones for the United States, Noel Coward for great Britain, Romain Gary for France, and Remarque for Germany. Noel Coward did not agree to review the script because he said he was too busy. However, the others accepted. According to film biographer Mel Gussow who tells the story "Remarque commented briefly on the script and his agent followed it up with a bill for $5,000.00. Jones and Gary agreed to participate without compensation."[1] If the report is accurate, it should not have come as a surprise to Zanuck that Remarque would expect compensation for his contribution, unnecessary as it likely was, to a commercial enterprise. The wonder is that Jones and Gary didn't.

In mid-January of 1963 the Remarques left their home at Ascona and flew to Berlin's Tempelhof airport for their third post-war visit to the former German capital. Their first visit had been in 1956 before their marriage when they came to attend the initial performance of the play *Die letzte Station*. The second visit was for the filming of "A Time to Love and a Time to Die".

The 1963 visit came as the result of an invitation by Friedrich Luft for Remarque to appear on his television program "Das Porträt" (the portrait). On this visit the Remarques stayed at the Hilton Hotel. During their week in Berlin, before returning to Ascona, they attended three theatre performances and attracted wide-spread media interest. Remarque also took advantage, after a thirty-year hiatus, of the opportunity to attend the famous Berlin Press Ball. One can only speculate whether his thoughts turned occasionally to his former wife Jeanne who had accompanied him to the last Press Ball he attended.

While in Berlin the aging Remarque was unusually accessible to the press for interviews. He held court in the Hilton bar and talked with several journalists on a number of subjects ranging from the Berlin he remembered to his new book *Die Nacht von Lissabon*. Many interviews were given jointly by both Remarques because Paulette was just as popular a subject as her husband.

In the interview they gave to Liz Hiller for the January 18, 1963 issue of *Bild* they were forthcoming and charming in responding to questions of a light, general nature. After describing Paulette's Dior outfit and accessories, Hiller reported Remarque's answer to her question as to what the secret was that enabled a film star and an author to live together so amicably. Remarque answered: "Well, in our case the parts are well assigned. We never quarrel."[2] He went on to say: "You see, fortunately my English-speaking wife can not read the manuscripts for my books, which I always write in German. She can only do that if she has the English translation before her, and then, after all, the book is printed—and nothing more can be done about it."[3] Remarque laughed after making the observation.

When asked if there was a formula for his success he replied: "No, there isn't. Above all, work is required. Luck and chance are only characteristics of this work. If someone says to me 'good, then I will begin working tomorrow,' then I would answer him, no do it today."[4]

Remarque also expressed his pleasure that the old Berlin newspaper quarter was being revived and recalled that he got his journalistic start as a local reporter for Scherl. Paulette told Hiller that she liked it so well in Berlin that she would like to stay until it was again warm enough to go swimming in Lake Maggiore.

In an interview for the *Berliner Zeitung* of January 17, 1963 Remarque admitted to a secret desire to act. Apparently the taste of it he had had in "A Time to Love and a Time to Die" had appealed to his ham instincts which were never far below the surface.

> "At that time I was asked whether I would like to act in my film. Idealistic as I now am, I only inquired about the pay. I liked it. It was a small role. But afterwards I got the best reviews. I would like to try it again as an actor. Also on the stage. But unfortunately I haven't received any more offers."[5]

Paulette also brought the interviewer up to date regarding her acting career. She reported that she had just completed filming in California the first program for a new television series "The Phantom." In answer to a question as to whether her husband liked her to work she said: "I will be careful not to ask him about it." As a concluding note she said she had looked in vain the previous weeks for good guide books to Berlin. "The only thing that I learned is that one can buy good cameras here. However, I don't want a camera. I would never take pictures, except for money. I also don't like pictures of me." She went on to say that "famous American painters have done portraits of me. Do you know where I keep their pictures? In the basement where I don't have to see them."[6]

In the *Bild* interview Remarque discussed his latest novel *Die Nacht von Lissabon* which had been published a month earlier in order to take advantage of the Christmas market. The first German edition of thirty thousand copies had already been sold by the time of Remarque's visit to Berlin. The 1964 Ralph Manheim English translation for Harcourt, Brace and World was dedicated to "Paulette Remarque." Remarque said of his penultimate book: "It is a novel about emigrants which is intended to show the loneliness of each of them. In this book I want to convince people that in all chaos there can be love, a very special deep love, between two people."[7]

In *Die Nacht von Lissabon* Remarque once again returns to the plight of refugees seeking escape from the Nazi terror. As was the case earlier in *Flotsam*, one finds the interweaving of two exile stories; in this instance the stories of two married couples. Again, as in *Flotsam*, one of the principal male characters, at the risk of his life, returns to his hometown in Germany to see his wife. *Flotsam* told the stories of two strong and enduring loves. *The Night in Lisbon*, however, has only one significant love story. The story of a second couple is of secondary importance and is of interest only as another example of a Remarque fictional marriage gone wrong.

The novel is set within a narrative frame provided by an unnamed refugee from Nazi Germany. The refugee and his wife Ruth are in Lisbon in 1942 with Portuguese residence permits which are due to expire in a few days. They have no American visas and are three hundred dollars short of the steamer fare for America. A desperate attempt to increase their funds through gambling fails, leaving them with six dollars.

As the refugee stands alone on the dock staring at the boat which was the last hope of escape for him and his wife, but which now appears to be an unattainable goal, he notices a man who also appears to be a refugee. This man has also become aware of the narrator and tries to speak with him. But the refugee, because of the ingrained fear that any stranger might be a policeman, walks away quickly. However, the stranger perseveres, overtakes him, and asks him if he would like to go to New York. And then, mirabile dictu, he holds out two steamer tickets with the offer to give them, free of charge, to the refugee-narrator. The only thing he wishes in return is to have company for the night and an opportunity to tell his story to someone. The refugee eagerly accepts the offer and takes the stranger to a restaurant where the story is told.

The stranger identifies himself as Josef Schwarz although he says that is not his real name but only the name on his passport. It is only much later in the story that the reader learns that his true name is Josef Baumann. His true name doesn't really matter, however, because in the world of the exile one name serves as well as another. The only real concern is the possession of valid papers; with the individual's true name or that of another.

Through the long night Schwarz-Baumann told the story of his exile which began in Osnabrück in 1934. After leaving Germany he went to Paris and, after his arrest for lack of proper documentation, spent time in French and Swiss prisons as a punishment for illegal entry as he went back and forth from one country to the other. Inspired by a dream in which he returned to his home of Osnabrück to see his wife, he managed to acquire a valid passport which was previously owned by a deceased exile named Schwarz. Now he could make the dream come true and carry out the dangerous return to Osnabrück to see his wife.

When he arrived he did not contact his wife, with whom he had had no contact for five years, but got in touch with Dr. Rudolf Martens, a friend from childhood days. Baumann was not certain how he would be received by Helen but he was certain about the reception he would get from her storm trooper brother Georg Jürgens who had already denounced him. Rudolf arranged a meeting of Josef and Helen which led to a reaffirmation of their love and Helen's resolution to leave Germany and Josef. Their exile took them to Switzerland and then France where Georg Jürgens followed them in a vain attempt to get Helen to return to Germany with him. During his confrontation with Josef he mentioned that Helen was sick and should return to Osnabrück. The disease, Josef finally learned, was cancer which she had wished to conceal from him.

When the war began, and the French closed their borders, Josef and Helen were interned along with hundreds of other foreign refugees. They were together briefly and then assigned to separate camps. When France was defeated Josef escaped from his camp and went to find Helen. When he reached the camp in which she was reportedly interned, circumspect inquiries revealed that there was—or had been—a Helen Baumann (only at this point in the story does the reader learn that Josef's surname is Baumann). Their eventual reunion led to Helen's escape and a flight to freedom which took them to Bordeaux, Bayonne, Marseille, and finally, Lisbon. However, Remarque, with typical irony, cheated them of the potential rewards of their escape. Helen took poison to escape the cancer she had steadfastly sought to ignore—and also to escape the necessity to board a ship for America. Josef, crushed by the unexpected loss of the only person he cared about, lost all interest in making a new life in America and briefly entertained thoughts of suicide. That mood did not last long, however, because Baumann had suffered too much at the hands of the Nazis to kill himself when he could more profitably remain alive to fight them. At story's end he was making his way to join the French Foreign Legion to begin that fight.

Before he left, Josef Baumann gave the exile-narrator Josef his passport and Helen's passport which enabled him and his wife Ruth to escape to America. The gift did not bring with it any real happiness, however, because Josef and Ruth were divorced within six months and she was married to a wealthy American who had befriended them. Josef returned to Osnabrück at the end of the war and made inquiries concerning Josef Baumann without success, leaving the reader to speculate about the fate of the Nazi-hunter.

In this novel Remarque adds to his credentials as a chronicler of the exile plight. He is expert at capturing the mood of that desperate situation and in telling the story of many people by concentrating on the fate of a few. As one might expect, there are characters and situations the Remarque reader has previously encountered in other guises. The most striking of which is Baumann's self-defense murder of his storm trooper brother-in-law Georg Jürgens which immediately brings to mind the execution of Haake by Ravic in *Arch of Triumph*. Also strongly in evidence are such recurrent themes as Nazi brutality and torture, art, the infidelity of wives, and the solitary nature of man. All in all, there is a strong sense of deja vu.

At the heart of the novel, however, is the love story of Josef and Helen. *The Night of Lisbon,* when stripped of the trappings of the exile novel is really just another in Remarque's series of true, but tragic, loves.

34

Recognition from the Germans

Die Nacht von Lissabon was the last novel published during Remarque's life. The later *Schatten im Paradies (Shadows in Paradise)* was published posthumously. By the time of the 1962 publication of *die Nacht von Lissabon* his creative well had largely gone dry. And even loyal Remarque readers have a saturation point for war novels, exile novels, and bitter-sweet love stories.

However, given Remarque's industry and his successful formula approach to writing, he might have continued his literary output for several more years if the condition of his health had not declined rather suddenly. Apparently, apart from some arthritic complaints which he had mentioned as early as 1946, his health was generally good until the early 1960's. By this time he had begun to suffer from heart problems and advanced arteriosclerosis. It is likely, given his age and physically rather inactive life, that he had other problems. That remains sheer speculation, however, because of his intense desire for privacy. His heart and circulatory problems became known only when they had progressed so far that it was impossible to maintain secrecy. Those health problems necessarily curtailed many of his activities and also made it impossible for him to travel to accept the belated official recognition his former homeland offered.

Except for the Nazi years after the book burnings, Remarque's books always were best sellers in Germany. In other countries the popularity of his books was always dependably high. The reading public in all countries gave him a warm acceptance. Literary critics were often less enthusiastic. This was particularly true of German critics who, for the most part, consigned his work to the category of "Unterhaltungsliteratur"—recreational reading. Persistent friends and admirers of Remarque's principles and literary works kept pressing for official recognition of his literary accomplishments and the honor he had brought to a newly democratic Germany.

The first of the significant honors to come to him was from his hometown of Osnabrück which awarded him the Justus Möser Medal in 1963. The undoubted catalyst for this action was Remarque's long-time friend Hanns-Gerd Rabe who was tireless in his struggle to obtain the proper recognition for him. Because Remarque was unable to make the trip to Osnabrück to receive the award, a delegation of eight city officials and dignitaries, including Hanns-Gerd Rabe, traveled to Remarque's home at Ascona to present it to him. According to Rabe's account, Oberbürgermeister Willi Kelch presented the Möser Medal and read the award, the text of which may be translated as follows:

> "Erich Maria Remarque in his rich life's work has at all times stood for peace, freedom, and human dignity; he has portrayed war in its cruelty and senselessness and has summoned people to act in the sense of true humanity; in addition, he has lovingly remembered his native city in works which have become known far beyond the borders of Germany. In grateful recognition of this service the council of the city of Osnabrück on the 17th of December, 1963 unanimously decided to honor Erich Maria Remarque by the conferring of the Justus Möser medal."[1]

Oberbürgermeister Kelch also presented Remarque with an old engraving of the city of Osnabrück from the year 1630. Remarque was very touched by the honor and in his response told the group that he still regarded himself as an Osnabrücker even though he no longer had German citizenship. He further assured them that it was his fond hope, indeed an inner need, to return to Osnabrück. He even expressed the hope that he could remain there for a while to work as he had done during the writing of *Der Weg zurück*. This despite the fact that, as Hanns-Gerd Rabe reminded, Remarque had been advised by some persons obviously unfavorably impressed by *Im Westen nichts Neues,* "Am besten nichts Neues mehr."—an amusing play on the title of his first successful novel, which may be translated as "Best of all nothing more new."

In the cheerful, bantering mood of the occasion, Remarque pointed out to Rabe, who was taking notes for an article in the *Osnabrücker Tageblatt,* that in addition to the *Tageblatt* the *New York Times* also wrote about him. He also mentioned that he hoped it had been forgotten that he had published his first poems in the *Tageblatt* and further assured them that he was no longer writing poetry.

It was a wonderful occasion for Remarque as well as for old friend Rabe and the other Osnabrück visitors even though it was made bitter-sweet by the unspoken awareness that the honoree would almost certainly never return to their hometown.

With the decline of his health Remarque made fewer trips to New York and more to Rome because that required a far less arduous journey. He and Paulette spent the winter of 1965–66 in Rome at the Hotel Flora on the via Veneto to escape the cold of Porto Ronco. In a letter to Rabe dated January 24, 1966 Remarque indicated that Porto Ronco was too lonely for his wife in the winter. He also mentioned that a short time before a landslide had caused considerable damage to his property. Fortunately his hillside home was not affected. However, his garden, garage, and automobile were heavily damaged. He further reported that his own health was essentially unchanged. He tired easily and was visited by the doctor every other day. There was some comfort in the fact that he could take short walks and enjoyed the view of Monte Pincio and the Borghese gardens which he had from his balcony.

By March of 1966 he and Paulette had returned home after the months spent in Rome. In a letter dated March 26, 1966 he wrote Hanns-Gerd Rabe that his health had been better during the last weeks and they were going to venture a trip by boat from Genoa to New York at the end of April. It was a mode of travel which appealed to Remarque's patrician tastes and was also less physically demanding for him. There was really no choice in view of the fact that his physician had forbidden him to travel by air. It was an uneventful crossing and his boat, the Italian liner "Raffaelo", docked in New York harbor May 1, 1966. He indicated to Rabe that he urgently had to return to New York, after an absence of six years, because many matters had accumulated which he had to attend to. Before their return in the summer, Remarque renewed his acquaintance with one of his favorite cities, did a little writing, and was involved in planning for the American production of his play. Unfortunately the play was not to appear until after his death.

In 1967 the Federal Republic of Germany gave Remarque its highest official recognition when it conferred on him "das Grosse Verdienstkreuz des Verdienstordens der Bundesrepublik Deutschland" (The Distinguished Service Cross of the Order of Merit of the Federal Republic of Germany). The award was officially granted on April 25, 1967 by the then president Heinrich Lübke but was actually presented to Remarque in Porto Ronco on July 20, 1967 by the German ambassador. The award was given to Remarque in the presence of Paulette and his friend and attorney Robert M. W. Kempner.

A translation of the "Vorschlagsbegründung" (rationale for the proposal) is as follows:

> "The author Erich Maria Remarque, despite the loss of his civil rights at the hands of the national socialist government, his exile fate and the tragic events in his family—his sister was executed during the Third Reich—has vigorously sought a reconciliation with today's Germany. His attitude has not been without effect on numerous German literary personalities who, like him, chose Switzerland as an exile.
>
> If one takes as a basis the number of copies sold, no German-language author in this century has had a greater success than Remarque with "All Quiet on the Western Front" and a few other of his novels (estimated total publication — Ca. 15 million).
>
> Among the great survivors of German Literature of the Exile Period, who live in Switzerland today, Remarque, in addition to Zuckmayer, occupies a prominent position."[2]

After reading the rationale for the award one is struck by the remarkable lack of enthusiasm on the part of the person writing it. It appears to be an excellent example of damning with faint praise. The only positive note in the statement is the reference to Remarque's status as the best-selling German-language author of the century. That, however, is merely recognition of incontrovertible fact and hardly qualifies as praise. However lukewarm the praise in the citation statement may have been, the Cross of Merit did represent an official recognition of Remarque's career and as such was welcome. It is perhaps better that we do not have Remarque's reaction to the rationale for the award.

Any awards which need bureaucratic approval require effective advocates to serve as catalysts in achieving the recognition of merit which might otherwise go unrewarded. Robert M. W. Kempner was Remarque's advocate for this award just as Hanns-Gerd Rabe had been for the earlier Justus Möser award. A letter written to Dr. Kempner January 9, 1967 by a representative of the German Embassy in Bern in response to his letter contained assurances that an award for Remarque would likely be forthcoming soon. This certainly proved to be the case. There were, however, other parts of the letter of even more interest. One learns, for example, that the representative in Bern had advocated an award for Remarque as early as 1963 but the failure to do so lay in the presidential office in Bonn. It is also mentioned that a large dossier exists regarding the matter. Of most interest perhaps is a reference to the obstacle posed by the fact that in the circle of Remarque's colleagues, prominent men who had also shared the exile fate and who, like him, had lived for many years in the Tessin, many an unfriendly comment, many an "innuendo", had been made against him. Evidently snide and even slanderous comments were part of the price Remarque had to pay for his fierce independence and his failure to associate himself with any sort of exile movement. There also certainly was jealousy of the "popular" and commercial success which had brought him affluence. The attitude of his literary peers might have been somewhat different if the man whose charm could even make Garbo smile had cared enough to cultivate them.

The Remarques spent the 1967–68 winter and the spring of 1968 in Rome. Then they returned to their home in Porto Ronco so that Remarque could "survive", as he put it, his seventieth birthday enjoying the beauty of the lake from his hillside home. His return home was marked by a pleasant surprise when he learned that the towns of Ascona and Ronco wished to make him an honorary citizen on his birthday. This recognition from his adopted home touched him deeply. He did not fail to take note of the fact that Germany in more than twenty years had not seen fit to restore to him the citizenship the Nazis took away.

His final literary recognition came in his seventieth year when he was elected to membership in "Die Deutsche Akademie für Sprache und Dichtung" (The German Academy for Language and Literature). This additional example of belated recognition may have been influenced by the outpouring of journalistic and literary articles which used the occasion of his seventieth birthday to recognize his accomplishments and his importance as a literary chronicler of the last fifty years of German history.

35

"All Quiet"

Remarque, who always prided himself on being a survivor, was running out of time. During the last two years of his life he devoted much of his failing strength to the completion of *Schatten im Paradies*. The book had no publicly announced title while he was working on it because of his conviction that things which are discussed prematurely are likely to remain unfinished.

By August 29, 1970 Remarque's health had deteriorated to the point that he had to be admitted to the Saint Agnese hospital in Locarno. He was reportedly suffering from the results of two previous infarctions and a stroke. Lengthy hospital care could not change the inevitable result but only delay it. Remarque died approximately at noon on Friday, September 25, 1970 and Paulette was with him when he died. Heart failure was given as the cause of death.

Funeral services were held two days later on Sunday, September 27 in the Roman Catholic church of Ronco. At Paulette's request the services were private. There were also no eulogies.

One of the persons at the funeral service was the author Hans Habe. Habe, who lived in Ascona, was Remarque's closest friend during the last years of his life. In a short essay about Remarque he described the funeral service.

> "It was a quiet funeral, with many flowers and no speeches. The priest spoke Italian, a language which Remarque, who lived more than thirty years in the 'Italian' Tessin, had never learned. Not a single one of his colleagues was present, no government was represented, and which one should it have been anyhow—the German, the American, or the Swiss? Nevertheless, it was a long procession which followed the hearse up to the village cemetery of Ronco above Ascona, between the

> walls with their autumn colors. All the craftsmen of the town were there and the baker's boy and the shopkeepers and the shop girls and the pharmacist and the innkeepers. They said afterwards that it had been a nice funeral. None of them thought of the fact that they had carried a great German writer to his grave."[1]

Remarque's grave is marked by a black granite monument, attractive in its stark simplicity, which has inscribed on it only his name and the dates of his birth and death. The visitor will be pleased to see that in death, as in life, Remarque still has a splendid view of his beloved Lake Maggiore.

36

Posthumous Events before *Schatten im Paradies*

Among the many expressions of condolence received by Paulette Goddard Remarque was one from the chancellor of the Federal Republic Willy Brandt. In a telegram sent September 26, 1970 Brandt expressed the view that Remarque understood, as few others had, how to express, and give artistic expression to, contemporary problems.

Osnabrück also paid tribute to its native son in two additional ways. *Die Welt* for September 30, 1970 carried a large memorial notice which read:

> "We mourn for Erich Maria Remarque, recipient of the Justus-Möser-Medal of the City of Osnabrück.
>
> With his great literary works which have become familiar in almost all countries of the world, the Osnabrück-born author addressed the conscience of the world. Because he had always retained close emotional ties to his native town, it had been his great wish for years, despite a long, serious illness, to see once more the places of youth. This hope remained unfulfilled.
>
> With the death of Erich Maria Remarque Osnabrück lost a great son whose memory will always be honored."[1]

The city of his birth paid him a second, more lasting honor when the city council approved a proposal to name a street for him. The former "Karlsring" was renamed the "E. M. Remarque Ring" and bears that name today.

Berlin also made its contribution to the memory of Remarque. On April 26, 1971 Heinrich Lummer, the CDU party chairman and legislator, recommended that a school in the Wilmersdorf section of the city be named for him and a plaque placed on his former residence at number 5 Wittelsbacher Street in Wilmersdorf. Remarque was living there at the time he wrote *Im Westen nichts Neues*. Lummer's suggestion regarding the school could not be implemented until a new school was built. However, the suggestion of a memorial plaque was approved. The plaque was dedicated in a ceremony which took place on Tuesday, June 22, 1972, a date which would have been Remarque's seventy-fourth birthday. Paulette had been invited to the dedication but declined on the basis that other memorial ceremonies for her dead husband's birthday prevented her from attending.

37

Schatten im Paradies

Remarque's last novel was published posthumously in the summer of 1971 by the Droemer Knaur Verlag of München. The book was given the title *Schatten im Paradies (Shadows in Paradise)* by Paulette Goddard Remarque. The English translation by Ralph Manheim was published by Harcourt Brace Jovanovich in 1972.

The publication of the German edition was preceded by an intensive publicity campaign featuring Paulette. The campaign opened with a media reception at the Droemer Knaur publishing firm in München. The invitations indicated that Paulette would turn over the manuscript for the novel to publisher Willy Droemer at the reception. More than one hundred persons from the press, television, politics, and the literary world were in attendance. The occasion was strictly ceremonial because the book had already been purchased and announced for summer publication.

Paulette, who had taken on the role of literary representative, had acquired a new Paris wardrobe for the publicity tour in Germany. "No widow's weeds, Erich would not have liked that. Pink, white, and brown dresses and coats."[1] The Remarque who wrote *Heaven has no Favorites* and created such memorable and fashion-loving characters as Lillian Dunkerque and Lydia Morelli would certainly have approved.

She also revealed at the Droemer reception that seven publishing houses had bought the novel sight unseen and speculated that "even the Russians will surely print it, Erich's books are bestsellers in the Soviet Union."[2] She did point out, however, that "the Russians never pay royalties."[3]

A later interview with Associated Press newsfeatures' writer Joy Stilley soon after the publication of the English translation of *Shadows in Paradise* provided a few more personal observations from Paulette regarding the book, Remarque, and herself. She may have wanted to put to rest any fears that the posthumous publication might raise regarding whether the novel had really been completed before her husband's death. Her statement was unequivocal in this regard. "Erich finished the book the night before he went to the hospital for the last time."

To no one's surprise she said: "This is my favorite of all his books. - - - It's definitely the most personal and most powerful. It's so natural; the characters are so alive you think you're sitting in the scene." She also had these comments to make concerning Remarque and his writing: "He was never satisfied with his work - - - He worked on each of his books five years or more and did six complete rewrites on this one. He said he never finished a book—he always abandoned it. Otherwise he would have rewritten it a thousand times."

Her estimates of the time Remarque expended on each novel were true for some but not for others. There is a strange distribution pattern for the publication dates of his novels with greatly varying periods between works. Including the unfortunate first work *Die Traumbude*, which he later disclaimed, Remarque wrote twelve novels. The years of their publication were: 1920, 1929, 1931, 1937, 1939, 1946, 1952, 1954, 1956, 1961, 1962, and 1971. With intervals of 9, 2, 6, 2, 7, 6, 2, 2, 5, 1 and 9 years between novels the obvious conclusion to be drawn is that Remarque was a writer of somewhat sporadic inspiration and/or industry.

Remarque readers who had been cheered by the prospect of a new work had little to cheer about in his last novel. *Schatten im Paradies* is the exile experience revisited. The only thing unique about this work is that the experiences take place in the United States during the last years of the war. The first-person narrator is a former German journalist whose passport name is Robert Ross. Remarque makes the novel to some extent a continuation of *Die Nacht von Lissabon* by bringing Ross by freighter from Lisbon to New York and allowing him to make his way in an exile situation removed from the European locales his readers know so well.

After an internment at Ellis Island, reminiscent of the experience of Remarque's former wife Jeanne, Ross left with a residence permit good for three months and instructions to obtain a visa from some other country which would accept him. Almost of equal importance was a name he was given by another detainee of an old Russian emigre living in New York to whom he might turn for help. The emigre was named, or used the name, Vladimir Melikov and worked in the Hotel Reuben, a seedy hotel off Broadway. Melikov took a liking to Ross and got him a room at the Hotel Reuben. More importantly, he served as an advisor and guide to Ross in introducing him to New York and the quaint customs of the residents. The relationship of Ross and Melikov brings to mind that of Ravic and Boris Morosow in *Der Triumphbogen*. The comparison must remain very general, however, because Melikov is a good friend to Robert but is a shady character who, by book's end, has received a prison sentence for drug dealing.

Robert Ross is a Remarque survivor who needs very little help to adapt to and, indeed, prosper in his new surroundings. Drawing on his experiences in France "as a salesman for a dealer in dubious paintings and phony antiques",[4] as well as on knowledge he gained from a Belgian museum curator, Ross soon was coping financially through employment with the Lowy brothers antique dealers and later with the shady art dealer Silvers. Ross' work with the Lowys and, particularly, Silvers provides Remarque an opportunity to display his impressive knowledge in a number of areas ranging from Chinese bronzes to French impressionist paintings. In his descriptions of the business practices of the shady Silvers he throws light on some of the more unattractive aspects of many commercial art transactions. Silvers surely must be a composite representation of some of the many art dealers Remarque knew in his long association with commercial art.

Ross' business relationship with Silvers also serves as a way for Remarque to get him to California and introduce him to the Hollywood producers and actors who are Silvers' clients. Ross is not only successful as Silvers' salesman but is offered the job of technical consultant on an anti-Nazi movie. Here Ross is treated to the ironic spectacle of Jewish-German exiles playing the parts of Gestapo officials and S.S. officers. California is pleasant and diverting for Ross but not capable of holding him long. Ross probably spoke for Remarque when he said: "For all the local excitement, I felt as if I were living in a strange vacuum somewhere between Japan and Europe. Besides, I realized that I couldn't stay in America forever and was eager to spend as much as possible of the time I had left in New York."[5]

Ross' most compelling reason to return to New York was his desire to be reunited with Natasha Petrovna, a fashion model to whom he had been introduced by Melikov. Natasha, who was born in France of Russian parents, is described as slender, tallish, pale, with ash-blond hair and gray eyes. She introduced Ross to a world in which Remarque was very much at home: a world of fashion, Rolls Royces, night-clubs (in particular Remarque's favorite, "El Morocco") and high-society types. Theirs was a volatile relationship marked by highs of great passion and lows of antagonistic withdrawal. There is, however, no evidence of any real tenderness. It is a relationship which appears to be most similar to that of Ravic and Joan in *Der Triumphbogen*. The essential difference is that the vulnerability of those characters has changed. Ravic has become a somewhat less confident Ross who is more vulnerable in his love for Natasha than in other aspects of his life. Natasha and Joan are both narcissistic survivors who use men to achieve that survival. Natasha, however, seems less attractive because of the harder edge of her character. Ravic and Ross both give more love than they receive.

Schatten im Paradies contains several vignettes of exile life as well as descriptive portraits of a number of interesting European exiles. One of Remarque's literary strengths is his journalistic ability to capture exile experiences through descriptions of individuals. The most flamboyant of these characters is Harry Kahn, a Jewish refugee who has made his way to New York after enjoying a legendary career harassing the Nazis in Europe. Kahn, because of his connections with the French underground, was able to save several refugees from the Germans, particularly the Gestapo. When he came to America, however, he was out of his element and chose suicide to end his painful realization that life no longer held any acceptable prospects.

An exile more poignantly appealing in her love for her homeland, specificially her native city of Berlin, is the character named Betty Stein. Remarque appears to have modeled her in part on Mrs. Betty Stern who was well-known for her literary salon at number 16 Barbarossastrasse in Berlin. Mrs. Stern left Germany and became a refugee in Paris where she later died. The fictional Betty Stein was described as "a mother to all refugees, just as she had been a mother to every unsuccessful writer, painter, and actor in Berlin. Her affection for her proteges was unquestioning, wholehearted, and mildly tyrannical."[6] Betty's home served as a rallying point in New York City for German refugees and a clearing house for refugee information. She became a symbol of the refugees' fervent hope that someday the Nazis would be defeated and that the exiles could return to the Germany of a gentler age. For most of them the dream did not end as they had hoped. That was particularly true of Betty Stein who died of cancer before she could see the overthrow of Hitler. She had resisted the disease as long as it appeared the Nazis were on the run. Their last-gasp offensive, with its temporary gains, was just enough to take away her will to live. With Remarque's customary irony, she was deprived of the opportunity to see the ultimate triumph of the Allied forces.

In an apparently sentimental gesture, Remarque has brought into his last book a character from the past. Ravic, the exile protagonist from *Arc de Triomphe,* has now made his way to America and collaborates with another surgeon on Betty Stein's cancer surgery. Unfortunately, he has no better luck with her operation than with the one he performed on Kate Hegstroem in his own novel. Ravic, who now goes by his real name Fresenberg, is obviously one of Remarque's favorite characters. At least Remarque likes the name. Spelled either Fresenburg or Fresenberg it is used for sympathetic characters in three novels. Ravic-Fresenberg is permitted by Remarque to remain in the new "paradise" and practice his profession. His former alter ego from *Arc de Triomphe* is therefore making the total commitment to the United States that Remarque himself was not able finally to make.

Robert Ross, however, feels driven to return to a Germany he no longer knows. He was ultimately forced to agree with Kahn's appraisal. "It was a return to a strange country, a return to indifference, cowardice, and concealed hatred."[7]

In his final observations as he looked back on his "futile searchings and bitter disappointments"[8] Ross belatedly recognized "that Natasha had been the most important experience of my life."[9] There were no real regrets, however, for the decision made. There were only the usual human speculations made after the fact.

"Sometimes I reflected that if I had known what awaited me in Europe, I might have stayed on in America. . . . I also knew that there was no going back. One can never go back; nothing and no one is ever the same."[10] The novel's last sentence seems particularly poignant in its implications for Remarque as well as for Robert Ross. "All that remained was an occasional evening of sadness, the sadness that we all feel because everything passes and because man is the only animal who knows it."[11] The poignancy is shared by Remarque's readers who understand the significance the sentence had for an author fully aware that those would be his last published lines.

The literary legacy left by Remarque is not enhanced by *Schatten im Paradies*. Indeed, this last work is not even the best of his exile novels. That honor should probably be claimed by *Arc de Triomphe*. The idea of treating the subject of exile in an American setting was refreshingly different and promising. However, the finished product fails to offer anything new other than new settings, and much of the plot is simply Remarque revisited.

38

Full Circle

Another Remarque work which enjoyed a brief revival in a slightly different guise was his only play *Die letzte Station*. The play, with the title changed to *Berlin, 1945*, had its premiere performance on September 20, 1956 in the Renaissance Theatre during the West Berlin Cultural Festival. Although the play was well received, Remarque was never really satisfied with it.

An English adaptation of the play was planned and the task entrusted to the eminent writer Peter Stone. It seemed an excellent choice. Stone had won numerous awards for his work in theatre, motion pictures, and television. The only problem was the lack of agreement between Remarque and Stone regarding Stone's adaptation which "differed considerably from the original - - - ".[1] Apparently no artistic agreement was reached at that time. As Stone put it: "In the end, that first attempt at an American production went by the boards instead of on them."[2]

Stone's adaptation did not get on the boards until 1973. In that year the play, under its new title *Full Circle*, was performed in Washington, D.C. and New York City. It was produced and directed by Otto Preminger who was making a return to the theatre after a period of professional emphasis on film making.

Full Circle is a very lean play of only two scenes with a marked economy of dialogue and characters. The action is limited to a third-floor room in Berlin during the afternoon and evening hours of April 30, 1945 and the morning of May 1 at a time when the Russian army was completing its conquest of Berlin and the Hitler regime was ending with his suicide in his Berlin bunker. Eleven characters appear on stage although only three of them are of major importance. Those three characters are: Anna, the attractive twenty-eight year old widow of the resistance leader Otto Wilke; Erich Rohde, a political prisoner escapee from the concentration camp; and the clever, opportunistic Gestapo Captain Schmidt.

At the beginning of the play Rohde and his fellow inmates from Oranienburg had been moved to Berlin and were to have been executed at the zoo. However, they were saved by a timely air raid. In the ensuing confusion Rohde escaped. Because the name of Otto Wilke had been whispered among the concentration camp prisoners as a source of possible assistance, Rohde immediately made for Wilke's address.

When he arrived at Wilke's apartment he learned that Wilke had been caught and killed by the Nazis. Wilke's widow, Anna, reluctantly agreed to help him, or at least tolerate his presence for a while. Since it was a question of whether the Gestapo or the Russians would arrive first, Rohde burned his arm in an attempt to remove his concentration camp number tattoo. The desperate act succeeded chiefly in winning Anna's unqualified sympathy and support. The first evidence of her changed attitude was the gift of a lieutenant's uniform for him. The uniform had belonged to her friend Hans Vollmer who had been killed in North Africa.

Anna's neighbor Grete came to the room to tell her that a Gestapo patrol was searching the building looking for escaped prisoners. Soon after that two uniformed Gestapo soldiers burst into the room, followed by Gestapo Group Leader Captain Schmidt. Schmidt interrogated Anna and Rohde and tried to call Hedwig military hospital to verify Rohde's story that he had only recently been discharged from there. Fortunately for Rohde, verification was impossible because the area, only two miles away, had fallen to the Russians.

At this point one of the escaped prisoners, Joseph Katz, a man in his middle fifties, was brought by a Gestapo man to see Captain Schmidt. Katz was asked the whereabouts of the escaped prisoner Erich Rohde. He was further asked if he knew anyone in the room. Katz denied any knowledge on both points. When a radio announcement diverted the group's attention, he leaped up on the window sill. Under threat of being shot, Katz jumped the three floors to his death just before the radio announced the death of Hitler.

Scene Two took place the next morning in the same setting. As the scene opened Rohde was standing alone at the window looking at the rubble and at the white sheets and towels at the windows which indicated surrender. The block warden Körner entered, demanded to know Rohde's identity, and tried to intimidate him. However, in typical Remarque fashion, Körner was intimidated instead and escaped only when Anna returned to the room from a food-foraging expedition.

The peaceful interlude which followed provided Rohde and Anna an opportunity to attempt an understanding of the growing affection between them. Because of her residual resentment at her former husband for losing his life in what she regarded as a needless and tragic display of heroics, Anna was less willing than Rohde to make another emotional commitment. She did, however, finally give him some hope after she had exacted a promise that he would never leave her. She wanted no repetition of the heart-break she had experienced with Wilke's loss.

Their interlude was interrupted by the appearance of Anna's neighbor Grete who had come to get her to assist another neighbor, Mrs. Zandler, who was having a baby. Rohde also left to check on Koerner to make certain that he was not up to mischief. In their absence Gestapo Captain Schmidt returned to the room. This time, however, Captain Schmidt had undergone a change. He was in civilian clothes and had brought for Anna presents such as Scotch whiskey, Swiss Cheese, Westphalian ham, and even Beluga caviar. Schmidt, who obviously intended to settle down comfortably with Anna for the remainder of the battle for Berlin, had meanwhile equipped himself with false identity papers in the name of the dead prisoner Katz. To complete the effect, he had even acquired a concentration camp tattoo. With his false identity meticulously documented, Schmidt awaited the arrival of the Russians, secure in the bureaucrat's belief that proper papers can overcome all difficulties.

Because she could see no immediate alternative, Anna appeared to agree to his plan to move in with her. However, she asked for an hour to allow time to make some arrangements. Rohde's sudden return to the room made it instantly clear to Schmidt that Rohde was the reason for the time request. Anna tried to get Rohde out of the room but Schmidt's suspicions were now aroused and his drawn pistol prevented Rohde's departure. Schmidt's plan was to kill Rohde to ensure his secrecy and then hope for the approval of the Russians for his killing of a German lieutenant. Rohde, with great presence of mind, managed to postpone his execution by pointing out to Schmidt that the first arrivals might be from the Gestapo rather than the Russians. In that event, Schmidt-Katz would find it rather difficult to explain the murder of a German officer. Schmidt immediately saw the logic in the observation and decided to wait to see which way the battle would go.

As they awaited those developments, Schmidt poured a drink and relaxed. Rohde took advantage of the opportunity to reach under the pillow on the bed and produce a pistol. Even though the pistol was empty, Rohde succeeded in bluffing Schmidt and disarming him. He then forced him over to the window where the real Katz had leaped to his death and asked that Schmidt demonstrate by jumping from the window that he had as much courage as a Jew. As Schmidt tried to bargain for his life, Anna urged Rohde to shoot him because otherwise the evil he represented would triumph. However, Rohde had no intention of killing him. He had merely intended to give him a taste of the abasement Schmidt had caused the real Katz to suffer. At that point, Grete burst into the room and told them that the Russians were in the street outside. Before he could be stopped, Schmidt called to the Russians for help.

Two Russian soldiers came up to the room to investigate the disturbance. One of them, a sergeant, listened to the stories of Schmidt-Katz and Rohde and, on the basis of Schmidt's spurious tattoo, made the decision to shoot him. Fortunately,

Rohde's execution was prevented by the appearance of a young Russian captain named Korovkin who was displeased with what he had heard of the sergeant's interrogation. The captain gave Rohde and Schmidt-Katz an opportunity to tell their stories. He was apparently leaning toward believing Schmidt-Katz's story when Rohde made the point that only a man who could put someone in prison would be able to present such impeccable documentation—not the man who had actually been the prisoner. With this, Schmidt's composure began to disintegrate. Finally, he bolted for the door and was shot down.

The feeling of relief and happiness felt by Anna and Rohde at Schmidt's death was short-lived. Even though Captain Korovkin had told Rohde he could live, his questions about a future role for the former journalist Rohde in the building of the "new Germany" indicated the potential for trouble with Berlin's new masters. Korovkin was a completely dedicated communist and failed to understand Rohde's unwillingness to trade one form of dictatorship for another. Despite Korovkin's insistence on Rohde's participation in the new Socialist order, Rohde was adamant in his refusal. Anna urged him to go along but Rohde continued to refuse the Russian's suggestion that he "go with the tide."[3] "No! That's what I did the last time! I went with the tide until it was too late! I'll never do that again!"[4]

In view of Rohde's refusal to contribute to the new order, Korovkin determined that it would be necessary for him to have "guidance" in an "information center."[5] Anna pleaded again with Rohde to reconsider and to stop trying to become a martyr. However, Rohde had made the decision that he could not work for the Russians and compromise his principles. After a hurried goodbye to a sobbing Anna, and a promise to return, Rohde was led away to an uncertain fate. Because of his new resolution not to yield to tyranny, the prospects of that return seemed unlikely.

Except for the novelty of seeing Remarque's familiar ideas presented in a stage production, *Full Circle* is of limited interest to anyone already acquainted with his novels. Once again the theme of survival predominates with the emphasis on identity being a close second. Perhaps the most significant aspect of the play is its unequivocal statement about what can be expected from the Russian "new order." Remarque had already made clear in *Der Funke Leben* and *Zeit zu leben und Zeit zu sterben* that he had no illusions that Russian tyranny represented an improvement on Nazi tyranny. Each system was equally abhorrent to Remarque the great defender of individual freedom.

For most audiences whose knowledge of Remarque might well be limited to an awareness that he was the author of *Im Westen nichts Neues*, the choice of *Full Circle* would be a good one. The Remarque-Stone play is both entertaining and thought-provoking. It is easy to understand why Otto Preminger chose it to make his return to the theatre.

Preminger also selected a fine cast which could do justice to the play. The escaped prisoner Rohde was played by Leonard Nimoy, who was perhaps best known to the general public as Mr. Spock in the television series "Star Trek". Nimoy was also a veteran of dozens of other television series and movies. However, it was his performance during the summer of 1973 as King Arthur in *Camelot* which attracted the attention of Otto Preminger and resulted in an offer to play Rohde.[6] The part of Anna was given to the distinguished Swedish actress Bibi Andersson who had first gained acclaim for her work in the films of Ingmar Bergman. She had also played in a large number of international films and received acting awards from France, England, and her native Sweden. *Full Circle* was to be her first stage performance in English. The role of Schmidt was given to Josef Sommer who had appeared as a leading player in a number of major repertory theatres. Linda Carlson, also a veteran of regional and repertory theatre, played Grete. The small but important roles of Katz and Captain Korovkin were played by James Tolkan and David Ackroyd respectively. The cast was completed by Max Brandt as Koerner, Stan Wiklin in the roles of Maurer and the Russian soldier, and Peter Weller as Mack and the Russian sergeant.

The Preminger production of *Full Circle* was first presented in the Eisenhower Theater at the Kennedy Center in Washington, D.C. in October, 1973. There were preview performances on Friday evening, October 5 and a Saturday matinee on October 6. The regular engagement ran from the evening of October 6 through the last performance on October 27.

Paulette Goddard was in Washington to attend the October 5 preview showing and gave an interview to *Washington Post* writer Henry Mitchell.[7] Very little of the printed interview concerned the play. Paulette did express surprise that when she brought the play from her home in Switzerland to make arrangements for its production, only six days had been required to do so instead of the months she had anticipated. She also indicated her view that "the whole play is about survival."[8] Mostly, however, the interview touched on a number of topics ranging from the egos of husbands Chaplin and Remarque to Goddard's interest in Zen.

The play was reviewed by Richard Coe in the October 8, 1973 edition of *The Washington Post*. Coe gave high marks to the acting and praised particularly the performances of Andersson, Nimoy, and Sommer. He was dissatisfied with what he perceived as the inconsistency between the title and the play's ending. He was particularly concerned with "waffling the Communist similarity to the Nazis. Whether the fault is in Remarque or Stone I don't know, but the implied full circle is not closed. Instead of being a counterpart to the ruthlessly self-serving Gestapo boss, the Russian is presented with almost Chekhovian sympathy."[9] Coe concludes his point by writing, "Somewhere in Act II, with the arrival of the Russians, I stopped believing. 'Full Circle' is Remarque's own title; I can only assume the subject has been changed during Act II. So Stone's adaptation drifts away into sentiment without hardening into irony."[10]

Coe was not wrong in expecting to find in the play the irony that Remarque undoubtedly intended by the title. The only question is whether the adaptation makes the point strongly enough—or in a manner to satisfy the individual viewer. There is no doubt that the Russian Captain Korovkin is portrayed as a more sympathetic character than the Gestapo Captain Schmidt. However, to Rohde, the potential victim of both men, there might have been slight comfort in being killed by a fanatic believer in Communism rather than by a self-serving opportunist who would serve any master to keep his skin intact. For Remarque, both Korovkin and Schmidt are reprehensible because they wish to enslave their fellow men. Tyrants can always find reasons to excuse their tyranny.

After its Washington run *Full Circle* moved to New York City for an engagement at the ANTA (The American National Theatre and Academy) on West 52nd Street. The play opened Wednesday, November 7, 1973. There were six previews and fifty-seven regular performances during the nine week run at the ANTA.

Clive Barnes' review of the play for *The New York Times* was in general very favorable. Barnes praised the casting as well as the acting. He had particularly high praise for Andersson and Nimoy as well as kind words for Josef Sommer and James Tolkan. Barnes described the play as a "philosophical melodrama" which was "rather more melodramatic than philosophic."[11] He commended the play for holding the interest and attention of the audience. On a less positive note, Barnes indicated his view that the ending was "too simplistic" and said it was "a play of no particular profundity."[12] However, having said that, he concluded his impressions of the play by stressing its "cinematic values" and terming it "redolent of Broadway" as well as of "old style Hollywood."[13]

It might be mentioned as a gentle rebuttal to Barnes' gentle criticism of the play's ending that Rohde's decision to reject the Russians was hardly "simplistic." It might be termed "simple," however, in the sense that it was the only decision possible given Rohde's integrity and experiences. The question as to whether *Full Circle* is "a play of no particular profundity" is moot. What is not at issue is the final message: One survives if possible but, whatever the cost, does not compromise with evil.

Remarque never saw the final form of Peter Stone's adaptation of his play. Therefore, the degree to which he might have approved of that final version must remain a matter of speculation. There can be no doubt, however, that Stone's skillful adaptation has remained completely faithful to the tone and spirit of former Remarque works.

39

The Death of Jeanne Remarque

For the last decade of her life Jeanne Remarque lived a quiet, almost reclusive, life in Italy and, finally, Monte Carlo. The financial support she received from Remarque had given her the freedom to live wherever she wished. However, her personal tastes and artistic needs dictated residence in the Mediterranean area.

From July, 1965 to July 1971 she lived in Ospedaletti (Imperia), Italy. Her home during that period was the Villa Paradiso at Via Aurelia Levante 5 which had previously acquired a certain celebrity status because it had been the residence of the New Zealand writer Kathleen Mansfield Beauchamp. Beauchamp, who wrote under the pen name of Katherine Mansfield, had lived there in 1920 and 1921.

Jeanne Remarque lived alone in the Villa Paradiso with her dogs. She had no close friends although she was seen occasionally with a gentleman during walks with her dogs along the village promenade by the sea.

In July, 1971 she moved from Ospedaletti a short distance down the coast to Monte Carlo. In Monte Carlo she lived in an apartment, described as deluxe, at 19 Boulevard de Suisse.

Jeanne Remarque died at the Princess Grace Hospital in Monaco on June 25, 1975. The cause of death was not released by her physician. She died with no known survivors.[1]

40

The End of a Collection

Many of the art treasures which had been such a joy for Remarque to collect and own were sold in the decade following his death. Although Paulette Goddard Remarque was also a collector, her interests did not always run parallel to those of her husband. In addition, Remarque's collections had become somewhat burdensome for his widow. One important reason was concern for the safety of the collections. In an interview with Henry Mitchell for the *Washington Post* she mentioned the robberies which had occurred at the Remarque home in Ascona and lamented the fact that - - - "I cannot go anywhere, not to New York or Rome, because people break in."[1]

When Paulette Remarque decided to dispose of some parts of the collections she not only reduced significantly her security worries but assured herself of a tremendous financial gain from their sale. Fortunately for her, Remarque's acquisitions had greatly appreciated in value over the years.

On the basis of the available information, the collection of Islamic rugs and carpets was the first part of Remarque's collections to go on the block. Mrs. Remarque consigned 31 rugs and carpets to Sotheby Parke Bernet and Co. in London to be sold at their "Autumn Islamic Week" sale on November 18 and 19, 1976. The items for auction ranged in age from the late sixteenth century to the late nineteenth century with the seventeenth, eighteenth, and nineteenth century items most in evidence. The Sotheby sale catalog uses the terms "antique" or "early" in reference to several items. The Remarque offerings included such pieces as: Ushak bird carpets, Mamluk carpets, Kuba dragon carpets, a Cairene Ottoman rug, a Kashan "Polonaise'' silk and metal thread rug, Ushak ''Lotto'' rugs, an Indo-Persian animal carpet, a Shirvan rug, and an Anatolian rug.

The Sotheby list of prices realized shows a wide range from the sale's lowest price of 100 British pounds for a Panderma carpet to the collection's most sought-after piece, a late seventeenth century Ushak medallion carpet which was auctioned off for 10,000 pounds. A total of 107,430 pounds was realized for the 31 carpets and rugs in the sale. An additional 9 Islamic rugs and carpets were reportedly sold in February, October, and November of 1977.

Two years later the heart of the Remarque collection, the Impressionist paintings, pastels and drawings, was put up for auction by Sotheby Parke Bernet, Inc. in New York. The works were on public exhibition from Friday, November 2 to 1:00 p.m. Wednesday, November 7, 1979. The auction began at 8:00 p.m. on the last day of the exhibition.

The sale catalog listed 28 works by six artists: Paul Cezanne (two), Honore Daumier (two), Edgar Degas (thirteen), Claude Monet (three), Camille Pissarro (two), and Pierre-Auguste Renoir (six). Several of the works represented had previously been on public exhibition in the United States and Europe during the Remarque ownership. During Remarque's lifetime various pieces from the sale group had been exhibited at the Los Angeles County Museum in 1942, the Knoedler Galleries in New York in 1943, the New York Museum of Modern Art in 1944, the Metropolitan Museum of Art from 1949 to 1956, the Gemeentemuseum in The Hague in 1956, and the Museum zu Allerheiligen in Schaffhausen, Switzerland in 1963. The Kunsthaus in Zürich, Switzerland also had the benefit of a long-term loan of four of the art works both before and after Remarque's death. A Degas, a Pissarro, and two Cezannes were on exhibit there from 1956 to 1979. Two Monets were on loan to the Kunsthaus by Paulette Goddard Remarque from 1973 until the 1979 sale.

The disposal of the major part of such an important individually held collection was a major event in the art world and interest ran high. The total amount realized was a reported 3.1 million dollars.[2] Paulette Goddard Remarque was quoted as having said: "Owning these masterpieces has become a tremendous responsibility because I have to travel so much - - - and I'm tired of having them stored away in crates - - - the public should have access to them."[3]

41

"All Quiet" Revisited

One week after the sale of many of the Remarque art masterpieces the American television audience had an opportunity to see a new movie version of Remarque's own literary masterpiece, *All Quiet on the Western Front*. The film was a Norman Rosemont production directed by Delbert Mann for Lord Lew Grade's Marble Arch Productions. The screenplay was written by Paul Monash.

Careful casting assured a company of actors which was of as high a caliber as the cast of the original 1930 movie. The pivotal role of Remarque's protagonist Paul Bäumer, which had been played with such distinction by Lew Ayres, was done no disservice by the fine acting of Richard Thomas. Although Thomas was only a youthful looking twenty-eight he already had impressive acting credentials. He had appeared in six films and was best known for his role as John-Boy in "The Waltons" television series although he had also starred in other important television productions. Richard Thomas co-starred with the veteran actor Ernest Borgnine who played the important role of the veteran soldier Katczinsky, the friend and mentor of Paul Bäumer. Borgnine was reunited with director Delbert Mann with whom he had worked in 1955 when he received the "Best Actor" Academy Award for the title role in the film "Marty". Paul Bäumer's mother was played by Patricia Neal who had made a gallant recovery from the debilitating effects of a stroke. Ian Holm was Himmelstoss, the former postman who, as a corporal, tyrannized Paul and his fellow trainees in camp. Paul's comrades Kantorek, Westhaus, Tjaden, Behm, Kropp, Müller, and Kemmerich were played by Donald Pleasance,

Colin Mayes, Mark Drewry, Mark Elliott, Dai Bradley, Mathew Evans, and George Winter respectively.

Norman Rosemont and Marble Arch Productions first considered, then rejected, the possibility of filming in England and West Germany. Fortunately they next explored the possibility of filming their production in Czechoslovakia. That appeared to be the ideal locale because there were not only suitable buildings of the proper age available but also Czech army troops to serve as extras.

The situation in Czechoslovakia could hardly have been better for the film makers. In addition to having the cooperation of the Czech government and the use of soldiers as extras, there was even a town which could be destroyed for the battle scenes. This fortuitous circumstance involved the small town of Most which was located a short distance from the West German border. Because of the discovery of a very rich coal seam under the town, the government had decided to relocate Most and strip mine the coal. A new town was built in the same area and the townspeople moved to it.

In addition to the battle scenes involving the old town of Most "the crew also filmed at the World War II concentration camp at Tarrazin which became the 'All Quiet' barracks, and at an old convent."[1]

However, at first there were unexpected difficulties blocking the company's plans to film at the convent. According to producer Norman Rosemont his production company was denied use of the convent because the nuns were still furious at the Communist government for refusing to allow a visit by the Pope. "It took three days of negotiations to convince them."[2]

The battle scenes showing the destruction of the town involved a cast of approximately 1,000 soldiers and townspeople from Most. These impressive figures were matched by equally impressive ones in the area of logistics. Despite that fact, however, the remake of "All Quiet" only involved approximately half the manpower and effort of Universal Pictures' 1930 original.

The original and the remake both contained a specific,

although different, depiction of Paul Bäumer's death in contrast to the novel's ending which was deliberately devoid of details. In the original film director Lewis Milestone decided to show Paul's death as being the result of a sniper's bullet as he was reaching out for a butterfly resting on a sandbag. Because this inspired touch was not a part of Remarque's book, it could not be used by Rosemont and Marble Arch Productions for the remake since they had bought film rights to the book. In the Rosemont version Paul's interest in a meadowlark proved to be his undoing.

Fortunately the Marble Arch production was blessed with the same determination to be true to the action and spirit of Remarque's novel that marked the 1930 Laemmle-Milestone production. Remarque's memory was well-served by the treatment his novel received in both films.

42

Arch of Triumph: The Television Movie

The success of the television movie "All Quiet on the Western Front" in 1979 generated a renewal of interest in Remarque's works. In 1980 filming began in France of Remarque's second best-known novel, *Arch of Triumph*. The roles of Ravic and Joan which were played by Charles Boyer and Ingrid Bergman in the 1946 movie were to be played in the television version by Maximilian Schell and Suzanne Pleshette. The production, however, was short-lived. A few days after work began a lack of funds brought an end to the project.

When filming of the adaptation of Remarque's novel again began in March, 1984, it was with different producers and different stars. The Newland-Raynor production which was shown on television on May 29, 1985 as the CBS "Wednesday Night Movie" was produced by Peter Graham Scott. The teleplay was written by Charles Israel.

The casting, particularly for the principal actors, was excellent. This time the role of Ravic was played by Anthony Hopkins and Lesley-Anne Down was Joan Madou. Ravic's confidant Boris Morosow was played by Frank Finlay. Richard Pasco was Ravic's French physician colleague and friend Dr. Veber.

Anthony Hopkins played Ravic with the proper blend of authority and compassion even though his portrayal made the character more taciturn and less outgoing than the novel's character. However, despite such relatively minor deviations from the model, Hopkin's Ravic was thoroughly credible.

Lesley-Anne Down also gave a fine, believable performance as the vulnerable, enigmatic, errotically attractive Joan Madou. Most of Joan's tiresome bitchiness and self-indulgence fortunately did not appear in the teleplay. The most problematic aspects of their relationship in the novel have been excised in the attempt to get a more simple and appealing love story.

Although the cinematic love affair of Hopkins and Down was quite convincing, there was reportedly some pique on the part of Hopkins during the filming. It seems that he did not share the amusement felt by Down "who frequently cracked up during their love scenes".[1]

The movie succeeded admirably in the difficult task of capturing the essence of Remarque's 455 page novel within a period of two hours, minus time for commercial messages. Given the time constraints, a surprising fidelity to the basic story line has been preserved. Adding to the film's credibility for any person who has read the novel is the creation of a strikingly authentic atmosphere made possible by careful attention to proper costumes and settings.

43

The Summing Up

It is self-evident that no completely accurate assessment of a human being can ever be made. The information on which to base such an assessment is always incomplete. Even within the closest relationships there are areas which must properly be termed "terra incognita". It is also true that celebrities, even more than lesser-known mortals, are evaluated on the basis of imperfect information and flawed perceptions.

Remarque is a prime example of a literary celebrity about whom there has been both a dearth of accurate information and some items of gross misinformation. Much of the original problem can be attributed to the sudden international prominence which was thrust upon him by the overwhelming success of *Im Westen nichts Neues*. Because it was his first successful novel very little was known about him. The situation was further complicated by the fact that the book deeply alienated influential ultra-nationalistic groups which then spread scurrilous misinformation with the intention of discrediting Remarque and diminishing the impact of his book's message. Although such misinformation failed to achieve its basic purpose, it did succeed in creating a degree of confusion about the fledgling author which persisted throughout his life. For example, even when he died the myth that his true surname was Kramer did not. Perhaps it never will.

Remarque himself did very little to supply information which could have provided insights into the private areas of his life. He was usually understandably reluctant to be interviewed for fear that his jealously-guarded privacy might be breached. As a consequence, most Remarque interviews tended to be bland

and dealt largely with subjects peripheral to the truly important concerns of his life. This is true in part because he was dealing with journalists who, by and large, came from a tradition in which it was not considered good form to probe too deeply into the privacy of public figures. An even larger part was played by the Remarque personality which could be intimidating as well as charming. However, when Remarque did consent to be interviewed his gracious manner usually made for a relaxed and friendly interview.

Remarque lived a success story which was worthy of a novelist's attention. He was a bright, ambitious boy from the traditionally humble beginnings whose aspirations kept him scrambling to even larger arenas in search of better opportunities to display his talent. His ability to write pithy, realistic material was sharpened by his years of journalistic work in Hannover and Berlin and paid off with the overwhelming successful *Im Westen nichts Neues*. The modest successes he had enjoyed in his previous work paled by comparison. Undreamed of financial security had suddenly been achieved along with the literary fame which ensured publication of all his future novels. The Good Life was at long last a reality. With fame went many disadvantages which were largely overridden by the advantages of the affluence which allowed him total independence. For the first time he was responsible only to himself and to the need to prove that he was not just a one-book author. Remarque felt that need for the rest of his life and continued his literary labors long after his declining health should have dictated an end to his efforts.

Remarque was an accurate chronicler of the chaotic times in which he lived. Millions of readers had the opportunity to see much of the horror of two wars, inflation, exile and totalitarianism through his eyes. More importantly, they also had the opportunity vicariously to experience the inspiring indomitability of the human spirit so often portrayed in his novels. Because of the strongly autobiographical nature of those works his protagonists tended to be either mirror images of the real Remarque or characters who reflect a Remarque interest, or even a wish fulfillment. His characters were always commoners who were quite uncommon in the nobility and fortitude of which they were capable.

Although Remarque never forgot his origins, and indeed drew strength and literary inspiration from them, he never wished to go back to them. His promises during the last years to friends in Osnabrück that he would return for a visit were destined to remain unfulfilled because of his illness. More likely the real reason was his unwillingness to debase his idealized memories of home by returning to a war-devastated Osnabrück which in his mind still bore the taint of the Nazi past.

In the public perception the former Osnabrück plebian was a cosmopolitan patrician completely at home in such settings as Berlin, Paris, Zürich, Rome, New York, and Los Angeles. The Remarque in public view was the handsome and debonair escort of such lovely ladies as Marlene Dietrich and Paulette Goddard and a bon vivant at home in all the most fashionable places. To a great extent the perception was accurate. The enjoyment of the tangible aspects of success in several areas of sensory indulgence was very important for him in part because it offered confirmation of his achievements. It represented the realization of his youthful dreams of literary recognition and affluence. Remarque's pursuit of the gratification of the senses did not ordinarily extend to license because of the pride he took in cultivating discriminating and refined tastes. The gourmet was rarely allowed to become the gourmand.

However, the tastes he cultivated as a connoisseur of alcoholic beverages were not as successfully restrained. Remarque's interest in things alcoholic was of long standing. As early as 1924 he caused a mild stir with his essay "Über das Mixen kostbarer Schnäpse" which was later pointed to by the enemies he made with *Im Westen nichts Neues* as evidence that he was not a serious writer. The work hardly proved that. It was, rather, merely one of the first proofs that he did have a serious interest in drinking. The emphasis on drinking found in his novels was reflected in his own life and alcohol was his reliable companion. It was also a companion which got out of hand occasionally in Ascona when late night solitary drinking in bars ended with taxi drivers depositing him at his home. However, the infirmities of age and other medical problems eventually put an end to the old excesses.

Although all of his novels confirm the importance that good food and drink had for him, none of them did as much missionary work for the consumption of alcohol, specifically Calvados, as *Arc de Triomphe*. Although the Normandy applejack Calvados was not a particular favorite of Remarque, he chose to emphasize the drink because it seemed appropriate for his story. The popularity of the book proved to be such a tremendous stimulus to sales of Calvados that suppliers' stocks were soon sold out. *Arc de Triomphe* must surely be one of the few novels to have been prominently displayed in the show windows of liquor stores.

No area of Remarque's private life was at once more on display and yet hidden from sight than his relationships with the women who were most important in his life. In the final accounting there were only three women who really mattered: Jeanne Zambona, Marlene Dietrich, and Paulette Goddard. Although they were not alike in appearance or background they were all strikingly attractive, sophisticated, and intelligent.

Jeanne Remarque, to whom he was twice married, was married to him for five years before their first divorce in 1930 after the success of *Im Westen nichts Neues*. Apparently it was marriage rather than the relationship which was too confining because after the divorce they continued to live and travel together much of the time. It was the first real evidence that Remarque needed a large amount of space in his relationships. It was certainly not evidence of animosity because not only did the relationship continue to exist but Remarque remarried Jeanne in 1938 to give her the protection of his name and residence status so that she would not have to return to Germany. Although in time the relationship lost its intensity and was replaced by newer interests a good case could be made that it was the most significant love of his life. Any reader of *Drei Kameraden* could not fail to understand the emotional importance to the author of the woman who served as the prototype for the memorable Pat Hollmann.

When Remarque's nominal second marriage to Jeanne ended with a Mexican divorce in 1957, the way was open for a final marriage to the actress Paulette Goddard, with whom he was to spend the rest of his life. The glamorous Goddard seemed a perfect companion for the wealthy and urbane Remarque who was impressed not only by her sophistication and beauty but also by her intelligence and business acumen.

Remarque's most publicized relationship was with Marlene Dietrich. Their appearances together at night spots usually found their way into print or were captured on film for the movie fan magazines so popular at that time. It was a press agent's dream; the dashing and handsome world-renowned author and the equally renowned actress whose name, in the public perception, was synonymous with sophistication, eroticism, and mystery. For Remarque, sharing the companionship of one of the most famous Hollywood screen stars surely was additional ego-satisfying confirmation of his celebrity status. For Dietrich it must have been equally satisfying to enjoy the attention of the internationally famous man of letters. There appears to be little doubt that for a while the emotional impact of the relationship was strong for both of them. However, only the principals could say to what extent, or if, that relationship caused any serious thought of terminating their respective rather enigmatic marital situations. When their close relationship ended, Remarque experienced some uneasiness that his letters to Dietrich might someday find their way into print. However, at least to date, the fierce loyalty for which Dietrich is noted has been confirmed by the non-publication of whatever Remarque letters may be in her possession.

A penchant for privacy on the part of each of the partners has been characteristic of Remarque's most important relationships with women. Jeanne had no literary pretensions and furthermore would have had no interest in making titilating and potentially embarrassing disclosures about their private life which possibly could have lead to a curtailment of Remarque's financial support. Marlene Dietrich's written and spoken comments about Remarque have tended to be laudatory and in general give the impression of being very carefully chosen. Paulette Goddard has been reported as having an interest in writing an autobiography but has also been quoted as being too busy for such a task. Because of Remarque's aversion to truly personal disclosures, one hopes that he is resting peacefully in Ronco, happy in the posthumous knowledge that thus far the two living women who have the most to tell have respected his, and their, privacy.

By most of the world's standards of measurement Remarque was an outstanding success. He was handsome, intelligent, generally healthy, rich, and extremely successful in his profession. He sought and achieved celebrity status and enjoyed the company of celebrities while at the same time jealously and successfully protecting his privacy. Although he had more than his share of irascibility, and a few of the eccentricities permitted particularly to the very rich, he was a man of great human understanding and warmth. He was also a courageous and idealistic man who was rigidly uncompromising regarding injustice and man's inhumanity to man. With friends he could be a delightful and witty companion, exhibiting the humor which unfortunately brightens the pages of his novels all too infrequently.

Remarque's greatest success is ultimately the lasting literary fame conferred on him by his readers. He was discovered by the reading public not by the critics who, as often as not, were hostile or indifferent. In Germany the critics have relegated his novels to the category of "Unterhaltungsliteratur" (recreational reading). Much of the criticism and deprecation can undoubtedly be attributed to the toplofty attitude of professional critics who find it difficult to grant literary merit to commercial success.

It is not difficult to understand the reasons for the success Remarque's novels have enjoyed and continue to enjoy. Readers have related to him because he tells a good story and because they see in his protagonists decent and courageous individuals who in many ways mirror their creator. His novels are stories of great human interest and emotional impact and reflect the turbulent times in which he lived. Remarque drew upon his knowledge of those times to tell the stories of individuals attempting to cope with circumstances dictated by outside events. He told those stories with such skill and uncompromising honesty that there was always a large and loyal readership eagerly looking forward to his next carefully crafted novel.

His success never caused him to forget the earlier Remarque. The remembrance of the past was his comfort, his strength, and his literary inspiration. His writing was his link to the past and the one way he could return home even in exile.

There is indeed much validity to his contention that one need only look in the novels to find the real Remarque. It is also true, however, that the literary portrait Remarque would have us accept is often highly idealized and doesn't tell enough about the real Remarque.

By the tests of birth, language, and culture, Remarque was a German author despite the ambiguity produced by the years of exile: involuntary and voluntary. Because of the theme of *Im Westen nichts Neues*, his first success as a German author also made him an international author. His international reputation made possible the lion's share of his commercial success but also blurred the clear national identification which is almost a requirement for literary awards. Unfortunately, whatever the combination of reasons might have been, there were to be no international literary awards for Remarque. After the first flurry of interest following *Im Westen nichts Neues* there was no more talk of a possible Nobel Prize for Literature for him. That is as it should be if he is compared with the very best recipients such as Hermann Hesse and Thomas Mann. However, in many cases the Prize has been awarded to individuals whose literary credentials were considerably less worthy than those of Remarque. Not even Hesse or Mann had a single novel with the international impact of *Im Westen nicht Neues*. With that work Remarque not only ensured the fulfillment of his personal hopes but gained for himself a secure place in world literature.

Notes

Chapter 1. Remarque Family Origins

[1] This is my translation. Subsequent English translations of German terms or titles will be placed in parentheses after the German the first time the term or title is used. All translations are mine unless otherwise noted.

[2] References to Erich Maria Remarque will use the spelling of his surname later adopted by him. References to other members of the Remark family will use the spelling (Remark) retained by them.

[3] I am indebted to Hanns-Gerd Rabe whose research provided most of the information concerning the early Remarque family. The information first appeared in his article "Remarque und Osnabrück," *Osnabrücker Mitteilungen*, LXXVII (1970).

Chapter 2. The Early Years in Osnabrück

[1] Hanns-Gerd Rabe, "Remarque und Osnabrück," *Osnabrücker Mitteilungen*, LXXVII (1970) 199.

[2] Erich Maria Remarque, *All Quiet on the Western Front* (Boston: Little, Brown, and Company, 1929) 119–20.

[3] Harry Kessler, *In the Twenties* (London: Weidenfeld and Nicholson Ltd., 1971) 366–67.

[4] Rabe, "Remarque und Osnabrück" 200–01.

[5] Erich Maria Remarque, *The Road Back* (Boston: Little, Brown, and Company, 1931) 259–60.

[6] *Ibid.*, 260–61.

Chapter 3. Military Service

[1] Rabe, "Remarque und Osnabrück," 211.

[2] Statistics concerning battle casualties are taken from: Leon Wolff, *In Flanders Field* (New York: The Viking Press, 1958).

[3] "Remarque und Osnabrück," 213.

Chapter 4. From Field Gray to Mufti

[1] My translation.

[2] *The Road Back*, 121–22.

[3] "Ingeborg," *Die Schönheit*, 15. Jahrgang 554. My translation.
[4] "Abschied," *Die Schönheit*, 15. Jahrgang 527. My translation.
[5] *The Road Back*, 219–20.

Chapter 5. The Reluctant Teacher

[1] Rabe, "Remarque und Osnabrück," 222.
[2] *Ibid*. My translation.
[3] *The Road Back*, 252–54.

Chapter 6. The Hand-to-Mouth Years

[1] D. A. Prater, *European of Yesterday* (Oxford: Clarendon Press, 1972) 140.
[2] "Erich Maria Remarque, the Violent Author—A Quiet Man," *Newsweek*, April 1, 1957, 108.
[3] Erich Maria Remarque, *The Black Obelisk* (New York: Harcourt, Brace and Company, 1957) 29.
[4] *Ibid.*, 30.

Chapter 7. The Young "Conti" Editor in Hannover

[1] *Echo Continental*, Jahrgang 1923, 57. My translation.
[2] *Ibid.*, 97. My translation.
[3] *Ibid.*, 24. My translation.
[4] *Ibid.*, 34. My translation.

Chapter 8. Up the Ladder of Success in Berlin

[1] Listed by Rabe on page 170 of his archival materials in Osnabrück. This is one of three Remarque references from Berlin police registration records. My translation.
[2] *Die Literatur* 1928–29 (Oct.–Oct.) 467.
[3] *Der Spiegel* Jan. 9, 1952, 25.

Chapter 9. The Spokesman of a Generation

[1] *All Quiet on the Western Front* (Boston: Little, Brown, and Company, 1929) Unnumbered page before the beginning of the text.
[2] *New York Times*, Sept. 22, 1929, 7.
[3] *Ibid.*
[4] *All Quiet on the Western Front*, 26.
[5] *The Living Age*, Dec. 1930, 347–48.
[6] *Die Literatur*, Vol. 32 (1929–30) 6. My translation.
[7] Harry Kessler, *In the Twenties* (New York: Holt, Rinehart and Winston, 1971) 367.
[8] *Ibid.*
[9] *Der Spiegel*, Jan. 9, 1952, 25.
[10] *Ibid.*, Jan. 9, 1952, 25.

Chapter 10. Coping With Success

[1] *The Living Age*, June 1931, 372–73.

[2] *Ibid.*, 374.

[3] *Ibid.*, 375.

[4] *Ibid.*

[5] *Ibid.*, 347.

[6] *Der Spiegel*, Jan. 9, 1952, 26.

[7] *Ibid.*

[8] *Ibid.*, 25.

Chapter 11. The Filming of "All Quiet on the Western Front"

[1] Statistical information regarding the movie comes from: *Souvenir Programs of Twelve Classic Movies 1927–1941*, ed. Miles Kreuger (New York: Dover Publications, Inc. 1977) 72–73.

Chapter 12. Enjoying the Good Life

[1] Robert Van Gelder, *Writers and Writing* (New York: Charles Scribner's Sons, 1946) 377–78.

[2] *Road and Track*, May 1972, 54.

[3] *Ibid.*, 55.

[4] *New York Times*, Sept. 22, 1929, 7.

Chapter 13. The Second Book and Film

[1] *New York Times*, Oct. 13, 1929, 8.

[2] *The Road Back*, 199–200.

Chapter 14. Prelude to Exile

No notes.

Chapter 15. Exile in Switzerland

[1] *Writers and Writing*, 380–81.

[2] Stefan Lorant, *I Was Hitler's Prisoner* (London: Victor Gollancz Ltd., 1935) 129.

[3] *Time*, Oct. 9, 1933.

[4] *Colliers*, July 1, 1939, 25.

[5] *Der Spiegel*, Jan. 9, 1952, 28. My translation.

[6] *Ibid.*, 27.

Chapter 16. *Drei Kameraden (Three Comrades)*

[1] Erich Maria Remarque, *Three Comrades* (Boston: Little, Brown and Company, 1937) 428.

[2] *Three Comrades*, 453.

[3] *Ibid.*, 456.

[4] *Ibid.*, 474.

[5] *Ibid.*, 17.

[6] Such a picture can be found on the cover of the *Saturday Review of Literature* for Saturday, May 1, 1937.

Chapter 17. The Film Version of *Drei Kameraden*

[1] *F. Scott Fitzgerald's Screenplay for Three Comrades by Erich Maria Remarque*, ed. Matthew J. Bruccoli (Carbondale and Edwardsville: Southern Illinois University Press, 1978) 251.

[2] Fred Lawrence Guiles, *Hanging on in Paradise* (New York: McGraw-Hill, 1975) 158.

[3] *New York Times Film Reviews* (New York: New York Times and Arno Press, 1970) 1505.

Chapter 18. A New Relationship Made and an Old Marriage Repeated

[1] *Madame*, July 1971. My translation.

[2] *Ibid.*, My translation.

[3] Charles Higham, *Marlene* (New York: W. W. Norton and Co., Inc., 1977) 184.

[4] Marthe Lemestre, *Madame Sphinx* (New York: Ballantine Books, 1975) 136–37. Translation by Gale Strom.

[5] *Der Spiegel*, Oct. 11, 1976, 186–189.

[6] *Marlene*, 182.

Chapter 19. Loss of German Citizenship

[1] I am greatly indebted to Remarque's friend and German attorney Dr. Robert M. W. Kempner who supplied copies of the Nazi documents pertaining to Remarque's loss of German citizenship. The translations are mine.

Chapter 20. The Beginning of the Second Exile

[1] Charles Higham, *Marlene* (New York: W. W. Norton and Co., Inc., 1977) 187.

[2] *Ibid.*, 187–88.

[3] *Time*, Jan. 5, 1931, 22.

[4] *New York Times*, March 24, 1939, 23.

[5] *Marlene*, 188.

[6] *Time*, Sept. 11, 1939, 36.

Chapter 21. California Interlude

[1] *Marlene*, 191.

[2] David Niven, *Bring on the Empty Horses* (New York: Dell, 1976) 103.

[3] *Writers and Writing*, 379.

[4] *Ibid.*

[5] Bernard Rosenberg and Harry Silverstein, *The Real Tinsel* (London: Collier-Macmillan Ltd., 1970) 351.

[6] *Marlene*, 195.

Chapter 22. Jeanne's Bureaucratic Welcome to America

[1] Records of the hearing before a board of special inquiry were released to the author June 30, 1978 by Mr. Stanley McKinley of the Immigration and Naturalization Service.

Chapter 23. *Liebe deinen Nächsten*: The Book and the Movie

[1] Erich Maria Remarque, *Flotsam* (Boston: Little, Brown and Co., 1941) 2.

[2] *Ibid.*, 390.

[3] *Ibid.*, 429–30.

[4] *Ibid.*, 430.

Chapter 24. The Last Years in Hollywood

[1] *Marlene*, 200.

[2] *Colliers*, May 14, 1954, 26.

[3] *Ibid.*

[4] *Ibid.*

[5] *Ibid.*

[6] A. E. Hotchner, *Papa Hemingway* (New York: Random House, 1966) 26–27.

[7] In a letter to the author dated Dec. 7, 1976.

Chapter 25. The Art Collection

No notes.

Chapter 26. The Tragedy of Elfriede Remark Scholz

[1] Dr. Robert M. W. Kempner made available to me copies of the Nazi material relating to the trial of Elfriede Remark Scholz. The translation is mine.

[2] *Osnabrücker Nachrichten*, Jan. 24, 1969. My translation.

Chapter 27. *Arch of Triumph*: The Novel and the Movie

[1] Erich Maria Remarque, *Arch of Triumph* (New York: Appleton-Century Co., Inc., 1945) 455.

[2] *Ibid.*, 294.

[3] *Marlene*, 183.

[4] *New York Times Film Reviews* (New York: New York Times and Arno Press, 1970) 2248.

[5] *Ibid.*

[6] *Ibid.*

[7] *Der Spiegel*, Jan. 9, 1952, 28. My translation.

Chapter 28. *Der Funke Leben (Spark of Life)*

[1] *New York Times*, Sept. 26, 1970, 32.

[2] *Newsweek*, April 1, 1957, 108.

[3] *Writers and Writing*, 381.

[4] *Ibid.*

[5] Erich Maria Remarque, *Spark of Life* (New York: Appleton-Century-Crofts, Inc., 1952) 274.

[6] *Ibid.*

[7] *Ibid.*

[8] *Ibid.*, 276.

[9] *Ibid.*, 265.

[10] *Ibid.*, 343.

[11] *Ibid.*, 344.

[12] *Ibid.*, 297.

[13] *Ibid.*

[14] *Ibid.*, 298.

[15] *Ibid.*, 364.

[16] *Ibid.*, 365.

[17] *Ibid.*, 273.

[18] *Ibid.*, 354.

[19] *Ibid.*

[20] *Ibid.*, 292.

[21] *Ibid.*

[22] *Ibid.*, 293.

[23] *Ibid.*, 280.

[24] *Ibid.*, 274–75.

Chapter 29. *Zeit zu leben und Zeit zu sterben*: The Novel and the Movie

[1] Erich Maria Remarque, *A Time to Love and a Time to Die* (New York: Harcourt, Brace and Company, 1954) 39.

[2] *Ibid.*, 66.

[3] *Ibid.*, 97.
[4] *Ibid.*, 118.
[5] *Ibid.*, 171.
[6] *Ibid.*, 171–72.
[7] *Ibid.*, 256.
[8] *Ibid.*, 338–39.
[9] *Ibid.*, 339.
[10] *Der Spiegel*, Dec. 15, 1954, 43. My translation.
[11] *Ibid.* My translation.
[12] *Ibid.*, 44. My translation.
[13] *Ibid.* My translation.
[14] *A Time to Love and a Time to Die*, 15.
[15] *Ibid.*, 352.
[16] *Ibid.*
[17] *Ibid.*, 274.
[18] *Ibid.*, 161.
[19] *Ibid.*, 163–64.
[20] *Ibid.*, 173–74.
[21] *Los Angeles Times*, July 21, 1957, part V, 1.
[22] *Ibid.*
[23] *Los Angeles Times*, Oct. 24, 1957.
[24] *Ibid.*
[25] *Los Angeles Times*, July 21, 1957, part V, 1.
[26] Telephone conversation with Ambassador Gavin on Feb. 22, 1974.
[27] *New York Times Film Reviews* (1913–1968) (New York: New York Times and Arno Press, 1970) Vol. 4/1949–1958, 22:1.
[28] *Ibid.*
[29] *Ibid.*
[30] *Ibid.*
[31] *Ibid.*
[32] *Ibid.*

Chapter 30. *Der schwarze Obelisk (The Black Obelisk)*

[1] *The Black Obelisk*, 99.
[2] *Newsweek*, April 1, 1957, 108–09.
[3] *The Black Obelisk*, 432.
[4] *Los Angeles Times*, July 21, 1957, part V, 1.

Chapter 31. The First Play, the Second Divorce, and the Third Marriage

[1] *El Paso Herald Post*, May 21, 1957, 1.
[2] *Ibid.*
[3] *Ibid.*

[4] *Ibid.*
[5] *New York Times*, Aug. 23, 1957, 11:2.
[6] *Newsweek*, Sept. 2, 1957, 19:108.
[7] *New York Times*, Nov. 29, 1957
[8] *The New Haven Evening Register*, Feb. 26, 1958

Chapter 32. *Der Himmel kennt keine Günstlinge (Heaven has no Favorites)*

[1] Erich Maria Remarque, *Heaven has no Favorites* (New York: Crown Books, 1961), 110.
[2] *Ibid.*, 111.
[3] *Ibid.*, 225.
[4] *Ibid.*, 235.
[5] *Ibid.*, 239.
[6] *All Quiet on the Western Front*, 291.
[7] *Heaven has no Favorites*, 239.
[8] *Ibid.*
[9] *New York Times Film Reviews* (New York: New York Times and Arno Press, 1970) 2181.
[10] *Ibid.*

Chapter 33. *Die Nacht von Lissabon (The Night in Lisbon)*

[1] Mel Gussow, *Don't Say Yes until I Finish Talking* (Garden City, New York: Doubleday and Company, Inc., 1971) 222–23.
[2] *Bild*, Jan. 18, 1963, My translation.
[3] *Bild*, Jan. 18, 1963, My translation.
[4] *Bild*, Jan. 18, 1963, My translation.
[5] *Berliner Zeitung*, Jan. 17, 1963, My translation.
[6] *Berliner Zeitung*, Jan. 17, 1963, My translation.
[7] *Bild*, Jan. 18, 1963, My translation.

Chapter 34. Recognition from the Germans

[1] My translation from Hanns-Gerd Rabe's article in the *Osnabrücker Tageblatt*.
[2] My translation.

Chapter 35. "All Quiet"

[1] Hans Habe, *Erfahrungen* (München: Wilhelm Heyne Verlag, 1975) 85. My translation.

Chapter 36. Posthumous Events before *Schatten im Paradies*

[1] My translation.

Chapter 37. *Schatten im Paradies (Shadows in Paradise)*

[1] *Der Spiegel*, 1971/18, 172. My translation.

[2] *Ibid*. My translation.

[3] *Ibid*. My translation.

[4] Erich Maria Remarque, *Shadows in Paradise* (New York: Harcourt Brace Jovanovich, Inc., 1972) 5.

[5] *Ibid.*, 241.

[6] *Ibid.*, 29.

[7] *Ibid.*, 304.

[8] *Ibid.*

[9] *Ibid.*

[10] *Ibid.*, 305.

[11] *Ibid.*

Chapter 38. *Full Circle*

[1] Erich Maria Remarque, *Full Circle* (New York: Harcourt Brace Jovanovich, Inc., 1974) vi.

[2] *Ibid.*

[3] *Ibid.*, 114.

[4] *Ibid.*

[5] *Ibid.*

[6] Anta Theatre "Playbill" magazine, 7.

[7] *Washington Post*, Oct. 5, 1973, B1, B8.

[8] *Ibid.*, B1.

[9] *Ibid.*, B3.

[10] *Ibid.*, B3.

[11] *New York Times*, Nov. 8, 1973, 58.

[12] *Ibid.*

[13] *Ibid.*

Chapter 39. The Death of Jeanne Remarque

[1] I am indebted to Mr. Edward M. Milburn, American Consul in Genoa, Italy, for many of the details concerning the last years of Jeanne Remarque's life.

Chapter 40. The End of a Collection

[1] *Washington Post*, Oct. 5, 1973, B8.

[2] *Pittsburgh Press*, Nov. 11, 1979, B3.

[3] *Ibid.*

Chapter 41. All Quiet Revisited

[1] *Pittsburgh Press*, TV Graphic, Nov. 11, 1979, 3.

[2] *Ibid.*

Chapter 42. Arch of Triumph: The Television Movie

[1] *Indianapolis Star*, May 20, 1985, 10.

Chapter 43. The Summing Up

No notes.

Selected Bibliography

Remarque Novels in German

Die Traumbude (Dresden: Verlag der Schönheit, 1920)
Im Westen Nichts Neues (Berlin: Propyläen Verlag, 1929)
Der Weg Zurück (Berlin: Propyläen Verlag, 1931)
Drei Kameraden (Amsterdam: Querido Verlag N.V., 1938)
Liebe deinen Nächsten (Stockholm: Bermann-Fisher Verlag, 1941)
Arc de Triomphe (Zürich: F. G. Micha, 1946)
Der Funke Leben (Köln: Kiepenheuer and Witsch, 1952)
Zeit zu leben und Zeit zu sterben (Köln: Kiepenheuer and Witsch, 1954)
Der schwarze Obelisk (Köln: Kiepenheuer and Witsch, 1956)
Der Himmel kennt keine Günstlinge (Köln: Kiepenheuer and Witsch, 1961)
Die Nacht von Lissabon (Köln: Kiepenheuer and Witsch, 1962)
Schatten im Paradies (Stuttgart: Droemer Verlag, 1971)

Selected Remarque Novels in English Translation

All Quiet on the Western Front (Boston: Little, Brown and Company, 1929)
The Road Back (Boston: Little, Brown and Company, 1931)
Three Comrades (Boston: Little, Brown and Company, 1937)
Flotsam (Boston: Little, Brown and Company, 1941)
Arch of Triumph (New York: D. Appleton-Century Company, Inc., 1945)
Spark of Life (New York: Appleton-Century-Crofts, 1952)
A Time to Love and a Time to Die (New York: Harcourt, Brace and Company, 1954)
The Black Obelisk (New York: Harcourt, Brace and Company, 1957)
Heaven has no Favorites (New York: Harcourt, Brace and World, 1961)
The Night in Lisbon (New York: Harcourt, Brace and World, Inc., 1964)
Shadows in Paradise (New York: Harcourt, Brace, Jovanovich, 1972)

Chronology

1898	(June 22) Born in Osnabrück. Son of the book printer Peter Franz Remark, and his wife Anna Maria (Stallknecht). Baptized Erich Paul Remark in the Roman Catholic faith.
1898/99	Lived at Jahnstrasse 15
1900/01	Lived at Jahnstrasse 21
1902	Lived at Schinkeler Strasse 2
1903/04	Lived at Herrenteichstrasse 16
1903	(March 25) His sister Elfriede Remark was born in the house at Herrenteichstrasse 16
1904	Attended the "Domschule" (a Catholic Volksschule). He attended this school until 1908—as long as his parents lived in the northern part of the city.
1905	Lived at Gertrudenstrasse 17
1906/07	Lived at Klingensberg 7
1908/09/10	Lived at Jahnstrasse 29
1908	From this time until 1912 he attended the Johannisschule (a Catholic Volksschule)
1911/12/13	Lived at Jahnstrasse 23
1912 (Easter)	Entered the "Katholische Präparande"
1914	Again lived at Jahnstrasse 29

1915/16	Lived at Luisenstrasse 28. Gave piano lessons to several students until he entered the army.
	Made the acquaintance of the Fritz Hörstemeier circle of enthusiastic idealists who were later depicted in his novel *Die Traumbude*
1916	"Aus der Heimat. Von den Freuden und Mühen der Jugendwehr." Published in *Heimatfreund* (Ein Blatt für die Jugend des Regierungsbezirks Osnabrück). This is very likely Remarque's first published work. He participated in a prize contest concerning the "Jugendwehr" and got a prize of 30 Marks for the work.
	(Nov. 21) Remarque and the other members of the group of 1898 were drafted from school into the army. Went to the Caprivi-Kaserne on the Westerberg for recruit training. Later training in the camp at Celle. Received leave often to return home to visit his mother who was suffering from cancer.
1917	The Remark family moved to Hakenstrasse 3 to an attic apartment in which they lived until 1935. The house was owned by the Prelle firm on Krahnstrasse with which Peter Remark was employed as a book binder and later master machinist.
	(June 12) Was sent toward the western front
	(June 14) Assigned to the "2.Kp. Feld-Rekr-Depot der 2. Garde-Res.-Division" which was located in Ham-Lenglet on the "Canal de la Sensee" behind the Arras front.
	(June 26) The unit marched to Aubigny-au-Bac from which they were transported by rail to the area between Thourout and the Houthulst forest where he was assigned to a sapper group.

(July 25) Rescued his friend Troske, who had been wounded by shell fragments, and carried him out of enemy fire. Troske was taken to a hospital but died on August 24.

(July 31) The Battle of Flanders began. Remark was wounded by shell fragments from English long-range artillery. One wound was in the neck. Another was in the left leg above the knee, and another in his right arm just above the wrist. He, with other wounded, was taken to a collecting point at Geite-Sankt-Josef.

(Aug.) Taken to Field Hospital 309 in Thourout. From here he was transported by hospital train to Duisburg. He was in the St. Vincenz hospital here from approximately the middle of August.

(Sept.) Remark's mother died in Onsbrück of cancer. He went to Osnabrück from the hospital in Duisburg.

1918 (March 6) His friend Fritz Hörstemeier died at the age of 36.

(March) Returned to Osnabrück from the hospital in Duisburg for the funeral of Fritz Hörstemeier and played the organ for the service.

Sketch "Aus der Jugendzeit" published in *Die Schönheit*

Short story "Die Frau mit den Goldenen Augen" was published in *Die Schönheit*

Poem "Ich und Du" published in *Die Schönheit*

(Oct. 31) Released from the hospital, declared fit for garrison duty, and transferred to the "I.Ers.-Batl.I.R. 78" in Osnabrück

(Nov. 7) Examined by the batallion doctor for fitness to return to the front

(Nov. 11) The end of the war found Remark in the replacement batallion in Osnabrück

(November) Christian Kemmerich met the "lance corporal" (Gefreite) Remark in Osnabrück. Remark was wearing the Iron Cross (first and second class) and the Oldenburg Cross (first and second class). Subsequently Kemmerich learned that the batallion commander had sent out a patrol from the local military headquarters to apprehend him in regard to the "promotion" and decorations.

(Jan.) Discharged Musketier Remark returned to the Catholic Lehrerseminar on Brinkstrasse. Approximately a week later he and his friend Hanns-Gerd Rabe were chosen as their comrades' representatives in a dispute with school authorities and traveled to see officials in Berlin.

Remark (according to the publisher Steegemann) was seen at this time in Hannover in the uniform of a lieutenant, wearing the Iron Cross (First Class) as well as a monocle.

Lived at Hakenstrasse Nr. 3.

Short story "Schöne Freunde" published in *Die Schönheit*

Poem "Abschied" published in *Die Schönheit*

(June) Arranged the "Rosenfest" (the ball for the seminary students)

(June 25) Passed his teacher's examination

"Ingeborg" (Ein Erwachen von Erich Remark) appeared in *Die Schönheit*

(Aug. 1) First teaching experience in Lohne, Kreis Lingen (Ems) as a substitute for the teacher Wulfern who was a French prisoner of war. Remark kept the job until March 31, 1920. Wulfern returned to his position April 1, 1920.

In Lohne Remark lived in the Gastwirtschaft Lambers.

Contributed theatre, music, and art criticism for the Osnabrück newspapers.

(December) The school officials in Osnabrück were given a report that Remark had been involved in Spartacist activities during his time in the teachers' seminar. Remark denied this. However, officials made a statement indicating disapproval of his activities there.

1920 (April 1) From this date until May 3 he was unemployed in Osnabrück between teaching jobs.

Die Traumbude was published by the "Verlag der Schönheit" in Dresden

(May 4) Took a teaching job in Klein-Berssen, Hümmling, as a replacement for the teacher Nieberg who was ill and on leave. Here he came into conflict with the strong-willed priest Brand who wished to control the school.

(July 31) Left Klein-Berssen when the teacher Nieberg returned from leave.

(Aug. 20) Took temporary teaching job in Nahne, on the outskirts of Osnabrück, replacing the teacher Elbert, who was ill. Kept this position until Nov. 20.

Poem "Cis moll" published in *Die Schönheit*

(approx.) Poem "Nocturne" published in *Jugend*

(Oct. 13) The "Osnabrücker Tageblatt" published one of his early poems, "Abendlied".

(Dec. 12) School authorities in Osnabrück agreed to his request not to be considered for future teaching assignments.

"Natur und Kunstwerk" (by Erich Remark) appeared in *Die Schönheit*

(Dec. 17) His tone in correspondence with the Osnabrück authorities in regard to his quarrel with Brand resulted in a written reprimand. This was on the basis of the disciplinary rules of 1852.

1921 Worked at various jobs—among them salesman for dry goods

"Flieder" published in *Die Schönheit*

Sent Stefan Zweig a letter of near-despair, along with some poems for his evaluation, "remember that this is a matter of life and death for me"

1922 Found employment with the Vogt Brothers, stone-cutting and grave stone firm at Süsterstrasse 2 in Osnabrück. Played the organ on Sunday at the Michaelis-Kapelle of the Landeskrankenhaus.

(Oct.) Moved to Hannover and took a job as editor and publicity director for the Continental Rubber Company. He had earlier contributed advertising articles for their magazine "Continental-Echo".

(Nov.) Became editor of the "Echo Continental", the advertising and trade journal of the Continental Rubber Company. Also traveled in

Italy, Switzerland, the Balkans, and Turkey. Kept this job through 1924.

(Nov. 16) Osnabrück government tried to bring him back into teaching. He wrote a letter informing them he was employed by the Continental Company. In his letter he uses the name "Maria" for the first time.

1923 Poem, "Einer Frau", published in *Die Schönheit*

1925 Became the picture editor of the newspaper "Sport im Bild" for the Scherl-Verlag in Berlin.

(Oct. 14) Married Frau Jutta Ilse Ingeborg Ellen Zambona (born Aug. 25, 1901 in Hildesheim). She was divorced from a man named Winkelhoff.

1926 In Berlin, with his first money (500 RM) he paid Freiherr von Buchwald to adopt him so that he could decorate his calling card with the five-pronged crown. Freiherr von Buchwald was an impoverished Rittmeister. Even after the appearance of *Im Westen nichts Neues* Remark was registered at the 152nd police station in Berlin-Wilmersdorf as "Ehemann Erich Freiherr von Buchwald gen. Remark".

However, it was in Berlin that he changed the spelling of his name back to the original name "Remarque" of his French and German ancestors.

1927 "Hymne auf den Cocktail" published in "Sport im Bild"

1927/28 *Station am Horizont*. This automobile-novel ran in serial form in "Sport im Bild".

1928 (Nov. 10 to Dec. 9) "Die Vossische Zeitung" printed *Im Westen nichts Neues*

1929 (Jan. 31) The "Propyläen Verlag" in Berlin published *Im Westen nichts Neues*

(March 9) Copies of *Die Traumbude* were bought up by Ullstein Verlag at Remarque's request

Remarque took a 3,750 mile automobile trip through France. He traveled through Normandy, Brittany, Limoges, and the Pyrenees.

Dr. Salomo Friedländer, under the pseudonym Mynona (Anonym), wrote a book *Hat Remarque wirklich gelebt?*

(Sept. 6) The German Officers' League, on the basis of a report that Remarque would be awarded the Nobel Prize, wrote to the Nobel Prize Committee to protest in advance any such course of action.

(October) Placed an anonymous ad in the Osnabrück newspaper requesting a quiet apartment. Frau Maria Hoberg on Johannisstrasse answered.

(Nov./Dec.) Stayed in the Hoberg home and worked on the novel *Der Weg zurück*.

(Jan. 4) Divorced Jutta Ilse Zambona. Although the decree was granted January 4, the divorce was not revealed until April because she remained a member of the household.

1930 (Jan.) Took some friends to the Avus race track in Berlin. His Bugatti slid along the wet asphalt, flipped over, hurting his nose and right leg, and shaking up his friends.

(Jan. 24) Arrived at Arosa, Switzerland for a vacation.

(Feb. 8) A Dr. Frick, a member of the Nazi party and recently elected Minister of Education, announced in Weimar that *Im Westen nichts Neues* had been banned in all schools in Thüringen. He called it "pacifist, Marxist propaganda".

Vacation in Davos, Switzerland with Ilse

(Summer) Returned to the Hoberg home for eight weeks to finish *Der Weg zurück*

(Dec. 6) Josef Goebbels was responsible for having a showing of *Im Westen nichts Neues* in Berlin broken up by using stench bombs and releasing white mice. A few weeks later the movie was banned.

1931 *Der Weg zurück*

Bought a Villa on Lago Maggiore from a Herr Meier from Offenbach. Meier had bought it from the Swiss landscape painter Hermann Rüdisühli. The Villa had formerly belonged to the painter Arnold Böcklin. It was called "Casa Monte Tabor".

(June) Was living in Berlin at 5 Wittelsbacherstrasse

(June 2) The Irish Free State banned six books, including Remarque's *The Road Back*.

(June 15) Remarque's American publishers, Little, Brown, and Co., announced that he had written a new novel especially for the screen which would be produced soon. The new story is called "Fate".

(July 10) His car knocked down a lamp-post in Leyden. The car was seriously damaged but Remarque escaped injury. He paid $48.00 in damages and gave the Dutch police copies of *Im Westen nichts Neues* in appreciation of their help.

1932	(Feb. 2) There was a report from Amsterdam that Remarque was going to remarry his former wife and live at Bussum, fifteen miles from Amsterdam.
	(April) German government seized his Berlin bank account of 20,000 Marks (4,760) and accused him of 1) establishing a residence in the Netherlands and 2) of banking outside Germany with his royalties.
1933	(Jan. 29) Went to Switzerland to live. Although his former wife had been divorced from him for three years she also went along.
	Thomas Mann didn't want to be seen on the streets of Ascona with Remarque because he didn't want to lose his German reading public.
	(May 10) His books were burned by the Nazis in front of Berlin University
1935	Peter Remark moved to Bad Rothenfelde. Lived there with his daughter Erna and her husband Walter Rudolph.
1937	*Drei Kameraden*
1938	(Jan. 22) Remarried Jutta Ilse (Jeanne) in St. Moritz, Switzerland to offer her the protection of his name so she would not have to return to Germany.
	Nazis took away his citizenship
1939	(March 23) Arrived in New York from Le Havre on the Cunard White Star liner Queen Mary. He was accompanied by a friend Otto Klement who often served as his interpreter.
	(Oct. 22) Jutta Ilse Remarque arrived in the United States aboard the S. S. Manhattan. She was detained at Ellis Island because her travel papers were not in order.

1941 (Oct. 8) Filed his declaration of intention to become a citizen of Los Angeles.

Liebe deinen Nächsten

1942 (Jan. 13) His art collection valued conservatively at $100,000 was loaned to the Los Angeles County Museum for an indefinite period and was to be on exhibition sometime in March. He turned over his collection to the museum when he decided to close his Westwood home and return to New York City. He had been in Hollywood for several months writing for the movie studios. The Remarque collection included 50 paintings by French artists of the post-impressionist and modern schools, oriental carpets, Chinese pottery, figurines of the Tang Dynasty (900 A.D.) and Chinese bronzes of the same period. Many drawings and water colors also were included.

1943 (Sept. 21) Settled an $8921.50 income tax dispute with the government for $3892.50. The government claimed the former amount as additional taxes on his 1939 income tax. It disputed deductions he had claimed for travel expenses. Federal Judge W. W. Arnold ordered payment of the $3892.50.

(Oct. 18 to Nov. 13) Loan exhibition of his paintings and pictures at the Knoedler Galleries in New York City.

(Oct. 29) Elfriede Remark Scholz was brought before the First Senate of the "Volksgerichtshof" and condemned to death by the notorious President of the court, Roland Freisler. She was called a "ehrlose, fanatische Zersetzungspropagandistin unserer Kriegsfeinde" who had made hostile remarks about the "Führer".

(Dec. 16) Elfriede Scholz was beheaded at 12:57 A.M. in Plötzensee prison in Berlin.

1946 *Arc de Triomphe*

1947 (Aug.) Became a U.S. Citizen in New York

1948 Returned to Switzerland to live

1949 (April) Went to court in Los Angeles to get a $10,000. installment from Enterprise Productions for rights to his "Arch of Triumph".

1952 *Der Funke Leben*

1953 (Summer) Moved from the Ambassador Hotel on Park Avenue into an apartment in the Ritz Towers on Park Avenue at 57th Street.

1954 *Zeit zu leben und Zeit zu sterben*

(March 19) Remarque was shaken up and bruised when his automobile crashed into a wall near Locarno. He had bought a new automobile in Italy and was returning to Ascona when the accident happened.

(June 9) Peter Remark died in Bad Rothenfelde and was buried there. Remarque and his sister Erna were present at the funeral.

1955 (Aug.) An Austrian movie "The Last Act", whose screenplay was written by Remarque, based on Michael Musmanno's book *Ten Days to Die*, was scheduled to open the annual film festival at Edinburgh, Scotland. The film depicted the last days of Hitler.

1956 *Der schwarze Obelisk*

(Sept. 20) His play "Berlin, 1945" had its world premiere at the West Berlin Cultural Festival. Remarque appeared on stage after the performance. There were more than thirty curtain calls. The play was directed by Paul Verhoeven with Heide Marie Hatheyer and Kurt Meisel in the principal roles.

1957 (May 9) In New York

(May 21) A newspaper report, datelined El Paso, Texas, stated that Mrs. Jutta Zambona Remarque of New York City obtained a divorce from her husband yesterday in Juarez on the grounds of incompatability.

(July 21) Living at this time in the Bel-Air-Hotel on Stone Canyon Road in Los Angeles.

(July 21) It was reported in a newspaper column from Los Angeles that Remarque had been at Universal-International Studios several weeks turning the novel *A Time to Love and a Time to Die* into a screenplay.

(Aug. 22) Paulette Goddard told friends in Hollywood that she and Remarque would be married next Christmas at St. Moritz, Switzerland.

1958 (Feb. 25) Married actress Paulette Goddard in Branford, Connecticut. They were married in the office of Judge Cornelius T. Driscoll in a simple, private ceremony which lasted ten minutes.

1961 *Der Himmel kennt keine Günstlinge*

1962 *Die Nacht von Lissabon*

1964 (Nov. 1) A delegation from Osnabrück, including Hanns-Gerd Rabe, visited him in Porto Ronco and gave him the Justus Möser Medal of the city of Osnabrück.

1966	(Jan. 24) In Rome
1967	(April 25) German President Lübke conferred on Remarque "Das Grosse Verdienstkreuz des Verdienstordens der Bundesrepublik Deutschland"
	(July 20) The German Ambassador presented to Remarque in Bern the documents and insignia pertaining to his award from the Federal Republic.
1968	(May 3) In Rome
	"Die Deutsche Akademie für Sprache und Dichtung" elected him a member in his 70th year.
1970	(Sept. 25) Died in Saint Agnese hospital in Locarno, Switzerland. He died at noon of heart failure. Paulette was at his bedside.
1970	(Sept. 27) Buried in the hillside village cemetery of Ronco, Switzerland. Only relatives and friends took part in the service.
1971	*Schatten im Paradies*
1973	(Oct. 5) "Full Circle" had its preview performance in the Eisenhower Theater at the John F. Kennedy Center in Washington, D.C. The play ran through Oct. 27. It was an adaptation by Peter Stone of "Die letzte Station" and starred Leonard Nimoy and Bibi Anderson.
	(Nov. 7) "Full Circle" had its premiere performance at the ANTA Theatre in New York City. The play ran nine weeks.
1975	(June 25) Jeanne died in Monte Carlo
1976	(Nov.) Sotheby Parke Bernet sold oriental rugs having a value of approximately 220,000 dollars.

1977	"Bobby Deerfield." A movie based on *Heaven has no Favorites*
1979	(Nov. 7) Sotheby Parke Bernet sold 30 french impressionist paintings for 3.1 million dollars.
1979	(Nov. 14) Marble Arch T.V. movie production of "All Quiet"
1985	(May 29) CBS presentation of T.V. movie version of "Arch of Triumph"

Filmography

Year	1930 (Reissued in 1939)
Title	All Quiet on the Western Front
Studio	Universal
Producer(s)	Carl Laemmle, Jr.
Director(s)	Lewis Milestone
Stars	Lew Ayres, Louis Wolheim, John Wray, George "Slim" Summerville, Raymond Griffith, and Ben Alexander

Year	1937
Title	The Road Back
Studio	Universal
Producer(s)	James Whale
Director(s)	John King, Richard Cromwell, Andy Devine, Spring Byington, Noah Berry, Jr., and George "Slim" Summerville

Year	1938
Title	Three Comrades
Studio	Metro-Goldwyn-Mayer
Producer(s)	Joseph Mankiewicz
Director(s)	Frank Borzagas
Stars	Robert Taylor, Margaret Sullavan, Franchot Tone, Robert Young, Guy Kibbee, Lionel Atwill, and Monty Wooley

Year	1941
Title	So Ends Our Night (from *Flotsam*)

Studio	United Artists
Producer(s)	David Loew and Albert Lewin
Director(s)	John Cromwell
Stars	Fredric March, Frances Dee, Glenn Ford, Margaret Sullavan, Ann Sten, and Erich von Strohheim

Year	1947
Title	The Other Love
Studio	Enterprise
Producer(s)	David Lewis
Director(s)	Andre DeToth
Stars	David Niven, Barbara Stanwyck, and Richard Conte

Year	1948
Title	Arch of Triumph
Studio	United Artists
Producer(s)	David Lewis
Director(s)	Lewis Milestone
Stars	Charles Boyer, Ingrid Bergman, Louis Calhern, and Charles Laughton

Year	1957
Title	A Time to Love and a Time to Die
Studio	Universal-International
Producer(s)	Robert Arthur
Director(s)	Douglas Sirk
Stars	John Gavin, Lilo Pulver, Keenan Wynn, Don Defore, and Erich Maria Remarque

Year	1977
Title	Bobby Deerfield
Studio	Columbia Pictures/Warner Brothers
Producer(s)	Sydney Pollack
Director(s)	Sydney Pollack
Stars	Al Pacino, Marthe Keller, Anny Duperey, Walter McGinn, and Romolo Valli

Year	1979
Title	All Quiet on the Western Front (Television Movie)
Studio	Marble Arch Productions
Producer(s)	Norman Rosemont
Director(s)	Delbert Mann
Stars	Richard Thomas, Ernest Borgnine, Patricia Neal, Ian Holm, and Donald Pleasance

Year	1985
Title	Arch of Triumph (Television Movie)
Studio	Newland-Raynor
Producer(s)	Peter Graham Scott
Director(s)	Warris Hussein
Stars	Anthony Hopkins, Lesley-Anne Down, Frank Finlay, and Richard Pasco

Index

Remarque (Remark) family members are indexed under: Remarque, Erich Maria (Erich Paul Remark)